The Guru Guide™
to Marketing

The Guru Guide™
to Marketing

A Concise Guide to the Best
Ideas from Today's Top Marketers

Joseph H. Boyett
and
Jimmie T. Boyett

John Wiley & Sons, Inc.

Published by John Wiley & Sons, Inc., Hoboken, New Jersey.
Published simultaneously in Canada.

Designations used by companies to distinguish their products are often claimed as trademarks. In all instances where John Wiley & Sons, Inc., is aware of a claim, the product names appear in initial capital or ALL CAPITAL LETTERS. Readers, however, should contact the appropriate companies for more complete information regarding trademarks and registration.

Corporate logos are used with permission from McDonald's Corporation, the Coca-Cola Company, Weyerhauser, and Starbucks Coffee Company.

Limit of Liability/Disclaimer of Warranty: While the publisher and author have used their best efforts in preparing this book, they make no representations or warranties with respect to the accuracy or completeness of the contents of this book and specifically disclaim any implied warranties of merchantability or fitness for a particular purpose. No warranty may be created or extended by sales representatives or written sales materials. The advice and strategies contained herein may not be suitable for your situation. The publisher is not engaged in rendering professional services, and you should consult a professional where appropriate. Neither the publisher nor author shall be liable for any loss of profit or any other commercial damages, including but not limited to special, incidental, consequential, or damages.

For general information on our other products and services please contact our Customer Care Department within the U.S. at (800) 762-2974, outside the United States at (317) 572-3993 or fax (317) 572-4002.

Wiley also publishes its books in a variety of electronic formats. Some content that appears in print may not be available in electronic books. For more information about Wiley products, visit our website at www.Wiley.com.

Library of Congress Cataloging-in-Publication Data

ISBN: 0-471-21377-2

Printed in the United States of America.

10 9 8 7 6 5 4 3 2 1

Contents

Introduction

Peter Drucker, the guru of all management gurus, once wrote that marketing was the distinguishing, unique function that set businesses apart from all other human organizations. As a businessperson, you know how important the marketing function is to the success of any business. You also know that marketing is in the throes of change. The Internet has altered the dynamics of customer and business-to-business relations. Regardless of medium, advertising doesn't seem to work quite as well as it once did. Once-strong brands seem to be less potent. Of course there is no shortage of explanations for what is happening to marketing and advice for remedying its ills. Amazon.com lists over 13,000 books on marketing and a search on Google.com yields over 22 million Internet sites devoted to the topic. Therein lies the problem.

If you are like most people, you simply have too much to do and too little time to sift through hundreds of books, thousands of articles, and millions of web sites on marketing to uncover the latest trends and revelations. Which books should you read? What articles could provide you with insight into emerging marketing issues? Whose writings should you seek on the Internet and in your library? Who are the leading authorities on brand management, customer relationship management, and other hot marketing topics? What advice do they give? How do the ideas of one authority complement or conflict with those of another? You need a guide to answer your questions. Congratulations: you have just found it.

This *Guru Guide™ to Marketing* has been designed to provide you with a clear, concise, and informative digest of the best thinking about marketing in the new global, high-tech world of business. You are holding in your hands a highly opinionated but informative guide to ideas of the world's top marketers and marketing consultants. Like the original *Guru Guide™* (Wiley, 1998), we have designed this guide to be more than just an overview of current thinking. We go further to link and cross-link the ideas to show where the experts agree and disagree. We show how the gurus' ideas have evolved. Finally, we provide an evaluation of their strengths and weaknesses.

OUR GURUS

In selecting our gurus, we began by making a list of established marketing gurus, such Philip Kotler, who have dominated marketing thinking for decades. Then, we went looking for the newcomers. We browsed the on-line and off-line bookstores. We consulted the marketing journals, both popular and academic. We cruised the Internet. We searched for those who were making a splash with new marketing ideas. What journal articles and books on marketing were people reading and talking about? Who did the popular media—TV, radio, business periodicals—cite on emerging marketing issues? Who was widely recognized as THE marketing authority? Who was being quoted? Whose ideas were being discussed? Whose were being cussed?

Because the economy and marketing's challenges have changed so dramatically in the last few years, we focused our search primarily on the most significant books and articles that had been published over the last three years. We checked the best-seller lists to see what people were reading, and we asked our friends, clients, and associates to recommend people they thought had unique marketing insights. We ultimately narrowed our list down to the 62 gurus listed here.

David Aaker	Marc Gobé	Chuck Martin
Harry Beckwith	Seth Godin	Regis McKenna
Robert Blattberg	Ian Gordon	Mary Modahl
Neil H. Borden	Sam Hill	Adam Morgan
Marc Braunstein	Robert Hisrich	Frederick Newell
Darren Bridger	Arthur Hughes	Don Peppers
Kevin J. Clancy	Erich A.	Faith Popcorn
Steven Cristol	Joachimsthaler	Stan Rapp
Adam Curry	Guy Kawasaki	Frederick Reichheld
Jay Curry	Duane Knapp	Al Ries
David d'Alessandro	Philip Kotler	Laura Ries
Frank W. Davis Jr.	Peter C. Krieg	Martha Rogers
Scott M. Davis	Chris Lederer	Emanuel Rosen
George S. Day	Katherine Lemon	Roland Rust
Laura Day	Edward H. Levine	Bernd Schmitt
Frank Delano	Jay Conrad Levinson	Don E. Schultz
Gary Getz	David Lewis	Evan I. Schwartz
Malcolm Gladwell	Karl Manrodt	Peter Sealey

Patricia Seybold	Daryl Travis	Fred Wiersema
Alex Simonson	Jack Trout	Valarie Zeithaml
Jacquelyn Thomas	Lars Tvede	Sergio Zyman

Our gurus are drawn from leading research and teaching centers such as the Harvard Business School, the London Business School, the Wharton School of the University of Pennsylvania, and the Kellogg Graduate School of Management at Northwestern University. Our gurus also represent some of the world's largest and best-known management consulting firms, including Forrester Research, and they include marketing pioneers in the high-tech industry such as Seth Godin of Yahoo!

Our gurus are the best and/or most popular marketing writers and thinkers. You won't agree with everything they have to say—we don't either—but we are confident that they will stimulate your thinking, point you in new directions, and challenge many of your best-loved assumptions about what is wrong with marketing and how it can be fixed.

ORGANIZATION OF THE BOOK

We have designed this book to be your reference manual to the current challenges marketing faces. It is organized around key marketing issues. We cover each issue in a separate chapter and present a summary of the best thinking of a panel of gurus about that issue. We show where the gurus agree and disagree. When our gurus offer different approaches—such as a different sequence of steps to follow in addressing an issue or solving a problem—we use tables, charts, and exhibits to illustrate the similarities and differences.

We have organized our gurus' ideas into six chapters.

Chapter 1, The Future of Marketing, provides an overview of some of the most critical challenges our gurus say marketers face today including the increasing difficulty in creating relevant and distinctive product differentiation, the impact of the Internet on consumer/business and business-to-business relations, the declining effectiveness of advertising, and attacks on traditional pricing schemes.

The five remaining chapters of *The Guru Guide™ to Marketing* cover five different approaches our gurus offer to address marketing's problems and challenges.

Chapter 2, All You Need Is a Brand, and **Chapter 3, All You Need Is Brand Management,** present the arguments a vocal group of gurus make for addressing marketing's problems through improved branding and brand management. Among other things we cover our gurus' recommendations for improved product positioning, building a strong brand, and managing portfolios of brands that extend, in some cases, across companies.

Chapter 4, All You Need Is a Customer Relationship, covers one of the hottest marketing topics of the day—customer relationship management (CRM). We examine what our gurus say is the key concept underlying CRM and its principal advantages over other approaches to marketing, such as branding; four steps our gurus say companies should take to implement CRM; how they say companies must reorganize the marketing function and the company in general to make CRM work; and key questions they say you should ask to determine if CRM is right for your company.

Chapter 5, All You Need Is Customer Equity, presents the arguments of another group of marketing gurus who say that neither branding nor CRM offer a real cure for marketing's ills. Instead they say companies should treat customers as financial assets and marketers should focus their efforts on building what the gurus call "customer equity." In this chapter, we compare and contrast two competing approaches that our gurus offer to both measuring and building customer equity.

In **Chapter 6, All You Need Is Buzz,** we present the arguments of a fourth group of gurus who say that the key to solving marketing's problems isn't more branding or relationship and equity building but rather just more "word-of-mouth" buzz. We explain why they say buzz is critical now, the questions you should ask to determine if you have a "buzzable" product or service, and the steps they say you should take to create genuine street-level excitement and "infectious chatter" about your product or company.

We conclude the book with biographies for all of the gurus, including in many instances postal addresses, phone numbers, and e-mail addresses.

SOME GUIDANCE ON WHAT FOLLOWS: HOW THE CHAPTERS ARE ORGANIZED

Throughout the *Guru Guide™ to Marketing* we have tried to summarize as clearly, succinctly, and objectively as possible the gurus' key ideas. Our personal opinions are expressed in sections entitled "Our View" and preceded by the following icon:

OUR VIEW

At the beginning of each chapter, we use the icon below to identify the gurus whose ideas are covered in that chapter. For example, the chapter on customer relationship management begins as follows:

THE CUSTOMER RELATIONSHIP GURUS

At the end of each chapter, we provide a summary of the key ideas presented in that chapter. Key ideas are identified by the following icon:

KEY POINTS

You can read this book straight through, from beginning to end, covering the topics in the order we present them, or you can go directly to a topic that interests you. You can read the chapters in any order you wish, since each has been designed to stand on its own. Therefore, we encourage you to start with whichever topic is of most interest to you at the moment. If you are interested in specific gurus, check the index or the guru lists at the beginning of each chapter to find out where they appear in the book and proceed accordingly. You are in control of how you read this book.

So here it is—an unbiased but highly opinionated look at the best and worst the most notable marketing gurus have to offer. We wish you good reading and success in meeting your company's marketing challenges. If you have comments about *The Guru Guide™ to Marketing* or would like to learn about other *Guru Guides™* as they become available, please visit our web site at http://www.jboyett.com or e-mail us at Boyett@jboyett.com.

Joseph H. Boyett
Jimmie T. Boyett

The Guru Guide™
to Marketing

Harry Beckwith, author of *Selling the Invisible*
Neil H. Borden, author of *The Economic Effects of Advertising*
Marc Braunstein, coauthor of *Deep Branding on the Internet*
Darren Bridger, coauthor of *The Soul of the New Consumer*
Kevin J. Clancy, coauthor of *Counterintuitive Marketing*
George S. Day, author of *The Market Driven Organization*
Seth Godin, author of *Permission Marketing*
Ian Gordon, author of *Relationship Marketing*
Robert D. Hisrich, author of *Marketing*
Philip Kotler, author of *Kotler on Marketing*
Peter C. Krieg, coauthor of *Counterintuitive Marketing*
Edward H. Levine, coauthor of *Deep Branding on the Internet*
Jay Conrad Levinson, author of *Mastering Guerrilla Marketing*
David Lewis, coauthor of *The Soul of the New Consumer*
Chuck Martin, coauthor of *Max-e-Marketing in the Net Future*
Mary Modahl, author of *Now or Never*
Frederick Newell, author of *Loyalty.com*
Faith Popcorn, coauthor of *EVEolution*
Stan Rapp, coauthor of *Max-e-Marketing in the Net Future*
Don Schultz, author of *Communicating Globally*
Evan I. Schwartz, author of *Digital Darwinsim*
Lars Tvede, coauthor of *Marketing Strategies for the New Economy*
Fred Wiersema, author of *The New Market Leaders*
Sergio Zyman, author of *The End of Marketing as We Know It*

The Future of Marketing

Peruse the marketing literature of the last few years and you will find some extraordinary statements.

- The age of mass marketing is dead.[1]
- Marketing is, for all practical purposes, dead.[2]
- Forget everything you know about mass marketing—it's over. . . . Stick a fork in it—it's done. Mass marketing is over.[3]
- Brand . . . is the refuge of the ignorant . . . [Today] brand has absolutely no hold on the loyalty of a customer.[4]
- The marketing function is being marginalized to advertising and PR.[5]
- Traditional marketing is not dying—It's dead! . . . Old style marketing is dead. It is as dead as Elvis.[6]

What's going on here? Is marketing really dead? Of course not. Otherwise, this would be a very short book.

Death-of-marketing gurus rationalize their hyperbole by explaining that marketing is in the throes of fundamental change. For example, David Lewis and Darren Bridger, authors of *The Soul of the New Consumer,* say that marketing is going through what the American author and poet Shel Silverstein called a *Tesarac.*

During a Tesarac, society becomes increasingly chaotic and confusing before reorganizing itself in ways that no one can accurately predict or easily anticipate. It is an era when, in the words of MIT's Shelley Turkle: "Old things are dead or dying and one cannot easily make out what will happen next."[7]

Lewis and Bridger note that "the changes taking place as society travels through the Tesarac are so profound that nobody born on one side of this 'wrinkle in time' will ever be able to understand fully what life was like before it occurred."[8] And, they continue, if you get caught on the wrong side of the wrinkle, you will be increasingly overwhelmed by the vastness of the changes that occur while your competitors who make it through the Tesarac are swept onward to an undreamed-of level of success. In short, Tesaracs are heavy things, serious things, things not to be taken lightly, things to be understood. This chapter examines the phenomenon of Tesaracs. What is the marketing Tesarac that we are seeing? What's causing it? What does it portend?

Let's start with the word "marketing" itself. If we want to understand the death or Tesarac of marketing, it is important to get straight just exactly what is said to have died or, at the very least, crossed over a great chasm of history.

> Every few hundred years in Western history there occurs a sharp transformation. . . . Within a few short decades, society rearranges itself—its worldview; its basic values; its societal and political structure; its arts; its key institutions. Fifty years later, there is a new world. And the people born then cannot even imagine the world in which their grandparents lived and into which their own parents were born.
>
> We are currently living through just such a transformation.
>
> *Peter Drucker*[9]

WHAT IS MARKETING?

Quick now. Give us a definition, and no fair running to your closest marketing textbook. What is marketing?

Write your answer here: _____

Need some help? Try these. The American Marketing Association defines "marketing" this way:

> Marketing is the process of planning and executing the conception, pricing, promotion and distribution of ideas, goods, and services to create exchanges that satisfy individual and organizational goals.[10]

Not happy with that definition? Well, how about this rework of the definition offered by Robert D. Hisrich, Mixon Chair and Professor, Weatherhead School of Management at Case Western Reserve University:

Marketing is the process by which decisions are made in a totally interrelated changing business environment on all the activities that facilitate exchange in order that the targeted group of customers is satisfied and the defined objectives accomplished.[11]

Still not satisfied? Boy, you're tough. Okay, we think you'll like this one:

Marketing is about creating satisfactory exchanges via effective and integrated communication with consumers and building relationships with customers and with other publics who could impact organizational performance (the investors, analysts, employees, pressure groups, and so on) by means of effective corporate communication.[12]

Now do you understand what marketing is? No? Well, you are not alone. Pick any marketing textbook and you will probably get a different definition for the term. As one writer put it, "a shelf-full of textbooks on the subject produces a shelf-full of differences."[13]

> Marketing has always been one of the most despised aspects of business.
>
> Seth Godin[14]

Okay. Let's say we can't come up with a definition for marketing that everyone will accept, much less one everyone can understand. Maybe we can at least agree on what marketing is not.

One thing that marketing is not is selling. Who says that? None other than the guru of all marketing gurus, Philip Kotler. Kotler is the S.C. Johnson & Son Distinguished Professor of International Marketing at the Kellogg Graduate School of Management at Northwestern University and author of 15 books including *Marketing Management,* which the *Financial Times* called one of the 50 best business books ever written. Kotler says that the belief that marketing and selling are the same is a common and mistaken view held by both the public and many businesspeople.

Selling, of course, is part of marketing, but marketing includes much more than selling. Peter Drucker observed that "the aim of marketing is to make selling superfluous." What Drucker meant is that marketing's task is to discover unmet needs and to prepare satisfying solutions. When marketing is very successful, people like the new product, word-of-mouth spreads fast, and little selling is necessary.

Marketing cannot be equivalent to selling because it starts long before the company has a product. Marketing is the homework that managers undertake to assess needs, measure their extent and intensity, and determine whether a profitable opportunity exists. Selling occurs only after a product is manufactured. Marketing continues throughout the product's life, trying to find new customers, improve product appeal and performance, learn from product sales results, and manage repeat sales.[15]

Harry Beckwith, author of *Selling the Invisible,* says that equating sales with marketing is particularly problematic in the service sector.

In a free-association test, most people—including most people in business—will equate the word "marketing" with selling and advertising: pushing the goods.

In this popular view, marketing means taking what you have and shoving it down buyers' throats. "We need better marketing" invariably means "We need to get our name out"—with ads, publicity, and maybe some direct mail.

Unfortunately, this focus on getting the word *outside* distracts companies from the *inside,* and from the first rule of service marketing: The core of service marketing is the service itself.

I am not suggesting that if you build a better service, the world will beat a path to your door. Many "better services" are foundering because of rotten marketing. Nor am I suggesting that getting the word out is enough. Getting the word out and attracting people to a flawed service is the preferred strategy for killing a service company.

This is what I am saying: The first principle of service marketing is Guy Kawasaki's first principle of computer marketing:

Get better reality.[16]

Jay Conrad Levinson, author of *Mastering Guerrilla Marketing,* adds that not only is marketing *not* sales, it is *not* a lot of other things.

- **Marketing is not advertising.** Don't think for a second that because you're advertising, you're marketing. There are more than one hundred weapons of marketing. Advertising is one of them. But there are ninety-nine others. If you are advertising, you are simply advertising—you are doing only 1 percent of what you can do.

- **Marketing is not direct mail.** Some companies think they can get all the business they need with direct mail. Mail order firms may be right about this. But most businesses need a plethora of other marketing weapons to support direct mail, to make direct mail succeed. . . .

- **Marketing is not telemarketing.** For business-to-business marketing, few weapons succeed as well as telemarketing—with scripts. You can dramatically improve your telemarketing response by augmenting it with advertising—yes, advertising—and direct mail—yes, direct mail. Marketing is not telemarketing alone.

- **Marketing is not brochures.** Many companies rush to produce a brochure about the benefits they offer, then pat themselves on the back for creating a quality brochure. Is that brochure really all there is to marketing? It's an important aspect of your plan when mixed with ten or fifteen other important parts—but all by itself? Forget it.

- **Marketing does not mean advertising only in the Yellow Pages.** Most, and I do mean most, companies in the U.S. run a Yellow Pages ad and figure that it takes care of their marketing. Advertising in the Yellow Pages only is sufficient for 5 percent of all businesses. For the other 95 percent, it's a disaster in the form of marketing ignorance. Use a Yellow Pages ad as part of your arsenal—but only as part.

- **Marketing is not show business.** There's no business like show business, and that includes marketing. Think of marketing as sell business, as create-a-desire business, as motivation business. [Marketers] aren't in the entertainment business—marketing is not meant to entertain.

- **Marketing is not a stage for humor.** If you use humor in your marketing, people will recall your funny joke, but not your compelling offer. If you use humor, your campaign will be funny the first and maybe the second time. After that, the humor will be grating and will hinder the very concept that makes marketing successful—repetition.

- **Marketing is not an invitation to be clever.** You don't want potential customers to remember the cleverness of your marketing—it's your offer they should remember. Cleverness is a marketing vampire, sucking attention away from your offer. . . .

- **Marketing is not a miracle worker.** More money has been wasted because marketers expected miracles than because of any other misconception. Expect miracles, get ulcers. Marketing is the best investment in America if you do it right, and doing it right requires planning and patience.[17]

> Anything that doesn't get results isn't really marketing, it's B.S. . . . and very expensive B.S.
>
> *Sergio Zyman*[18]

To sum up, we know so far that marketing is hard, some would say nearly impossible, to define, but that it is not sales, advertising, direct mail, telemarketing, brochures, Yellow Pages, show business, a stage for humor, an invitation to be clever, complicated, or a miracle worker. So, what is it? Let's take a different approach. If we can't define marketing, maybe we can specify key marketing activities and then see how our gurus say they have changed. These key marketing activities include the "Four Ps," or what is commonly known as the "marketing mix."

THE FOUR PS

In the late 1940s, a professor at the Harvard Business School by the name of Neil Borden coined the phrase "marketing mix" to refer to a number of activities that, he said, marketers could employ to influence a customer's purchasing decision.[19] For example, a marketer in a pharmaceutical company might undertake a number of activities to try to influence physicians' choices of prescriptions ranging from print and media advertisement, to direct sales calls, to offering product samples, to sponsoring medical conferences, and so on. Obviously, there are a large number of such marketing activities, and the specifics vary by company and industry. The important thing, said Borden, is that marketers identify the activities in their "marketing mix" and coordinate them to achieve maximum results. (See Exhibit 1.1 for a list of elements of the marketing mix for manufacturers and Exhibit 1.2 for a list of forces that Borden said governed the mixing of the marketing elements.) In short, said Borden, it is useful to think of the marketing executive as essentially "a 'mixer of ingredients,' one who is constantly engaged in fashioning creatively a mix of marketing procedures and policies in his efforts to produce a profitable enterprise."[20]

As you might expect, marketing professors and assorted gurus got excited about this idea of companies having a marketing mix, maybe because it was easier to explain to students and corporate clients than their defini-

---

EXHIBIT 1.1. Elements of the Marketing Mix for Manufacturers

1. **Product Planning**—policies and procedures relating to
   a) Product lines to be offered—qualities, design, and so on.
   b) Markets to sell—whom, where, when, and in what quantity.
   c) New product policy—research and development program.
2. **Pricing**—policies and procedures relating to
   a) Price level to adopt.
   b) Specific prices to adopt (odd-even, etc.).
   c) Price policy—for example, one-price or varying price, price maintenance, use of list prices, and so forth.
   d) Margins to adopt—for company, for the trade.
3. **Branding**—policies and procedures relating to
   a) Selection of trademarks.
   b) Brand policy—individualized or family brand.
   c) Sale under private label or unbranded.
4. **Channels of Distribution**—policies and procedures relating to
   a) Channels to use between plant and consumer.
   b) Degree of selectivity among wholesalers and retailers.
   c) Efforts to gain cooperation of the trade.
5. **Personal Selling**—policies and procedures relating to
   a) Burden to be placed on personal selling and the methods to be employed in
      1) Manufacturer's organization.
      2) Wholesale segment of the trade.
      3) Retail segment of the trade.
6. **Advertising**—policies and procedures relating to
   a) Amount to spend—that is, the burden to be placed on advertising.
   b) Copy platform to adopt.
      1) Product image desired.
      2) Corporate image desired.
      3) Mix of advertising—to the trade, through the trade, to consumers.
7. **Promotions**—policies and procedures relating to
   a) Burden to place on special selling plans or devices directed at or through the trade.
   b) Form of these devices for consumer promotions, for trade promotions.
8. **Packaging**—policies and procedures relating to
   a) Formulation of package and label.

(continued)

EXHIBIT 1.1. **(continued)**

9. **Display**—policies and procedures relating to
   a) Burden to be put on display to help effect sale.
   b) Methods to adopt to secure display.
10. **Servicing**—policies and procedures relating to
    a) Providing service needed.
11. **Physical Handling**—policies and procedures relating to
    a) Warehousing.
    b) Transportation.
    c) Inventories.
12. **Fact-Finding and Analysis**—policies and procedures relating to
    a) Securing, analysis, and use of facts in marketing operations.

Source: Neil H. Borden, "The Concept of the Marketing Mix," Journal of Advertising Research, June 1964, p. 4.

EXHIBIT 1.2. **Market Forces Bearing on the Marketing Mix**

1. **Consumers' Buying Behavior,** as determined by their
   a) Motivation in purchasing.
   b) Buying habits.
   c) Living habits.
   d) Environment (present and future, as revealed by trends, for environment influences consumers' attitudes toward products and their use of them).
   e) Buying power.
   f) Number (i.e., how many).
2. **Trade's Behavior**—wholesalers' and retailers' behavior as influenced by
   a) Their motivations.
   b) Their structure, practices, and attitudes.
   c) Trends in structure and procedures that portend change.
3. **Competitors' Position and Behavior,** as influenced by
   a) Industry structure and the firm's relation thereto.
      1) Size and strength of competitors.
      2) Number of competitors and degree of industry concentration.
      3) Indirect competition—that is, from other products.
   b) Relation of supply to demand—oversupply or undersupply.
   c) Product choices offered consumers by the industry, that is, quality, price, service.
   d) Degree to which competitors compete on price vs. nonprice bases.
   e) Competitors' motivations and attitudes—their likely response to the actions of other firms.
   f) Trends, technological and social, portending change in supply and demand.

(continued)

EXHIBIT 1.2. **(continued)**

---

4. **Governmental Behavior**—controls over marketing:
   a) Regulations over products.
   b) Regulations over pricing.
   c) Regulations over competitive practices.
   d) Regulations over advertising and promotion.

Source: Neil H. Borden, "The Concept of the Marketing Mix," Journal of Advertising Research, *June 1964, p. 5.*

---

tions of marketing. The downside of talking about marketing mix was that there were literally hundreds, maybe even thousands, of activities that could be included in the mix. It was easy for students and company executives to get so absorbed in the details that they missed the point of the marketing gurus' beautiful theory, as was often the case. What the gurus needed was a good old-fashioned classificatory schema—a way of boiling all the details down into a simple little phrase, preferably one consisting of words all beginning with the same letter.

Jerome McCarthy, an award-winning marketing professor and consultant, proposed a decidedly simple and, most important, easily remembered solution. The marketing mix in every company, he said, consisted essentially of the four Ps: *product, place, promotion,* and *price.* Those were the marketing activities that had to be planned and executed in concert if a company were to reap the maximum return for its marketing buck.

Each P in the Four Ps stood for a number of specific marketing activities as follows:[21]

Product—choosing the right one for the target customer
    Accessories
    Brand name
    Breadth and depth of line
    Design
    Features
    Guarantee
    Installation
    Instructions
    Packaging
    Product variety
    Quality
    Returns

Services
Sizes
Warranties

Place—reaching the target customer
Assortments
Coverage
Distribution channels—retailers,
    wholesalers, representatives
Inventory
Kinds of middlemen
Locations
Market exposure
Transportation
Warehousing

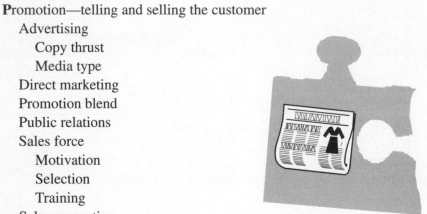

Promotion—telling and selling the customer
Advertising
    Copy thrust
    Media type
Direct marketing
Promotion blend
Public relations
Sales force
    Motivation
    Selection
    Training
Sales promotion

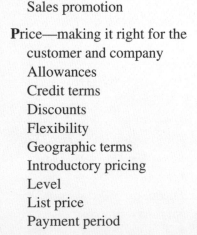

Price—making it right for the
customer and company
Allowances
Credit terms
Discounts
Flexibility
Geographic terms
Introductory pricing
Level
List price
Payment period

So, there you have it. What do marketers do? They "mix" the:

Product—its characteristics, functions and benefits.
Place—how the product should be distributed.
Promotion—what should be spent on advertising, publicity, etc.
Price—how much to charge and whether there should be sales or discounts.

It couldn't be simpler. Of course, not all of our gurus are happy with the Four Ps. Kotler notes that some critics of the schema argue that it underemphasizes important marketing activities as follows:

1. **Where are services?** Just because they don't begin with a P doesn't justify omitting them. The answer is that services such as taxi rides and haircuts are products too. They are called *service products*. And services accompanying a product, such as delivery, installation, and training are also components of the product. Some scholars and practitioners prefer the word "offerings" to "product." Offerings would convey a more general meaning.

2. **Where is packaging?** Isn't packaging one of the key competitive elements in consumer marketing? Marketers would answer that packaging is also part of the product and doesn't need to be listed as a fifth P.

3. **Where is personal selling?** Isn't the sales force of key importance in business marketing? Marketers treat the sales force as a tool in the promotion **P**. Their argument is that promotional tools are numerous and often can substitute for each other. For example, a direct-mail sales letter could be described as a "salesman with wings."[22]

Not only do Kotler and others feel that the Four Ps underemphasize certain activities, but they also argue that since the 1960s additional Ps have become important. For example, Kotler suggests the addition of a fifth and sixth P—**P**olitics and **P**ublic opinion.

- **P**olitics. Political activity can greatly influence sales. If laws are passed banning cigarette advertising, this hurts cigarette sales. If laws require steel companies to install pollution control equipment, this will increase the sale of pollution control equipment. Therefore marketers may want to use lobbying and political activity to affect market demand.

- **P**ublic opinion. The public moves through new moods and attitudes that can affect their interest in certain products and services. At different times, the U.S. public turned away from beef consumption, milk consumption, and other activities. Companies selling beef and milk do not stand idly by. They finance campaigns to influence people to feel safer in buying and consuming their products.[23]

Faith Popcorn, author of *EVEolution,* adds that if you market to women—and she notes that women make 80 percent of all purchasing decisions today—then you should consider adding a seventh P to your marketing mix—**P**olicy—which she says includes any and all of the following activities that women, in particular, care about:

The personal ethics of your owners and managers.

How you treat all your employees.

How you treat women and minority employees.

The number of women and minorities who hold corporate offices.

How much money top executives make.

What kind of perks top executives receive.

The salary gap between the highest paid man and woman.

How much money your CEO gives to political campaigns. And to which candidates.

Who you give charitable donations to and how much.

Your environmental record.

The origin of the materials you source and how you source them.

Your distribution policies (for instance, not opening locations in tough inner-city neighborhoods).

The policies of your outside resources, like your bank and law firm.

Whether you give reporters and consumers on-demand access to inspect your factories and offices.[24]

Lars Tvede, coauthor of *Marketing Strategies for the New Economy,* suggests that an eighth P might be **P**ace:

Pace refers to the crucial time dimension. We live in the economy of speed. We can order custom configured computers and receive them hours later, or custom configured cars, which arrive by the end of the same week (in Japan, at least). Product development cycles are collapsing, and everything is moving closer and closer to real time as we install chips and networks everywhere.[25]

Next we have Seth Godin, vice president of direct marketing at Yahoo! and author of *Permission Marketing.* In a 2001 article in *Sales & Marketing Management,* Godin offered four new Ps for our consideration. They were:

PERMISSION is the art of marketing to people who want to be marketed to, and doing it with anticipated, personal, and relevant messages. Companies that recognize that the consumer has more power than ever before will consistently defeat those that resent the power of the consumer and do everything they can to diminish it.

PARADIGM is the scary practice of busting the rules of your industry and inventing new rules; rules that make your competition obsolete. While some have turned this into a hackneyed generalization that means nothing, there's actually an imperative facing all smart marketers today: Destroy your industry or watch someone else do it.

PASSALONG (the Ideavirus) involves recognizing the fact that the single best way to grow your business is to help your customers tell other people about your product. Set the stage and get out of the way. The Razor scooter is just one example of a product that grew far faster than traditional marketing would have ever predicted.

And finally, PRACTICE is the scary idea that by testing, measuring, and evolving your product offering, you can grow and change much more quickly than your competition, which is stuck in an old way of doing business. Take a look at your product line, your sales techniques, and your marketing materials. Are they all as good as they could be? How are they going to get better?[26]

Finally, we have Stan Rapp and Chuck Martin, authors of *Max-e-Marketing.* They say that today we need four more Ps—these would be Ps 13 through 16 by our count.

Addressability: How do you identify and reach the best prospects and customers?

Accountability: How easy is it to measure results?

Affordability: How cost effective is it to interact with the customer?

Accessibility: How can you locate the people you want to reach, and are they ready, willing, and able to receive your message?[27]

◆ OUR VIEW

Yes, we recognize these aren't really Ps but more like As. Blame Rapp and Martin. Anyway, there you have it—all you need to know about marketing is contained in these 16 words: **P**roduct, **P**rice, **P**lace, **P**romotion, **P**olitics, **P**ublic opinion, **P**olicy, **P**ace, **P**ermission, **P**aradigm, **P**assalong, **P**ractice, **(P)**addressability, **(P)**accountability, **(P)**affordability, and **(P)**accessibility. Once you get past **P**roduct, **P**rice, **P**lace, and **P**romotion, however, we wonder to what extent our gurus' additions to the schema actually improve it and to what extent they just make it more complex. Still, we can't help but empathize with these gurus' efforts. Things have changed since the 1960s, and the Four Ps don't really work in the same way today. There are problems with every P, as we shall see.

THE PROBLEM WITH THE PS

Product

Place

Promotion

Price

Earlier in this chapter we introduced the Four Ps of marketing. They included:

Product—characteristics, functions, and benefits.

 Place—how the product should be distributed.

 Promotion—what should be spent on advertising and publicity.

 Price—how much to charge and whether to discount.

Our gurus say every P today is a troubled P. Let's look at these problems one by one.

The Problem with *Product*

In the Four-Ps world, marketers conceive of products, research them with customers, undertake various development activities, and then orchestrate product rollouts. Products are bundles of tangible and intangible benefits created by companies for customers. The marketer's task is to put together a product bundle that target customers not only will favor but will be willing to pay a premium price to obtain. To achieve this, the marketer's challenge is to create *relevant* and *distinctive* product differentiation according to one or more of the following types of differences as listed by Kotler:

- **Physical differences** (e.g., features, performance, conformance, durability, reliability, design, style, packaging).
- **Availability differences** (e.g., available from stores or orderable by phone, mail, fax, Internet).
- **Service differences** (e.g., delivery, installation, training, consulting, maintenance, repair).
- **Price differences** (e.g., very high price, high price, medium price, low price, very low price).
- **Image differences** (e.g., symbols, atmosphere, events, media).[28]

Of course, notes Kotler, marketers who were successful in differentiating their products would eventually draw the attention of competitors who would simply copy the product, usually at a lower price. The innovator would then be faced with three choices:

- Lower the price to protect market share and accept lower profits.
- Maintain the price and lose some market share and profits.
- Find a new basis to differentiate the product and maintain the current price.[29]

The latter option, according to Kotler, was the preferable one since it offered the best hope of maximizing long-run profitability.

The biggest challenge facing marketers was dealing with commodity products like fruit, vegetables, salt, sugar, and so on, that did not lend themselves to differentiation as easily as products such as automobiles, furniture, or buildings. In other words, it is much more difficult to show a relevant and distinctive difference between two brands of salt than between two brands of office chairs. Still, says Kotler, smart marketers found a way even to differentiate commodities. He cites five examples:

- **Perdue Chicken:** Frank Perdue decided some years ago to breed chickens in such a way that he could guarantee their tenderness. "It takes a tough man to breed a tender chicken," he would say in his TV ads. Today Perdue branded chicken has a 30 percent market share on the East Coast and sells at a 10 percent premium over unbranded chicken. Perdue's conclusion: "If you can differentiate a dead chicken, you can differentiate anything."
- **Colombian coffee:** Whenever a coffee manufacturer or retailer wants to advertise good coffee, it advertises that it used Colombian coffee. At one time Colombian coffee beans may have been among the best; but cof-

fee beans from Brazil, Argentina, and other places are probably on a par. Nevertheless, the idea still persists, aided by advertising, that Colombian coffee is still the best coffee in the world. Other "commodities" that are differentiated in the mind and earn a premium are Hawaiian pineapples, Idaho potatoes, and Wisconsin cheese.

- **Marlboro Cigarettes:** The flavors of most well-known brands of cigarettes are pretty similar. Many cigarette smokers would not be able to identify the brand of cigarette they are smoking in a blindfold test. This suggests that differentiation often exists in the mind, not in the physical product, which seems to be confirmed by the fact that one brand, Marlboro, enjoys a 30 percent market share worldwide. The chief difference seems to be based on the long-lived advertising campaign identifying the brand with rugged cowboys. By overlaying cigarettes with a strong universally appreciated image, Philip Morris established Marlboros as the world's leading cigarette brand.

- **Absolut Vodka:** By legal definition, all vodka is the same. In a blindfold test, most people would not be able to identify the brand of vodka they drank. Yet one of the world's leading selling brands is Absolut, a brand that comes from Sweden, not from Russia, where vodka consumption is highest. How did Absolut build such a preference for its version of a "commodity"? Primarily through a brilliant advertising campaign where every few months a new Absolut ad appears, created by a different artist showing the famous Absolut bottle lurking somewhere in the picture. Lovers of art and culture want to serve their evening dinner guests with vodka poured from an Absolut bottle. What Absolut did was to enlist the power of "marketing aesthetics."

- **DuPont dacron, nylon, orlon:** DuPont deserves credit for creating brilliant new fibers displaying different properties. In each case it gives them memorable names. After they go off patent, competitors introduce their own version of the fibers, which are essentially similar and typically priced lower. But they cannot give them the brand name DuPont created. And customers still prefer to order dacron, nylon, orlon, etc., even though equivalent and cheaper fibers are available.[30]

So, what is wrong with Product today? Two things, say our gurus. First, consumers don't want products or services, even differentiated ones; they want to blend the two into "prodices." Second, consumers don't want these "prodices" made for them; they want to participate in their cocreation.

Prodices

Frederick Newell, author of *Loyalty.com,* credits the term "prodices" to Lester Wunderman, then chairman of Wunderman, Cato, Johnson, the world's largest direct marketing advertising agency.[31] Wunderman's message essentially was that people want "the service, not the stuff."[32] They want the ability to communicate, not telephones; meals, not foodstuffs; entertainment, not CDs; clean clothes, not laundry detergent; healthy teeth, not toothpaste. Instead of products or services, said Wunderman, people wanted "prodices"—things that look like products but act like services. Newell predicts that this demand for prodices will only increase and that it means trouble for the tradition-minded marketing Ps. He says:

> In this era of souped-up, stressed-out, overscheduled, high-stress living, Lester Wunderman's prodices will become more and more vital for the winners who want to develop long-term customers. . . . Today's customer wants the service, not the stuff. Winners will find it's the quarter-inch holes, not the quarter-inch drill bits that will develop long-term customers.[33]

Cocreating Value

A second problem for our product **P**, say our gurus, is that marketers are losing control over the products they create. Customers aren't content to have companies create the prodices and shove them out the factory door. Consumers today increasingly want to participate in designing, developing, testing, piloting, providing, installing, and refining the prodices they purchase. Ian Gordon, author of *Relationship Marketing,* explains the new role of customers in product creation this way:

> The product is . . . the output of a process of collaboration that creates the value customers want for each component of the product and associated services. Products are not bundles of tangible and intangible benefits the company assembles because it thinks this is what customers want to buy. Rather, products comprise an aggregation of individual benefits customers have participated in selecting or designing. The customer thus participates in the assembly of an unbundled series of components or modules that together comprise the product or service. The "product" resulting from the collaboration may be unique or highly tailored to the requirements of the

customer, with much more of their knowledge content incorporated into the product than was previously the case.[34]

Gordon asks us to imagine the way GE works with Boeing in designing and developing the jet engines Boeing will buy. "General Electric works with . . . Boeing from the outset of the concept of the plane, to make jet engines capable of Boeing's specification. GE's engines for one Boeing plane differ from another, in part because Boeing's knowledge and direction is incorporated in the design and development process."[35] Now, say our gurus, imagine such customer/company collaboration not just in business-to-business marketing but in all marketing. It changes the nature of the product **P**.

The Problems with *Place*

The place **P** is all about channels of distribution. It used to be that the marketers' and consumers' options about channels were fairly limited, and perhaps more importantly, were almost totally the choice of the marketer. As Kotler notes, every seller really had two basic options—sell the goods directly or sell them through middlemen. For example, if you were a cosmetics company you could sell your product to retailers and have them resell them like Revlon does, or you could sell them directly like Avon does. The same was true of most other products and services. Then something happened in the mid-1990s. Levinson, author of *Mastering Guerrilla Marketing*, calls it "the newest, biggest, most mysterious, most misunderstood, and most promising marketing opportunity in history."[36] Godin adds that it will change marketing forever and that old style marketing will die in its path.[37] This new and mysterious opportunity that will destroy old marketing in its path, as you have probably guessed, is the Internet. The Internet has an impact on all of the Ps (for example, see our later discussion of the pricing **P**), but it most significantly impacts the place **P** because it opens up an entirely new distribution channel. That represents an opportunity but also a threat to marketers. It's an opportunity because it presents marketers with a powerful new channel to pursue to open up sales that might be limited by current distribution methods. For example, Marc Braunstein and Edward Levine, coauthors of *Deep Branding on the Internet,* note that the Internet could help some manufacturers gain more control over the distribution of their goods:

In retail, the trend toward consolidation and large-scale superstores means that relatively few trade buyers, whose loyalties and interests are in deepening their *own* store brands, control the big wholesale purchasing decisions. For manufacturers, who refuse (or are unable) to make the sacrifices these big stores require, the Internet provides an opportunity to wrest back some control by dealing more directly with end users.[38]

On the other hand, say our gurus, the Internet is a threat because it gives the consumer more channel options. Kotler writes that because of the information revolution and Internet, "today's consumers face more ways to obtain a good or service than at any time in history."[39] Competition between these channels becomes intense, as illustrated in the following example from Kotler of a shopper who wants to buy a laptop computer. Today's shopper has multiple channels to access, including the following:

Retail store channel. The shopper can visit a retail store, such as Circuit City or CompUSA, which carries one or more laptop brands. This channel offers the advantage of letting the shopper see and touch each brand and obtain information and advice from the salesperson. It has the disadvantage of imposing travel and time costs on the shopper and normally charging a higher price than might be available through other channels.

Catalog channel. The shopper can examine catalogs from some electronics catalog houses, such as Microcomputers Warehouse or J&R Computer World. The catalogs describe and price different laptops. The shopper can make a toll-free phone call and place an order. . . . The catalog channel has several advantages: ease of ordering; phone service twenty-four hours a day, seven days a week; choice of loaded software; and typically a lower price than buying the same laptop in a retail store. The lower price results from the fact that the catalog house does not rent a retail facility, carry much inventory, or charge a sales tax for out-of-state orders.

Home shopping TV channel. The shopper may view a laptop offering on home shopping TV and place an order. This channel offers ease of demonstrating and ordering the product and possibly a lower price. It has the disadvantage of showing only one brand and a price that must be accepted at that moment, leaving no time for comparison shopping.

Direct manufacturer channel. The shopper may visit the web page of a direct marketer like Dell Computer and order a model equipped with the shopper's desired software. Dell Computer is now selling over $3 million worth of Dell computers a day over the Internet, not counting its sales over the telephone. This direct channel offers a lower computer price than brands sold mainly through retailers, as well as customer-chosen and loaded software. It has the disadvantage that the shopper sees the brand of only one manufacturer at a time.

Electronic intermediary channel. The shopper can go to the web page of an information middleman who presents and compares the features and prices of all the available brands and indicates where they can be bought for the best price. The electronic middleman may receive income from advertisers, a subscription, or a charge per view. The effect of the electronic middleman is to lower the prices of manufacturers, increase customer welfare, and make middleman profit in the process.[40]

More channels—more ways to get the **P**lace right. More channels—more ways to get the **P**lace wrong.

The Problem with Promotion

The promotion **P** is about communicating with the customer through sales promotions, public relations, the sales force, direct marketing, and advertising. The latter is undoubtedly the most glamorous, most exciting, most expensive, and, if you believe our gurus, the most problematic for the promotion **P**. Why? Because, say our gurus, most advertising today, particularly television advertising, just doesn't work. Lewis and Bridger, authors of *The Soul of the New Consumer,* say that the consensus of opinion among researchers over the last decade is that "the power of many television commercials to affect sales ranges from the **insignificant** to the **nonexistent.**"[41] "Christopher Columbus," they write, "would have made a perfect television advertising executive. After all, he set off with no clear idea where he was going, when he arrived he didn't know where he was, and when he returned he didn't know where he'd been—what's more, he did it all on someone else's money!"[42] How bad are many television ads? Here is an example of the results one company obtained from its expensive television ad campaign, as reported by Kevin Clancy and Peter Krieg in their book *Counterintuitive Marketing.* Our gurus would argue that this might be extreme, but it is certainly not atypical.

Three years ago a multinational marketer, concerned about declining sales of its flagship brand, the leading brand in its category for decades, decided to develop and launch a major turnaround campaign. They invited us to help by undertaking a large-scale marketing strategy project, which within five months revealed insights into new and very profitable market targets and a bold and powerful positioning. At this point they asked their advertising agency to create a number of rough commercials that would execute the strategy in different ways. For reasons we'll explain later, the agency came back with only two ideas, which were tested and found wanting. Both were very entertaining, but neither communicated a clear message about the brand or why it was superior to competitors. Not surprisingly, the purchase interest needle, a measure we use to forecast sales, did not move.

We reported our finding to the client and agency and expressed our belief that, while the executions might win a Clio Award for advertising creativity, they were unlikely to win a David Ogilvy Award for advertising effectiveness. They were too ethereal, too image oriented—and their connections to the recommended targeting and positioning strategies were remote at best. To be frank, we couldn't figure out what they were trying to say.

The client, like many, was in a rush to launch the campaign, to put something on the air. He picked one of the two commercials, executed it in finished form, produced a pool-out, and ran the campaign, spending $32 million on television over the next six months.

A year after we had tested the commercials, the client invited us back to his marketing war room to hear a presentation by a well-known advertising tracking company. The client had commissioned the firm to measure the campaign's performance over a six-month period. Both the client and the agency executives were surprised at the tracking report results, and even we were taken aback. Consumer awareness of the company's positioning message after the $32 million investment was not 50 percent, not 5 percent, not even 0.5 percent. It was 0 percent. There was simply no awareness. The tracking firm found no one, not a single person, able to recall anything about the client's brand that reflected the advertising's positioning/message strategy.[43]

Clancy and Krieg write that the advertising agency's management supervisor, who had been listening to the dismal results, never missed a beat, proving that he was undoubtedly the world's most clever spinmeister. Our gurus say they were so amazed at his response that they wrote it down verbatim. It went like this:

THE FUTURE OF MARKETING

If you remember, before we ran the campaign, copy testing suggested that this was a transcendental, image-laden execution. It did not pound home a message for the brand. This kind of advertising probably produces a subliminal, sleeper effect, in which case zero percent awareness may be a good thing. It suggests that the campaign is really working.[44]

Obviously, the company executives were convinced. They continued running the ad for another six months.

So what's the problem with advertising, besides the point that it is often poorly done, as in the above example? Don Schultz says maybe advertising is less effective because consumers have created a 29.8 hour day. That's right. Schultz says many of us, if not most, now pack 29 plus hours into our 24 hour day. How is that possible and how does it impact marketers and advertisers? Here is how Schultz explains it:

The impossible becomes possible because consumers multitask across media.

Most of us multitask. We sit in front of the television with a newspaper, magazine or the current day's mail in hand, glancing occasionally at each. Or, we log onto the Internet with the radio or CD player on at the same time while we flip through Web addresses in a magazine. . . .

Today, media isn't just pervasive; it's all-encompassing and fed by our desire to keep up, be in touch and stay current. . . . [A]ll this media and communication has created a "continuous partial attention" situation among consumers, where sounds, sights and sensations simultaneously invade the senses of all consumers, who try to keep up with the avalanche of input by paying partial attention or scanning the media. As a result, we **don't** pay full attention to any of it and less attention to most of it.[45]

So, even when the ads are well done, we only give them partial attention. That's a big problem for the promotion **P**.

The Problem with *Pricing*

Kotler notes that **P**rice differs from the other elements of the marketing mix in that it is the only one of the four that generates revenue. The others generate costs. Because **P**rice is the revenue generator, marketers obviously want to get it right, and right in this case means setting prices as high as their level of product/service differentiation will allow without impacting volume. In short, writes Kotler, "the firm seeks the revenue level (price times volume) that, when the costs are subtracted, results in the largest profits."[46]

In setting prices, most marketers rely upon one of two methods—cost-based pricing or value-based pricing. Those who use cost-based pricing arrive at the price by adding a markup to their estimated costs of making and marketing the product or delivering the service. Those who use value-based pricing first estimate the most they think the buyer will be willing to pay for the offering and then set the price at just a little less, thereby giving the customer a little "consumer surplus." Kotler notes that management consultants frequently use the cost-based method and set their fees at two and one-half times the consultant's cost figuring that will be enough to cover their total costs and still leave a nice profit. Gurus, on the other hand, use value-based pricing in setting their speaking fees. Otherwise, why would companies pay $15,000, $50,000, or even $100,000 to hear them blather on for an hour or so. (Note: On the other hand, the "consumer surplus" from **our** speaking fees is said to be substantial. Or so we are told.)

Under the P schema, pricing is an art and not a science, but it is relatively straightforward. Essentially, you price by cost or price by value. The problem for the pricing **P**, say our gurus, is that the world has changed. Pricing isn't as straightforward as it used to be. At least three changes have occurred. First, consumers now want to collaborate on setting the price the same way they want to collaborate on developing the prodices. Second, while this may not be new, it is increasingly evident that consumers are decidedly illogical when it comes to price. Finally, consumers have more information about supply and demand and thus are more capable of exercising their logic or illogic when it comes to price.

Pricing Problem #1: Consumers Demand Collaborative Pricing

In his book *Relationship Marketing,* Gordon notes that customers today are no longer satisfied when given a price for a product and told essentially to "take it or leave it." If they participate in the design and development of the product or service offering as increasingly they are insisting upon doing, then consumers also want to participate in setting the price for that product or service. Gordon explains it this way:

> Consumers want to participate in decisions regarding the value they receive and the prices they pay. Give them a standard offering and they will

expect to pay a single price. But offer them options in the product and they will want some more than others, and will pay more for these. Give them a chance to have an even more tailored solution and they might pay more again. Give them options they don't want and they will expect these to be removed and deleted from the price. If the clothes don't fit, don't charge for alterations—just make the clothes fit.[47]

In short, writes Gordon, "just as the product and services are secured in a process of collaboration, so too will the price need to reflect the choices made and the value created from these choices."[48] Not only do customers want to collaborate on price thanks to the Internet and electronic commerce but they have more information at their disposal than ever. That makes them smart negotiators, which is the second problem for the pricing **P**.

Pricing Problem #2: The Dawn of Dynamic Trade

In his book *Digital Darwinism,* Evan I. Schwartz says that the Internet is profoundly changing the pricing models for most businesses.

[The Internet] creates a market in which the value of each piece of merchandise will fluctuate freely and continuously, and buyers and sellers will wield every tool available to them in their struggle to prevail over one another.

This is very different from walking into a store, or any marketplace, seeing a price tag, and deciding whether you want to buy at the posted price. We tend to take this notion of *fixed* retail pricing for granted, as if this was the only way to do things. But fixed pricing, as a practice, is fairly recent and very Western. In the United States, fixed pricing dates back only 125 years, when mass retail pioneers such as Aaron Montgomery Ward and Frank W. Woolworth popularized the practice. And in the marketplaces and bazaars of Turkey, Indonesia, and India, things haven't changed much over time—if there is any posted price at all, it's usually just the starting point for a negotiation.[49]

Schwartz notes that developments in transportation and communication have always affected pricing schemes. It was the growing network of railroads and canals in the mid-1800s that made the mass distribution of mass-produced goods feasible and Ward's and Woolworth's fixed pricing schemes plausible. "Meanwhile," writes Schwartz, "the telegraph became a pervasive business-to-business medium among traders, bankers, investors, merchants, entrepreneurs, and captains of industry. Whereas prices for retail goods became fixed, products such as coal, wheat, and pork bellies became dynamically priced commodities because information about them, especially current prices, could be relayed quickly for the first time."[50]

Communications technology is now allowing a shift in pricing schemes once again. Haggling, bidding, custom costing, and rapid-response pricing are becoming a fixture of e-commerce. While Schwartz and our other gurus don't expect fixed pricing to go away, at least for less expensive mass-produced merchandise, they expect dynamic pricing in which buyers and sellers negotiate in real time to become much more prevalent. As a consequence, say our gurus, in market after market there will be a tendency for prices to fall to their lowest competitive point. E-commerce is creating a business environment that is much more competitive and fluid. Mary Modahl and her colleagues at the e-commerce research firm Forrester Research call this new competitive environment *Dynamic Trade* and warn that companies that fail to understand and adjust to it "will lose control of their prices, revenue streams, and profits as more consumers shop on-line."[51]

In Dynamic Trade, writes Modahl in her book *Now or Never,* both the supply and demand for products and services become more apparent. As a result, prices tend to fall to their lowest competitive point and vary as demand shifts. Modahl says the Internet has two key impacts:

1. It increases the consumers' perception of the available supply of goods and services.
2. It allows e-commerce companies to collect more accurate and timely information about demand.

Let's look at each of these two impacts.

Pricing Impact #1: The Internet Increases Apparent Supply

Modahl points out that in the traditional marketplace there is a difference between actual supply and the supply that is apparent to the customer.

> When a buyer seeks a product, whether it is information such as news or hard goods like groceries, they go to the market. But the market is only as large as the one that a consumer can reasonably address. To an isolated villager, the "market" is limited to what is piled up in the stalls of local mer-

chants. Similarly, when a woman drives in her sedan to the mall, she chooses a blouse from among the stores in the mall. If she wants to, she can drive another forty-five minutes to a discount store like TJ Maxx or Frugal Fannies, where it is possible (though she can't be sure beforehand) that she'll find the exact same blouse at 50 percent off. But most women won't take the time to go find out.

In the cases of both the villager and the mall shopper, the actual supply of whatever they were seeking is many times larger than the supply around which they must make their purchase decisions. However, it simply isn't practical for consumers to locate and include all of the actual supply when making their decisions. Instead, consumers make their purchases from the supply they can easily find—the apparent supply.

While there is no evidence that the Internet increases the actual supply of goods in any consumer market, it clearly increases the apparent supply. . . . Once on-line . . . consumers can visit both upscale shops and discounters without moving an inch. In addition, new price-comparison engines sift through hundreds of web sites, searching for the best price on a given item. As a result, the Internet is driving up the quantity of goods that consumers can see and driving down prices.[52]

The actual difference in prices for identical products charged by e-commerce and traditional retailers can be considerable, says Modahl. For example, she reports on an experiment undertaken by Forrester in which the researchers used price-comparison software readily available to consumers to check prices on a CD, a kitchen appliance, and a personal digital assistant. On average the e-commerce sites were quoting prices 15 percent below their brick-and-mortar counterparts. The CD was available on-line for 37 percent less. Price differences such as these and, more importantly, writes Modahl, the ease with which consumers can discover these differences is certain to "cause real problems for companies whose products are sold at different rates in markets separated by geography or information. . . . Price differences based on poor information or geographic distance won't stand up very well in the Internet economy."[53]

Pricing Impact #2: The Internet Makes It Possible for Companies to Tie Prices Closer to Demand

According to Modahl, most traditional companies have sought to measure demand for their products and services. For example, grocery stores and other retailers regularly collect point-of-sale data in an effort to monitor what is selling and what is not. The problem for traditional businesses has always been one of getting such information in a timely manner. In many companies, even today, point-of-sale data may not show up in printed reports until weeks after the sales have occurred.

In contrast, many or most e-commerce companies collect and make available to decision makers point-of-sale data as the sales occur. Companies like Amazon.com actually measure demand in advance of sales by taking prepublication orders for books and music CDs. Others, such as Priceline, let consumers submit a kind of "request for proposal"—"I would like to purchase a one-way coach ticket from New York to LA on this airline for $$$$"—and allow companies to respond—"At this airline we have a seat available on this flight for $$$$." Modahl predicts that the availability of such current information will force all companies to change the way they measure demand and set prices.

> In the past, suppliers set the market agenda, determining which products to sell and at what price. The successful companies were those that did a good job of estimating future demand. Of course, no company ever estimated demand exactly right, so gaps existed. Sometimes, companies missed the opportunity to sell, when demand ran higher than available supply. Other times, they made more than the market wanted and had to write off inventory. Using primitive tools like monthly retail reports, companies tried to adjust to demand, but their ability to react was limited. . . .
>
> On the Internet, companies will measure and respond to current demand: what consumers want now. As they do, they will change the dynamics of competition. When consumers set the agenda, it is more important for companies to be able to respond quickly than it is for them to predict well. In Dynamic Trade, companies that can adjust the prices and quantities of goods—their supply—more closely to consumers' current demand will succeed. This eliminates the gaps between what consumers want and what companies can offer them.[54]

Modahl predicts that the consumer industries most vulnerable to these demand affects will be the ones that are characterized by temporary hits or fads (such as movies and music), focus on events (such as sports and entertainment), or operate on a seasonal pattern (such as fashion and toys). Regardless, they represent a capital P problem for the pricing **P**.

BLEAK REALITIES, NEANDERTHAL PRACTICES, AND OTHER THINGS THAT GO BUMP IN THE MARKETING NIGHT

Discouraged? Want to feel even worse? Well, read on. We'll close out this uplifting chapter with some more of what our gurus call marketing's bleak realities before looking at the more positive future of marketing. We will start by debunking some very popular winning marketing practices courtesy of Kotler. Then we will review five market transitions that George Day says you may not like but that you can't avoid.

"Winning" Formulas that Don't Win

Here are nine popular "winning" marketing practices that you have probably heard some guru advocate. All of them sound good—one-liner guarantees of marketing success. The problem, says Kotler, is they just don't work today.

#1. Winning through Higher Quality

So, what's wrong with that? Customers like quality products. Wasn't that what the Total Quality Management stuff was all about? Surely quality still works, but Kotler maintains that there are four problems with this approach:

> First, quality has a lot of meanings. If an automobile company claims good quality, what does it mean? Do its cars have more starting reliability? Do they accelerate faster? Do the car bodies wear better over time? Customers care about different things, so a quality claim without further definition doesn't mean much.
>
> Second, people often can't tell a product's quality by looking at it. Consider buying a television receiver. You go into Circuit City and see a hundred different sets with the picture on and the sound blaring. You look at a few popular brands that you favor. The picture quality is similar with most receivers. The casings may differ but hardly tell you anything about the set's reliability. You don't ask the salesperson to open the back of the set to inspect the quality of the components. In the end, you have at best an image of quality without any evidence.
>
> Third, most companies are catching up to each other in quality in most markets. When that happens, quality is no longer a determinant of brand choice.

Fourth, some companies are known to have the highest quality, such as Motorola when it touts its 6 sigma quality. But are there enough customers who need that quality level and will pay for it? And what were Motorola's costs of getting to 6 sigma quality? It is possible that getting to the highest quality level costs too much.[55]

#2. Winning through Better Service

Fine, says Kotler, but what is good service? You are in a restaurant. The waiter jumps to your table as soon as you sit down, takes your order, and rushes it to the kitchen. Before you have the chance to take a sip of water, he's back with your meal. Your glass gets half full. He's there in an instant to refill it. As soon as you finish a dish, he whisks the plate off the table. As you take your last mouthful of food, he deposits your check in front of you. Was it good service or did you feel rushed? The problem with winning through better service, says Kotler, is that customers define service differently.

#3. Winning through Lower Prices

IKEA does it and so does Wal-Mart. If you can't win through quality or service, why not just be the cheapest? Fine, says Kotler, but remember the Yugo automobile? It had a low price, but it also had low quality and disappeared. Low prices aren't enough. You still have to have a level of product quality and service. But what level?

#4. Winning through High Market Share

Market-share leaders make more money, right? Market-share leaders enjoy scale economies, right? Market-share leaders have higher brand recognition and an easier time attracting first-time buyers, right? Not so right, says Kotler. A&P was the largest supermarket chain in America but had low profits. IBM, Sears, and GM have all struggled at times, although they were the market-share leaders in their industries.

#5. Winning through Mass Customization

Advocates of mass customization maintain that if you tailor your product or service to meet each customer's needs he or she will beat a path to your door. Kotler counters that while mass customization has worked for some companies, it has been a costly and unprofitable strategy for others.

#6. Winning through Continuous Product Improvement

Make your laundry detergent a little better each year. Make your razor blade a little sharper or smoother. That's the ticket to marketing success! Maybe, says Kotler, but as far as the consumer is concerned that "little bit better" might not have much value. Some products just don't have room for much improvement, or at least for enough improvement to make a difference.

#7. Winning through Product Innovation

"Innovate or evaporate," or so the advice goes. Sure it works, says Kotler. Sony, 3M, and others do it, but Kotler maintains that product innovation doesn't work for all companies, or even for most, since 80 percent of new products fail. You may have to innovate to avoid evaporating, but chances are that innovating is going to lose you a lot of money.

#8. Winning through Entering High-Growth Markets

High-growth markets are the glamour markets—solid-state electronics, biotechnology, robotics, telecommunications, and so on. Companies have made fortunes in these markets, but Kotler warns that others have also lost fortunes. High-growth markets are fast markets, and you have to do a lot of running just to keep up. Don't expect to enjoy the profits from your current offering. Those will have to be invested in developing your next offering.

#9. Winning through Exceeding Customer Expectations

Don't just satisfy the customer, delight them—WOW! them. That'll work. Right, says Kotler, it will work this time, but what about the next time? The next time that customer does business with you, the delightful-level service becomes the expected level of service. The WOW! becomes the norm. Then what do you do, ask Kotler? Do you offer them "Delight-Plus?" How about "WOW" cubed? "The problem," he writes, "is that when a customer's expectations are exceeded, he has higher expectations next time. The task of exceeding the higher expectations gets more difficult and more costly. Ultimately, the company must settle for just meeting the latest expectation. Put another way, many of today's customers want the highest quality, added services, great convenience, customization, return privileges, guarantees—all at the lowest price. Clearly each company has to decide which of these many customer wants it can meet profitably."[56]

So much, then, for one-line, instant-fix marketing schemes.

Troubling Transitions

George Day holds the Geoffrey T. Boisi Professorship in the Department of Marketing at the Wharton School of the University of Pennsylvania. In his book *The Market Driven Organization,* he identifies five transitions that he says "are having—or will have—especially disruptive effects on the ability of companies to stay aligned with their markets and keep delivering superior customer value."[57] Think of them as transitions that are particularly troublesome for traditional marketing. (See Exhibit 1.3 for a similar list of "new realities" offered by Fred Wiersema, author of *The New Market Leaders.*) They are as follows:[58]

Transition #1: More Supply and Less Differentiation

Day says that weak demand, trade liberalization, cheap financing, and regulatory changes have resulted in an abundance of supply that is putting price pressures on every company. At the same time, the diffusion of technology is making it easier for competitors to copy each other quickly. In short, whether you are in automobiles, consumer electronics, athletic shoes, or almost any other market, you likely have a lot of competitors and you can be sure that they will watch every innovation you try whether in marketing or product/service design closely and, if it seems to work, will soon copy it.

Transition #2: More Global and Less Local

According to Day, we are seeing a steady and continuing progression from distinct and self-contained local or national markets to linked global markets. From books to CDs to mortgages, consumers are no longer tied to their local geographic area. They can now literally shop worldwide. As a result, says Day, local presence, geography, and real estate are becoming less important.

Transition #3: More Competition and More Collaboration

Chances are you have more competitors today than a decade ago, and, says Day, the competition that you experience is almost certainly more intense.

At the same time you are likely finding the need to develop more collaborative relationships with rivals. Your company's roles as customer, supplier, and rival are becoming increasingly blurred. Day cites the example of Sony and Philips, who worked together to develop common optical media standards and to supply components to each other. Such competitor/collaborator arrangements, writes Day, are becoming more common.

Transition #4: More Relating and Less Transacting

Day writes that as companies recognize the bottom-line benefits of customer retention we are seeing a major shift in marketing focus away from capturing new customers to keeping existing customers, particularly the most valuable ones. Companies are beginning to organize around customers rather than products or geographic markets in order to focus more on developing and maintaining customer relationships over the long term.

Transition #5: More Sense-and-Respond and Less Make-and-Sell

Markets today, says Day, are changing more quickly and behaving less predictably than in the past. As a result, traditional make-to-forecast firms with their hierarchical structures and command-and-control systems are finding it more difficult to compete. Day predicts that the future belongs to "sense-and-respond" organizations. He writes, "These market-driven companies win by establishing a dialogue with each customer and providing personalized responses to their unpredictable requirements. They have the ability to search out, capture and intercept clues about emerging customer requirements, and then build to order by deploying modular capabilities that can be combined and reused in many different ways. These firms also learn from each interaction . . . [so] . . . the relationship created through these interactions keeps getting smarter."[59]

EXHIBIT 1.3. Fred Wiersema's New Realities

In his book *The New Market Leaders*, Fred Wiersema offers six new realities that he says are causing a supply glut and customer shortage in most markets.

Competitors proliferate—Like George Day, Wiersema notes that most companies are facing increased competition. He adds that this competition often comes from unexpected sources. For example, Boeing is now loaning money to customers to buy its

(continued)

EXHIBIT 1.3. (continued)

planes, thus making Boeing a competitor of banks. In turn, banks are selling stock and stockbrokers are becoming financial advisors.

All secrets are open secrets—Don't expect your best practices to remain proprietary very long. Your competitors are becoming more adept at learning your secrets and adapting them for their own purposes. Everybody is imitating everybody else shamelessly.

Innovation is universal—Product life cycles keep getting shorter and innovation is now commonplace. Wiersema says it has gotten so frantic that customers are inundated with products (twenty-three thousand new packaged goods last year alone) and suppliers are dizzy from pursuit of the next best thing.

Information overwhelms and depreciates—We are all swamped with information, writes Wiersema. "Junk mail fills mailboxes; magazines stuffed with ads run as long as five hundred pages. . . . Advertisers stamp their logos on every conceivable surface, from cruising blimps and ski-lift towers to e-mail screens and bus roofs. Some television markets offer two hundred cable channels. An Internet surfer discovers a Milky Way or random data, much of it conflicting and some of it stupefying." Our problem today isn't how to generate information, it is how to digest it and make sense of it.

Easy growth makes hard times—Carmakers produce 30 to 40 percent more cars than can be sold. Airlines keep adding seats and packing more passengers on planes. The telecommunications industry invests frantically in network infrastructure to such an extent that bandwidth vastly exceeds demand. In industry after industry, technology makes it possible to make more things faster. In business today, writes Wiersema, growth is sacred. It also leads to overcapacity, a shortage of customers, fewer sales, lower prices, and falling margins.

Customers have less time than ever—"Of all the realities," writes Wiersema, "this may be the most important." After working, sleeping, eating, and doing chores people just have very little time left for such things as listening to your ad or even shopping for your product. Your biggest competitor, says Wiersema, might not be your rival but the demands on your customers' time. Pressed for time and overstimulated by too many choices, people cope by tuning out. Your marketing message has to catch their attention in a nanosecond because that's all the time they will give you. They are not paying attention. They are scanning.

Source: Fred Wiersema, The New Market Leaders: Who's Winning and How in the Battle for Customers (New York: Free Press, 2001), pp. 48–58.

So there you have it. Marketing is dead or dying. The Ps are in trouble. Quick-fix marketing schemes don't work, and we are in the middle of all kinds of troubling market transitions that turn everything inside out and upside down. It's enough to give any marketer a chronic case of indigestion and a migraine chaser. Need something to pick you up? How about this—

here are a few declarations from our gurus that we are sure all marketers will find comforting:

Marketing is important!

Marketing is essential!

Marketing is strategic!

Marketing is central to business!

Marketing is THE only path to growth!

Marketing is the engine that drives performance!

Clancy and Krieg, coauthors of *Counterintuitive Marketing,* are the source of those declarations, but they could just as well have come from any of our other marketing gurus. Like Clancy and Krieg, most of our marketing gurus quote Peter Drucker, the acknowledged guru of all business gurus. Drucker proclaimed over 30 years ago that there were only two basic functions of business—marketing and innovation and that "marketing is **the** distinguishing, unique function of the business."[60] (Emphasis ours.) In fact, said Drucker, marketing is so basic to business that an organization with no marketing or in which marketing is only incidental isn't really a business at all and shouldn't be managed as if it were. Our gurus would heartily agree. Of course that means that marketing can't be allowed to die, or even get sick, and that something must be done to save it from the evils we have just outlined. But what?

As you might guess, our gurus have some answers. Some say the road to marketing salvation is through branding; some say it comes through managing customer relationships; others say the path to righteousness is through building customer equity; and some say well-being is found in word-of-mouth buzz. We'll get to all of these in the remaining chapters, but for now let's sum up the key ideas we have discussed so far.

KEY POINTS

- Marketing may not be dead or even dying, but it is in the throes of fundamental change.

- Marketing is not selling, advertising, direct mail, telemarketing, brochures, and any of a number of other things people think it is.

- The key marketing activities are the Four Ps—**P**roduct, **P**rice, **P**romotion, and **P**lace.

- Additional marketing activities include **P**olitics, **P**ublic opinion, **P**olicy, **P**ace, **P**ermission, **P**aradigm, **P**assalong, **P**ractice, **(P)**addressability, **(P)**accountability, **(P)**affordability, **(P)**accessibility.

- People today want prodices—things that look like products but act like services, e.g., quarter-inch holes, not quarter-inch drill bits.

- Customers today want to be involved in cocreating value, so marketers have less control over their products.

- The Internet gives the customer more sales channels from which to purchase products or services.

- Most advertising today, particularly television advertising, doesn't result in increased sales. The affect of television advertising on sales ranges from insignificant to nonexistent.

- Consumers are demanding collaborative pricing and have much more information about supply and demand so that they are in a better position to negotiate prices.

- So-called "winning marketing formulas" such as the following no longer win:

  - Winning through quality.

  - Winning through better service.

  - Winning through lower prices.

  - Winning through high market share.

  - Winning through mass customization.

- Winning through continuous product improvement.

- Winning through product innovation.

- Winning through entering high-growth markets.

- Winning through exceeding customer expectations.

⊶ We are in the midst of five troubling transitions:

- More supply and less differentiation.

- More global and less local.

- More competition and more collaboration.

- More relating and less transacting.

- More sense-and-respond and less make-and-sell.

David Aaker, author of *Managing Brand Equity*

Harry Beckwith, author of *The Invisible Touch*

Kevin Clancy, coauthor of *Counterintuitive Marketing*

Steven Cristol, coauthor of *Simplicity Marketing*

David F. d'Alessandro, author of *Brand Warfare*

Scott Davis, author of *Brand Asset Management*

Frank Delano, author of *The Omnipowerful Brand*

Marc Gobé, author of *Emotional Branding*

Duane Knapp, coauthor of *The Brand Mindset*

Philip Kotler, author of *Kotler on Marketing*

Peter Krieg, coauthor of *Counterintuitive Marketing*

Adam Morgan, author of *Eating the Big Fish*

Bernd Schmitt, coauthor of *Marketing Aesthetics*

Peter Sealey, coauthor of *Simplicity Marketing*

Alex Simonson, coauthor of *Marketing Aesthetics*

Daryl Travis, author of *Emotional Branding*

Jack Trout, coauthor of *Differentiate or Die*

Sergio Zyman, coauthor of *Building Brandwidth*

2

All You Need Is a Brand

O kay, which would you rather market:

Coca-Cola or Joe's Cola?
Intel or Peter's Pretty Good Processors?
Walt Disney World or Wally World?

If you are like most marketers you said the former of each of these. If you chose Joe's Cola, Peter's Processors, and Wally's World, you might be considered—well, just a wee bit strange, and, say our gurus, you don't understand the power of **BRAND.** Brand is the Holy Grail, the road to salvation, and the way to triumph over all of the evils we outlined in the last chapter, according to one group of our gurus. One even described his book on branding as "a sure way to reach the 'promised brand.' "[1]

Of course, not everyone is so enthusiastic about brands. For example, Kevin Clancy and Peter Krieg in their book *Counterintuitive Marketing* decry those who would talk so reverentially about such things as "brand attitude," "brand emotions," "brand values," "brand voice," "brand statement," and just brand in general. "Listening to incoherent brandspeak," write Clancy and Krieg, "one might think that all you need to do is take a brand, product, service, maybe even an entire company, and dip it in brand juice. And voilà, something magical happens! You've transformed a nothing, through brand dip alone, into a powerful presence."[2] But enough of such criticism. We come here not to critique branding, but to revere it. We'll start with the most basic of questions, What is a brand?

WHAT IS A BRAND?

Here are a few examples of definitions our gurus offer for the term "brand." (See Exhibit 2.1 for some common misconceptions about the meaning of brand.)

- David Aaker, author of *Managing Brand Equity:*
  - □ A brand is a distinguishing name and/or symbol (such as a logo, trademark, or package design) intended to identify the goods or services of either one seller or a group of sellers, and to differentiate those goods or services from those of competitors. A brand thus signals to the customer the source of the product, and protects both the customer and the producer from competitors who would attempt to provide products that appear to be identical.[3]
- Scott Davis, author of *Brand Asset Management:*
  - □ *Brand* [is] an intangible but critical component an organization "owns" that represents a contract with the customer, relative to the level of quality and value delivered tied to a product or service. A customer cannot have a relationship with a product or a service, but may with a brand.
  - □ A brand is a set of consistent promises. It implies trust, consistency, and a defined set of expectations. A brand helps customers feel more confident about their purchase decision. A brand is an asset and, next to your people, no asset is more important.[4]
- Duane Knapp, coauthor of *The Brand Mindset:*
  - □ [A brand is] the internalized sum of all impressions received by customers and consumers resulting in a distinctive position in their "mind's eye" based on perceived emotional and functional benefits.[5]
- Adam Morgan, author of *Eating the Big Fish:*
  1. **Something that has a buyer and a seller**—the Spice Girls, but not the queen.
  2. **Something that has a differentiating name, symbol, or trademark**—Tide, but not sugar or bleach—but also something that is seen as being differentiated from other like products around it *for reasons other than* its name or trademark—the Los Angeles Police Department, but not the Fourteenth Infantry Division.

3. **Something that has positive and/or negative opinions about it** in consumers' minds for reasons other than its literal product characteristics—Cirque du Soleil, but not Concrete.

4. **Something that is created, rather than naturally occurring—** *The X-Files* and Las Vegas, but not Adam Morgan or the Blue Grass of Kentucky.[6]

- Daryl Travis, author of *Emotional Branding:*
  - □ A brand is an unwritten contract of intrinsic value.
  - □ A brand is an expectation of performance.
  - □ A brand is a covenant of goodness with its users.
  - □ A brand is predictable.
  - □ A brand is an unwritten warrantee.
  - □ A brand is a presentation of credentials.
  - □ A brand is a mark of trust and reduced risks.
  - □ A brand is a reputation.
  - □ A brand is a collection of memories.
  - □ A brand can be—*must be*—more than the sum of all these parts. . . .

  Perhaps the simplest way to think of a brand is to use the metaphor of a handshake. A brand represents the handshake that has been used by generation after generation of ordinary people as the sign of a deal well done.[7]

EXHIBIT 2.1. **Common Misconceptions about Brands**

Scott Davis, author of *Brand Asset Management,* says that many people think the following are appropriate definitions of a brand when in reality these are simply well-executed marketing and selling tactics. They may help bring the brand to life for consumers, but they are not the brand.

- A brand is a tagline like "We bring good things to life."
- A brand is a symbol like the Nike swoosh.
- A brand is a shape like the Absolut bottle or Coke bottle.
- A brand is a spokesperson like Bill Cosby for Jell-O.
- A brand is a sound like Intel's familiar four notes.
- A brand is an actual product or service—Kleenex tissue or Xerox copies or a Sony Walkman.

Source: Scott Davis, Brand Asset Management: Driving Profitable Growth through Your Brands *(San Francisco: Jossey-Bass, 2000), p. 4.*

- David d'Alessandro, author of *Brand Warfare:*
  - By definition, "brand" is whatever the consumer thinks of when he or she hears your company's name. Thanks to the information revolution, "whatever" now includes labor practices, quality controls, environmental record, customer service, and every rumor that wings its way around the Internet.[8]

In short, brand is a hot iron applied to the rump of the product or service that labels it, sets it apart from the herd, and signifies its value. It's what IBM, Coke, Intel, Disney World, Nike, Marlboro, and Martha Stewart have. It's what every company wants, or at least should want, say our gurus. You may ask, What difference can a brand make? A great deal, as it turns out.

WHAT IS THE ADVANTAGE OF HAVING A BRAND?

In his book *Emotional Branding,* Travis tells the story of his friend Harry who Travis says is so vain that "when he looks in the mirror to shave every morning, he blows his reflection a kiss and says, 'Thank you God!'"[9] In spite of failing eyesight and advice from his optometrist, Harry refused reading glasses, fearing they would spoil his perfect image, signal his entry into middle age, and greatly decrease, if not obliterate, his sex appeal. So Harry just went about his business, squinting until one day when he spied in an optometrist's display case a pair of frames with a tag reading "Giorgio Armani." What happened next, recalls Travis, was nothing less than magical:

> When [Harry] first tried on Armani's elegant spectacle frames, he decided that, far from being a handicap, they added a certain *je ne sais quoi* to his noble profile. Wearing them was like playing dress-up with his face. He could see that in a certain light, it wasn't stretching the truth too far to say his Armani's made him look like Gregory Peck in the classic movie *To Kill a Mockingbird.*
>
> The Armani's did the opposite of making him feel like a four-eyed geek. While he decided they gave him the *look* of a Gregory Peck, they made him *feel* like the debonair Marcello Mastroiani, nonchalantly accepting a steamy encounter with the young and nubile Sophia Loren. They might be the most expensive frames in the display case, but out of the dozens of options for sale, he could see no other choice than the Giorgio Armani's. He plunked down his Amex card and ordered four pairs—one for reading at the office, one for

reading at home, one for distance and watching TV, and one tinted for driving. Well over a thousand dollars later and with his Armani's carefully ensconced in their handsome brown, hard-cover cases, Harry was a happy man.[10]

So was Giorgio Armani. After all, Harry's glasses cost no more to make than the cheapest frames in the display case, and they didn't provide him with any better vision. They carried the Armani name, but, notes Travis, chances are that Armani didn't even manufacture them. Harry didn't care. He got his Armani's.

Oh, what a difference a brand makes, and it's not just the Armani brand.

A cup of coffee is a cup of coffee, but what is Starbucks?

A power tool is a power tool, but what is Black & Decker?

A motorcycle is a motorcycle, but what is a Harley?

And so it goes.

Ah, say our gurus, it's the power of **BRAND**, and if you doubt the value of brand, consider the following facts provided by Scott Davis:

- 72 percent of customers say they will pay a 20 percent premium for their brand of choice, relative to the closest competitive brand. 50 percent of customers will pay a 25 percent premium. 40 percent of customers will pay up to a 30 percent premium.
- 25 percent of customers state that price does not matter if they are buying a brand that owns their loyalty.
- Over 70 percent of customers want to use a brand to guide their purchase decision and over 50 percent of purchases are actually brand driven.
- Peer recommendation influences almost 30 percent of all purchases made today, so a good experience by one customer with your brand may influence another's purchase decision.
- More than 50 percent of consumers believe a strong brand allows for more successful new product introductions and they are more willing to try a new product from a preferred brand because of the implied endorsement.[11]

D'Alessandro, author of *Brand Warfare,* says that he frequently runs across people who say they don't pay attention to brands. When he meets these "brand immune" types, d'Alessandro says he gives them a small test. He asks them to imagine that they need to buy a list of things, such as a washing machine, a car, or even underwear. Then he asks them how they would go about making their purchase decision. Inevitably, says d'Alessandro, these self-proclaimed "brand immune" people say they purchase a major brand because that brand makes a good product. Rarely do these people mention doing any research. Instead, they rely on a brand to guide their choice. As d'Alessandro says, we all rely on brands whether we think we do or not.

> The truth is that no matter what is in question—where to send the children to school or what kind of potato chip to buy—no one is capable of pulling out the screwdriver and wrench every time and considering every case on its merits. Life is too complicated for that. So we're conditioned to respond to brands of all kinds. They help us organize our experience and tell us what to pursue and what to reject. And we use these brands not just to make purchasing decisions, but also to make life decisions. . . .
>
> We'd never survive without archetypes, pre-dispositions, and antipathies to give us at least a starting point for comprehending any given situation. Brands are simply the manufactured equivalent of the shorthand we use to interpret the world in general.[12]

What a difference a brand makes.

With a strong brand, writes Davis, all things are possible. You can:

- Charge a premium price.
- Launch new products more cheaply than your competitors.
- Recoup your development costs earlier.
- Cut your acquisition costs for new customers.
- Have higher profitability per customer.
- Exercise more control over your distribution channels. (Who's running things, Martha Stewart or Kmart?)
- More readily seek out cobranding and licensing opportunities. (Who is Disney more likely to license, Hallmark or Joe's "Not-So-Awful" Cards?)
- Leverage your brand across more target segments. (You can have a Marriott Marquis for the high-end business traveler and Courtyard by Marriott for the budget minded.)

And, continues d'Alessandro, there is another benefit to having a strong brand that people don't often think about. A strong brand can help you attract, retain, manage, and motivate the best employees. He says:

> If you ask most people what's most important when they're looking for a job, they'll probably say the following: the pay, the quality of the position they're

offered in terms of interest and prestige, and the character of the work environment. But the truth is, the most capable job seekers will probably sacrifice one of these—or all three—for a chance to work for the best brand.[13]

People know that a company with a strong brand is likely to be a demanding but good place to work. Perhaps more importantly, it is a good place to have worked. Having been part of making or keeping a strong brand strong looks awfully good on the old resume.

Of course, you have to have a strong brand to reap all these benefits. But what makes a brand strong, and how do you build one? It just so happens our gurus have given some thought to these questions.

> [A] white T-shirt . . . which is 100 percent cotton and of the highest quality can sell for $3 or for $30. It can be sold in a deep-discount retail store or a high-end prestigious boutique. How much that white T-shirt costs and where it is sold is directly linked to the brand name stitched inside its collar.
>
> Scott Davis[14]

WHAT MAKES A STRONG BRAND?

Before we talk about what our gurus say makes a brand strong, maybe we should begin by getting straight what it is that our gurus mean when they use the word "strong." Most are referring to something called brand equity. Your brand is strong if its brand equity is high. We know that doesn't help much, but bear with us.

Gurus Kevin Clancy and Peter Krieg say they first heard the term "brand equity" in 1991 during a board meeting at their former advertising firm Yankelovich Clancy Shulman. One of the firm's academic advisors was giving a presentation and used the term to refer to the financial value of a brand. For example, if a company wanted to buy Colgate's line of shaving cream, what would the brand be worth? What amount of equity has Colgate been able to build into its brand of shaving cream?

> The search for brand equity sometimes feels like whacking a piñata. It is blind; it is hit or miss. When you do hit, you don't know if you want what showers down.
>
> Kevin Clancy and Peter Krieg[15]

Since the early 1990s, there have been a plethora of definitions of the term "brand equity" but little agreement on how to measure it. For example, in his 1991 book *Managing Brand Equity,* David Aaker defined brand equity as follows:

> Brand equity is a set of assets and liabilities linked to a brand, its name and symbol, that add to or subtract from the value provided by a product or service to a firm and/or that firm's customers . . . The assets and liabilities on which brand equity is based will differ from context to context. However, they can be usefully grouped into five categories:
>
> 1. Brand loyalty.
> 2. Name awareness.
> 3. Perceived quality.
> 4. Brand associations in addition to perceived quality.
> 5. Other proprietary assets—patents, trademarks, channel relationships, etc.[16]

In spite of the efforts by Aaker and others, Clancy and Krieg say that by the mid-1990s they were convinced that there were so many conflicting definitions or indicators of brand equity being offered that the term was in danger of losing its usefulness. The two gurus say they decided to do something to bring order to this chaos. Like the saying goes, It was a tough job, but somebody had to do it. They write that they began a number of studies in 1995 designed to help them better understand the concept of "brand equity" and how it could be measured. They reviewed the brand equity literature and identified the following eight factors that they say form the basis of brand equity:

Brand permeation: A weighted combination of brand and advertising awareness and availability.

Brand distinctiveness: A weighted combination of measures indicative of brand differentiation/uniqueness and superiority.

Brand quality: An assessment of the brand as a whole and its line extensions in terms of its overall reputation for quality of product or service.

Brand value: A weighted combination of measures that reflect the extent to which the brand delivers what buyers pay for, often known as "price value."

Brand personality: The extent to which the brand's image is congruent with who the buyer is or wants to be.

Brand potential: The extent to which consumers will pay more for, go out of their way for, or are willing to try this brand's not yet introduced new products or line extensions.

Competitive inoculation: The extent to which the consumer would stick with the brand in times of adversity or competitive pressure.

Brand behavior: The extent to which buyers prefer, buy, use, or have bought this brand and its line extensions.[17]

(Note: The gurus say this factor is not used in calculating the brand equity score since it is redundant with market share. Instead, it is used to weight the importance of each of the other factors. See the following explanation they offer for calculating the brand equity score.)

To measure your brand's equity, the gurus say, you should develop an Internet, face-to-face, or mailed questionnaire with three to five questions for each factor. You ask respondents to rate your brand against that of several of your competitors on these questions. No, they do not tell you what these questions should be, although we suspect they would be willing to do so if you paid them large consulting fees. Clancy and Krieg explain that once you have the results of your survey, brand equity scores for your brand and those of your competitors can be calculated as follows:

Each item and factor is weighted by its contribution to the overall brand behavior and preference vector to produce one overall assessment of brand equity for every brand studied. Each brand, as a result, can be characterized by a single brand equity number. These numbers, in theory ranging from zero to infinity, are standardized from 0 to 100 within a category to express "share of equity."

Think of this as having in your pocket seven different kinds of currencies (French francs, Canadian dollars, Brazilian reals, and others), all of which can be totaled and expressed in their U.S. dollar value—a single number. If you are interested in brand equity across product categories (e.g., What's Amazon's equity in books, CDs, and movies?), this can be measured by weighting equity scores in each category [in which] a brand competes by the dollar size of the category.[18]

(Note: See Chart 2.1 for a comparison of four other efforts to develop a measurement of brand equity, including a set of 10 measures—the Brand Equity Ten—offered by David Aaker.)

CHART 2.1. Measures of Brand Equity

	YOUNG & RUBICAM'S BRAND ASSET VALUATOR	TOTAL RESEARCH'S EQUITREND	INTERBRAND'S TOP BRANDS	DAVID AAKER'S BRAND EQUITY TEN
Background	Measure of brand equity of 450 global brands and 8,000 local brands in 24 countries using 32 item questionnaire covering four sets of measures.	Annual survey of 2,000 respondents covering over 700 brands in 100 categories using questionnaire covering three sets of measures.	Measure of brand equity of 500 brands using seven "subjective" criteria.	Refinement of Young & Rubicam, Total Research, and Interbrand measures in context of Aaker's definition of brand equity as consisting of four major asset categories: awareness, loyalty, quality, and associations.
Measures	**Differentiation**—how distinctive the brand is in the marketplace. **Relevance**—how meaningful or personally appropriate the brand is to the respondent. **Esteem**—whether the brand is held in high regard and/or considered best in its class. **Knowledge**—extent to which respondent understands what the brand stands for.	**Salience**—the percentage of respondents who have an opinion about the brand. **Perceived Quality**—the average quality rating among those who have an opinion about the brand. **User Satisfaction**—the average quality rating of consumers who use the brand often.	**Leadership**—degree to which the brand leads its market in communication and distribution. **Stability**—length of time brand has been in existence. **Market**—degree to which brand is in a market that is growing or has stable sales levels and a profitable price structure.	**Loyalty Measures** Price Premium Satisfaction/Loyalty **Perceived Quality/ Leadership Measures** Perceived Quality Leadership/popularity **Associations/ Differentiation Measures** Perceived Value Brand Personality

Measures (continued)

International—breadth of the market scope of the brand—regional, national, international.

Trend—overall long-term trend of the brand in terms of sales growth.

Support—degree to which brand receives consistent investment and focused support from its company.

Protection—strength and breadth of the brand's trademark protection

Organizational Associations

Association Measures
Brand Awareness

Market Behavior Measures
Market Share
Market Price and
Distribution Coverage

Source: Adapted from David A. Aaker, Building Strong Brands (New York: Free Press, 1996), pp. 304–333.

OUR VIEW

As we were reading Clancy and Krieg we kept having this vision of two mad scientists huddled over a witches brew of survey results, stirring in statistical formulas until suddenly one midnight eight distinct vapors ascended to the heavens forming the words "you have found it, oh great and powerful gurus." Did they find it? Is the Clancy/Krieg eight-factor formula the definitive one? Is it better than the measurement schemes suggested by Aaker and others (see Chart 2.1)? Who knows? In our opinion, the Clancy/Krieg formula is as good as any and less mystical than some.

As Clancy and Krieg note, brand equity is just a number like an IQ or SAT score, and you know how reliable those are. But, as an overall estimate of the strength of a brand, it is probably as good as any. Luckily, the same brands typically come out as having the most equity—McDonald's, Coca-Cola, Disney, Kodak, Sony, Gillette, Mercedes-Benz, Levi's, Microsoft, Marlboro, and so on, regardless of whose formula you use for calculating brand equity.

HOW DO YOU DEVELOP A STRONG BRAND?

So, how did McDonald's, Coca-Cola, Disney, Kodak, Sony, and all the others get to be strong brands? How did they acquire their brand equity? More importantly, how can you build brand equity for your brand?

Philip Kotler says that there are two main steps in developing a strong brand. First, you must develop a *value position,* and second, you have to build the brand. The first step is largely about positioning or, if you prefer, differentiation. The second step involves choosing a brand name, developing rich associations with that brand name, and finally managing all customer contacts with the brand so that they are consistent with the brand image and meet or exceed the customers' expectations.

Step #1: Developing the Value Proposition—Differentiation

Sergio Zyman, the author of *The End of Marketing* and *Marketing Bandwidth,* says that "if you want to create a positive return on investment, there's one way to do it: Own the position of relevant differentiation in your marketplace. You've got to have meaning in your customers' lives, and you've got to be perceived as different from all competitors. Differentiation," he goes on, "is where value is created."[19] Jack Trout, coauthor of *Positioning* and *Marketing Warfare,* puts it even more succinctly: He says you must *Differentiate or Die,* which is not so coincidentally the title of one of his books. If having a strong brand is key to vanquishing the evils we outlined in chapter one, then differentiation, say our gurus, is the key to building that strong brand. It all has to do with choice—too much choice on the part of the consumer.

Choice, explains Trout, wasn't always a problem because consumers had fewer options. Dinner for the cave dweller was pretty much limited to the slowest animal in the forest. Dinner today means choosing from a seemingly endless array of meats—pork, beef, chicken, fish, shellfish—all diced, sliced, chopped, packaged, and even precooked. Or how about a vegetarian pasta with a salad and nice glass of cabernet, which would be much better for you. But we digress.

Choice hasn't just exploded on the dinner menu, continues Trout, it has exploded in every area of commerce. In the early 1970s there were no Internet sites (a really simple choice); now there are over 4.7 million and the number of sites is increasing every day. Colgate made 2 types of toothpaste in the 1970s; they produce 17 types today. It is the same in every industry.

- **Styles of sport utility vehicles (SUVs)**—8 in the 1970s, 38 today.
- **Over-the-counter pain relievers**—17 in the 1970s, 141 today.
- **Dental flosses**—12 in the 1970s, 64 today.
- **TV screen sizes**—5 in the 1970s, 15 today.
- **Styles of running shoes**—5 in the 1970s, 285 today
- **Guru Guides™**—0 in the 1970s, 4 and counting today. (Isn't this a great age?)

So, what must you do to protect your brand in this age of unlimited choice? Differentiate or die, insists Trout. Choice is a tyrant—harsh and cruel. "Just look at some of the names on the headstones in the brand graveyard," writes Trout. "American Motors, Burger Chef, Carte Blanche, Eastern Airlines, Gainesburgers, Gimbel's, Hathaway shirts, Horn & Hardart, Mr. Salty pretzels, Philco, Trump Shuttle, VisiCalc, Woolworth's."[20] If you don't want to end up being another burnt burger, crashed auto, or smashed pretzel then you better get busy differentiating your brand. And the way you do that is through "positioning."

Clancy and Krieg define "positioning" this way:

The positioning is simply a one- or two-sentence statement—even a word—that is not about vision and not about mission as such, but is a message you want to imprint in the minds of customers and prospects. It is about your brand, product or service and how it is different from—and therefore better than—the competition's.[21]

Davis puts it this way:

A brand's positioning is the place in consumers' minds that you want your brand to own—the benefit you want them to think of when they think of your brand. It has to be externally driven and relevant. It has to be differentiated from the competition and, most importantly, it has to be valued. A good positioning is a single idea to be communicated to your customers.[22]

Here are some examples of companies and products our gurus say have strong positioning statements or strategies:

Company/Product	Positioning Statement or Strategy
Apple	Ease of use
Charmin tissue	Softness
Coca-Cola	Authentic, real, original
Disney	Wholesome family fun entertainment
FedEx	Guaranteed overnight delivery
Hallmark	Caring shared
Healthy Choice	Nutritious, low-fat, low-calorie food
McDonald's	Food and fun
Nordstrom's	Highest level of retail service
Visa	Accepted everywhere
Volvo	Safety
Wal-Mart	Low prices and good values

In *Differentiate or Die,* Trout identifies eight ideas for differentiating, or if you prefer "positioning," a brand that will work today. He says you can do one or more of the following:

Be the first.	Be a specialist.
Own an attribute.	Be preferred.
Be number one.	Own a unique capability.
Have a heritage.	Be the latest.

Let's look at each of these differentiating ideas in more detail. (See Exhibit 2.2 for Philip Kotler's alternative list of possible sources of positioning.)

Differentiation Idea #1: Be the First

Trout notes that in general people don't like to change their minds or the way they go about doing things. In fact, being pigheaded is a fairly widespread trait. Being first, then, is a pretty good basis for long-term differentiation. Harvard is still considered the leading university. *Time* leads *Newsweek. People* leads *Us.* Hertz leads Avis. Chrysler minivans lead the pack. Hewlett-Packard (HP) leads in desktop laser printers, Sun in workstations, and Xerox in copiers. The one thing these brands have in common is that they were first in their category. Being first can sometimes work so well

---

EXHIBIT 2.2. **Possible Sources of Specific Positioning**

Philip Kotler suggests that you consider the following as possible sources of specific positioning for your brand:

- **Attribute positioning:** The company positions itself on some attribute or feature. A beer company asserts that it is the oldest beer maker; a hotel describes itself as the city's tallest hotel. Positioning by a feature is normally a weak choice since no benefit is explicitly claimed.
- **Benefit positioning:** The product promises a benefit. Tide claims that it cleans better, Volvo claims that its cars are safer. Marketers primarily work with benefit positioning.
- **Use/application positioning:** The product is positioned as the best in a certain application. Nike might describe one of its shoes as the best to wear for racing and another as the best to wear for playing basketball.
- **User positioning:** The product is positioned in terms of a target user group. Apple Computer describes its computers and software as the best for graphic designers; Sun Microsystems describes its workstation computers as the best for design engineers.
- **Competitor positioning:** The product suggests its superiority or difference from a competitor's product. Avis described itself as a company "that tries harder" (than Hertz, by implication); 7 UP called itself the Uncola.
- **Category positioning:** The company may describe itself as the category leader. Kodak means film; Xerox means copy machines.
- **Quality/price positioning:** The product is positioned at a certain quality and price level. Chanel No. 5 is positioned as a very high-quality, high-price perfume; Taco Bell represents its tacos as giving the most value for the money.

Source: Philip Kotler, Kotler on Marketing: How to Create, Win, and Dominate Markets *(New York: Free Press, 1999), p. 58.*

that the name of your brand becomes the generic term for the product or activity. Think about it. People ask for a Xerox of a document, a Band-Aid for their cut, Q-tips to clean their ears, Saran Wrap to cover the dish of leftovers, Jell-O for dessert, and that you FedEx the package to them overnight. They ask you to hand them a Kleenex from the box of Scott tissues and offer you Coke in a Pepsi can.

Trout does mention two caveats to being first as a differentiator. First, it can take a while for something new to catch on. It took 40 years for 35-mm cameras to get hot, 30 years for microwave ovens to become a rage, 20 years for people to discover VCRs, and 9 years to convince people that light beer wasn't so bad, although we think that is still debatable. So, it may take you some time to be first. Second, it is not enough just to be first, you have to stay ahead of the pack. Reynolds and Eversharp pioneered ballpoint pens. Bic made them super cheap and disposable and grabbed the lead. Gillette gained differentiation from being first with razor blades, but it has stayed that way through aggressive and smart innovation.

Differentiation Idea #2: Own an Attribute

Trout defines an *attribute* as "a characteristic, peculiarity, or distinctive feature of a person or thing."[23] Here are some examples of brands and the attributes he says they own:[24]

Brand	Attribute
Crest toothpaste	Cavity prevention
Ferrari	Speed
Heinz ketchup	Slowest (thickest)
Maker's Mark bourbon	Smooth, soft taste
Mercedes	Engineering
Target	Mass with class "tar-zhay"

Trout urges you to keep the following in mind if you use an attribute as a differentiator:

1. You can't own the same attribute as a competitor. Crest owns cavity prevention, so if you have a competing toothpaste brand, you should choose a different attribute like "whitening" or "tartar prevention."
2. Your competitor may turn your attribute against you. McDonald's owned the attributes "fast" and "a place for kids." Burger King emphasized "Have it your way" and that McDonald's was "kiddieland."

See Exhibit 2.3 for a list of possible brand attributes suggested by another of our gurus.

Differentiation Idea #3: Be Number One

People tend to associate "biggest" with "best." So, says Trout, one way to differentiate your brand is to emphasize that you are "Number One." That's what Hertz does.[25]

"The superstar in rent-a-car."
"The number one way to rent a car."
"Where winners rent."

EXHIBIT 2.3. Distinctive Brand Characteristics or Attributes

Duane Knapp, coauthor of *The Brand Mindset* suggest the following as possible brand attributes that can be used to differentiate a brand:

Sensory	Special/personal	The last one
Visual	Customized	**Communications**
Smell, aroma, scent	Personalized	Advertising/marketing
Touch	**Service**	**Value**
Sound	Speed	Price
Comfort	Fast	Time
Sense of arrival	Personal	Feelings
Understanding/education	Knowledgeable	**Personality, emotion**
Authoritative/expertise	Hassle-free	**(feelings)**
The leader	Convenience	Self-esteem
The innovator	**Guarantee**	Ego
Access	Unconditional	Sense of humor
Endurance, dependability	100% satisfaction	Sexuality
Craftsmanship	Hassle-free	**Design (aesthetics)**
Quality	**Source of origin**	Color
Packaging	**Consistency**	Fabric
Size	**Functionality**	Texture
Relevant	Versatility	Style
Healthy	Utilization	Typeface (font)
"Good for you"	**Ingredients**	Symbol
Natural	**Scarcity (uniqueness)**	"Look"
Pure	One of a kind	**Place**
Wholesome	The original	"Its own"
Preventative	The first one	Position (mind's eye)

Source: Duane E. Knapp and Christopher W. Hart, The Brand Mindset: Five Essential Strategies for Building Brand Advantage throughout Your Company *(New York: McGraw-Hill, 2000), p. 43.*

In short, if you can legitimately claim to be the leader—aka "Number One"—in anything, BRAG!! And remember that in any category there is more than one way to claim leadership. For example:

- Toyota Camry is the best-selling car in America.
- Lincoln is the best-selling luxury car in America.
- Dodge Caravan is the best-selling minivan in America.
- Ford Explorer is the best-selling sport utility vehicle in America.
- Ziat is the best-selling four-cylinder, two-door, minicar made in Zanzu, Michigan, on the third shift at the old Hudson plant by the Gargantula brothers and their friends in America.

See, it just takes creative wording.

Here are four words. In the space provided underneath each, write the name of the brand or company you most associate with each word. (To see how most people responded to the same question, see Exhibit 2.8 at the end of this chapter.)

Computer	Copier	Chocolate bar	Cola
_____	_____	_____	_____

How did you do? Did you think of the same brands and companies most people associate with these words? It's likely you did, but what's the point? The point, says Trout, is that if you can differentiate your brand as the leader in a product category, you have the chance of having your brand become synonymous with that product category. Your brand becomes the first thing people think of when they think about the category, and that's not a bad position to be in. In fact, it's great positioning.

Differentiation Idea #4: Have a Heritage

Suppose your brand isn't the biggest in a category. Maybe your brand has just been around longer than any other. That in itself, says Trout, can be a differentiator, although not necessarily for the reason that first comes to mind. Sure, if your brand has been around for a while people probably will give it some credit just for surviving. After all, they reason, you couldn't be that bad or you would have gone belly up long ago. But Trout argues that longevity says more about your brand than survival. It says your brand has a "heritage," and heritage is important. Trout quotes consumer psychologist Carol Moog on the psychological effects of heritage.

> The psychological importance of heritage may derive from the power of being a participant in a continuous line that connects and bonds one to the right to be alive, to a history that one carries forward from the living past, through death and on into the next generation. The link is a link to immortality. Without a sense of heritage, of known ancestors, people are vulnerable to feeling isolated, abandoned, emotionally cut off, and ungrounded. Without a line from the past, it is difficult to believe in a line to the future. The emphasis on heritage, then, is on continuity, on one's defeat of death by remaining part of the flow. Embracing companies and products with this kind of lineage allows people to participate in these powerful links to a continuous life.[26]

So it's immortality people are really after. Who would have thought it. Seriously, people do want to feel part of something enduring.

Suppose, however, that your brand hasn't been around long enough to have a heritage. Trout says you can connect your brand with something that does have a heritage, like a country. Let's play a game. Below we list some countries and some products. Your task is to match the country with the product that would benefit from each country's heritage by drawing a line from the country to the product.

Here is the list of countries and products. Match them by drawing a line from country to product or if your prefer product to country. It will work either way. See Exhibit 2.9 at the end of this chapter for the correct answers.

Product	Country
Airplanes	Argentina
Beef	Australia
Beer	France
Crocodile Dundee	Germany
Electronics	Italy
Lamb	Japan
Royalty	New Zealand
Shoes	Switzerland
Watches	United Kingdom
Wine	United States

Here is one final test of your "heritage as differentiator" knowledge. Which country best matches with automobiles:

A. Automobiles = Japan

B. Automobiles = Yugoslavia?

If you said "B," you have what we call the "Yugo" problem, and heritage as differentiator may not be right for you.

Differentiation Idea #5: Be a Specialist

What's wrong with the following list:	**Now, what's right with this list?**
Blockbuster's office supplies	Blockbuster's videos
Foot Locker's sexy lingerie	Foot Locker's athletic shoes
Ford sports drinks	Ford cars
Gatorade copiers	Gatorade sports drinks
Kraft jellies	Kraft cheese
Smucker's cheese	Smucker's jellies
Staples video rentals	Staples office supplies
Victoria's Secret's athletic shoes	Victoria's Secret's sexy lingerie
Xerox cars	Xerox copies

Get the picture? People are impressed by those who specialize. They are even more impressed by those who are so well known for their specialty that their name represents the specialty category. Tape = Scotch; Copy = Xerox; Sports drink = Gatorade.

Differentiation Idea #6: Be Preferred

We all want what other people want. Think sheep—herd—follow. One way to differentiate your brand, says Trout, is to find some way to claim that your brand is the brand of preference, ideally by people that matter. Here are some examples:

- Tylenol is the pain reliever hospitals prefer most.
- Nike is the shoe that basketball superstars can't live without.
- Lexus is the luxury vehicle participants in J.D. Powers surveys prefer.
- Midwest Express Airlines is the choice of sophisticated, affluent, in-the-know readers of *Condé Naste Traveler.*

Another way to think about this type of differentiation is that it involves being HOT. Your brand is the brand that everybody—at least everybody you consider your target customer—thinks is cool, or depending upon your generation, "rad," "spiffy," and "awesome," or "with it," "far out," and "groovy."[27] (Note: We will have more to say about this type of differentiation in our chapter on "buzz.")

Differentiation Idea #7: Own a Unique Capability

If your brand is made with a "magic ingredient," produced with a patented technology, manufactured with an exclusive process, or serviced in a special way, Trout says you may be able to turn that unique capability into a differentiator. He cites Batesville, the number one casket maker in America, as an example.

> Only Batesville offers "cathodic protection" on their metal caskets. This is the same science that protects the Alaskan pipeline and ships from the ravages of corrosion. They also offer "Monoseal," which is a system that keeps them from leaking. If you can believe it, each casket is vacuum tested for possible leaks. (That's impressive when you consider how easy it is for them to bury their mistakes.) They cap all this off by offering a warranty that guarantees some caskets up to seventy-five years. When Aunt Miriam is buried in a Batesville, her family knows they are burying her in the best and she will be heavily protected from the elements.[28]

We don't know about you, but that makes us feel better. Can you imagine what caskets without such protection must get to be like after a couple of decades?

Differentiation Idea #8: Be the Latest

We've been writing business books for well over a decade now, and we go through computers at the rate of about one per book. We've had a 286, 386, 486, Pentium, Pentium II, Pentium III, and have now moved on to Pentium IV. We've been through DOS, Windows, Windows 95, Windows 98, Windows ME, and now are faced with the prospect of Windows XP. We've been through Word for DOS, Word for Windows, Word for Windows 95, Word 2000, and so on. Why do we keep spending on computers? Simple:

Each time we are buying the "next generation" of computer or software, and we have to keep up.

Trout rightly notes that the "next generation" product is not just anticipated today; it is expected. Therefore, one way you can differentiate your brand from the pack is to be the latest and greatest. Just be sure, says Trout, that you avoid the following common "next generation" mistakes:

Don't solve a nonexistent problem. Your next-generation product must solve a real problem, not one that's unimportant. Dow Chemical introduced Dowtherm 209, a new antifreeze coolant which was billed as "doing no harm if it leaked into the crankcase" (and by the way, it cost twice as much as old-generation coolants). The trouble was that conventional coolants hardly ever leaked into the engine. Why pay twice as much for a nonexistent problem? Most people didn't.

Don't mess with tradition. There are real problems that people don't want solved. They like the old-fashioned way. Nothing is as traditional as eating unshelled peanuts at the ballpark. Unfortunately, everyone was up to their ankles in shells by the end of the game. To avoid the shell mess, Harry M. Stevens introduced pre-shelled peanuts in cellophane packages. People were outraged. Sales fell, complaints rose. Back to walking on shells.

It must be better. Why go for the next thing if it isn't a better thing? The United States mint brought out the Susan B. Anthony $1 coin as a replacement for the $1 bill. To the mint it was a big improvement, as they would save $50 million a year in printing and processing costs. To the public there were no perceived benefits. It looked like a quarter and many thought it was ugly. Good-bye, Suzy.[29]

A Ninth Differentiating Idea—Simplicity

Here is one more differentiating idea that Trout does not mention. It was suggested by Steven Cristol and Peter Sealey in their book *Simplicity Marketing*. What's interesting here is that while Cristol and Sealey begin with the same observation that Trout made about the proliferation of choice, they come to some very different conclusions. Rather than seeing positioning as an answer to the consumers' and brand builders' problem with the tyranny of choice, they see positioning, at least as it has been traditionally done, as the cause of the problem. They write:

Like capitalism itself, contemporary marketing has been based on an unflagging belief in giving customers more and more choices. The choice curve ramped up in the post–World War II economy, when packaged goods manufacturers set in motion a relentless juggernaut of product proliferation and line extensions. The cumulative result of a half century of bombarding customers with an overload of options is that their mental circuit breakers are beginning to trip—in both the consumer and business worlds. In a pressure-packed buying and selling environment, the line between choice and overchoice has become increasingly fine.

By the early 1970s, marketers were already desperately hungry for ways to ensure that their brands could stand out amidst the swelling marketing noise created by more choices and more media pervasiveness. It was then that the concept of *positioning* rippled through the marketing world. Positioning focused on the importance of differentiating a product, service, or company from its competition. It brought to the marketing planning process a new sense of focus on carving out a proprietary space in the customer's mind. During the three decades since, sustained success has come to those brands with a unique, relevant, and credible positioning consistently supported by aggressive marketing.

But many such successes are now threatened by overchoice. A new imperative for the positioning discipline has emerged: that marketers look for ways to connect their brands to *simplicity*. The interaction of two forceful tides—extreme choice proliferation and an exponentially increasing pace of change—creates a combustible combination that at once brings customers unprecedented opportunities and unprecedented anxiety . . . [In] the most developed economies of the twenty-first century, *the next generation of positioning successes will belong to those brands that relieve customer stress.* That means simplifying customers' lives or businesses in ways that are inextricably tied to brand and product positioning. It means *becoming the customer's partner in stress relief.*

Brands that do this will be the customer's heroes. Brands that don't will be nuisances.[30]

If you want to position your brand as a relief from stress, say Cristol and Sealey, there are four ways you can do so—**R**eplace, **R**epackage, **R**eposition, and **R**eplenish.

◉ OUR VIEW

Did you notice that there are four ways, not two, or six , or even nine? Did you notice that the words used to describe the four ways all begin with the same letter? Would you be surprised that our gurus refer to the four ways to position your brand as the "Four Rs"? We didn't think so.

Cristol and Sealey write that the Four Rs "encompass complementary approaches to excavating the 'simplification value' of a product, service, or even an entire company and incorporating that value into an effective positioning strategy."[31] They define the Four Rs as follows:

- **R**eplace—You position your brand as a replacement for a group of products or a more complicated product. For example, Procter & Gamble's Pert Plus is a combination shampoo/conditioner. It *replaces* two existing but separate products—shampoo and conditioner—and thereby offers the consumer *simplicity*—a single purchase rather than two.
- **R**epackage—You offer *simplicity* by bringing together in one offering products or services that previously were available as separate purchases and/or from multiple sources. For example, *Reader's Digest* aggregates or *repackages* stories, magazine articles, jokes, and book excerpts from a variety of sources, thus *simplifying* its readers' access to information and entertainment.
- **R**eposition—You make a direct promise of *simplicity*—"Honda. We make it simple"—or you reduce the number of brand relationships that the customer requires over time. For example, GM has 66 different subbrands of cars and trucks ranging from the Astro to the Venture. In contrast, BMW offers four subbrands—3 series, 5 series, 7 series, and 8 series—thus *simplifying* the car buyer's choice.
- **R**eplenish—You make readily available a continuous supply of products or services with zero defects. In his book *Permission Marketing,* Seth Godin identifies seven levels of "permission" marketing from the lowest *situational level*—the order taker at McDonald's takes advantage of the situation of you placing an order to suggest that you "supersize" your fries—to *Intravenous*—Poland Springs automatically replenishes the water cooler in your office and sends you a bill.[32] Cristol and Sealey's *Replenish* is positioning at the *Intravenous* level of permission.

Step #2: Building the Brand

Let's assume that you reviewed all the positioning options offered by our gurus and arrived at a short one-sentence positioning statement for your brand. Your next step, says Philip Kotler, is to build your brand by (1) selecting a brand name, (2) developing rich associations with that brand name, and (3) managing all contacts with your target customers to ensure that they are consistent with and supportive of the brand positioning. (Note: If you need more advice on how to arrive at a position, see Exhibit 2.4 for a

---

EXHIBIT 2.4. Kevin Clancy and Peter Krieg: Steps to Creating a Compelling Position

Here are the steps that Clancy and Krieg recommend following in developing a positioning for your brand. They begin with the assumption that you have clearly identified your target customers and that you have conducted research to determine your target customer's desires and problems and your competitors' strengths and weaknesses.

Step #1: Make a list of at least 200 tangible and intangible attributes and benefits that might motivate your target customers and thereby serve as the basis for a powerful positioning.

Step #2: Prioritize the list and combine redundant items to get the list down to between 50 and 100 items.

Step #3: Survey at least 200 and preferably 500 or more target customers on these 50 to 100 items on three dimensions: (1) how desirable each item is to them (dream detection), (2) the extent to which the product/service they are currently using contains that attribute or benefit (problem detection), and (3) the likelihood they would buy a product or service that had that attribute or benefit (brand preference detection).

Step #4: Average each respondent's scores for each item across the three dimensions to get the motivating power of each attribute or benefit. (Note: Clancy and Krieg say you may want to give more weight to the first dimension if the product is new and more weight to the second dimension if the product/service is an established one.)

Step #5: Examine the results of step four to identify highly motivating attributes and benefits that your brand enjoys relative to competing brands.

Step #6: Write three to seven different positioning statements and test them with 150 or more target customers to determine which is most powerful in terms of purchase interest, uniqueness, and product/brand superiority. Pick the winning positioning strategy.

Source: Adapted from Kevin J. Clancy and Peter C. Krieg, Counterintuitive Marketing: Achieve Great Results Using Uncommon Sense *(New York: Free Press, 2000), pp. 121–179.*

summary of advice offered by Kevin Clancy and Peter Krieg. Also, see Exhibit 2.5 for a brief summary of an approach to brand building proposed by David Aaker.)

EXHIBIT 2.5. David Aaker's Brand Identity System for Building Brands

Aaker argues that to build your brand you must develop a brand identity to provide direction, purpose, and meaning for your brand. "Brand identity," he writes, "is a unique set of brand associations that the brand strategist aspires to create or maintain. These associations represent what the brand stands for and imply a promise to customers from the organization members." In order to develop an identity for your brand, Aaker says you should consider how your brand could be portrayed from four perspectives: (1) as a product, (2) as an organization, (3) as a person, and (4) as a symbol.

Product Perspective

Product scope—with what product or products is the brand associated? For example, Visa = credit cards.

Product attributes—functional/emotional benefits.

Quality/value—is the brand a Mercedes, Buick or Ford?

Use or application—can the brand "own" a particular application? For example, Clorox bleach "owns" an association with whitening clothing and Gatorade "owns" an association with athletics and high performance.

Users—Gerber = babies; Weight Watchers = weight control and nutrition.

Country or region—Chanel = French, Swatch watches = Swiss, Mercedes = German.

Organization Perspective

Organization attributes—characteristics such as innovation, drive for quality, concern for the environment, and so on that result from the people, culture, values, and programs of the company. Aaker notes that organization attributes such as reputation for innovation and so on can be extremely valuable in building a brand because they are hard for competitors to copy.

Local vs. global.

Person Perspective

Personality—the humanlike qualities people attribute to the brand or should attribute to it such as competent, impressive, trustworthy, fun, active, humorous, casual, formal, youthful, intellectual, and so on.

Brand/customer relationship—how people view the relationship. For example, Saturn = friend, Levi Strauss = rugged outdoor companion, Hallmark = warm, emotional relative.

(continued)

EXHIBIT 2.5. **(continued)**

Symbol Perspective

Visual imagery and metaphors—Transamerica pyramid, Nike "swoosh," McDonald's Golden Arches, Quaker Oats man.

Brand heritage—U.S. Marines = the few, the proud; Amtrak = the heritage of first-class travel by rail.

Aaker says that by considering your brand from these four perspectives you should be able to arrive at both a "core" identity and an "extended" identity for your brand. The core identity is the essence of your brand; the associations that are essential to the meaning and success of your brand and that are likely to remain constant as you enter new markets and launch new products. Your brand's extended identity includes elements that provide completeness and texture to your brand's identity. These are the elements that flesh out the details of your brand. For example, Saturn's core identity, says Aaker, is that of a world-class car delivered by a company that treats customers with respect and as friends. Its extended identity is as a U.S. subcompact, a no-pressure/friendly buying experience with no-haggle pricing, and a personality that is thoughtful, friendly, down-to-earth, reliable, youthful, humorous, lively, and thoroughly American.

Source: David A. Aaker, Building Strong Brands (New York: Free Press, 1996), pp. 68–95.

Choosing a Brand Name

What's in a name? Our gurus say it's everything. Choose the wrong name for your brand and all the efforts you have made positioning it will be for naught. In fact, the wrong name can kill your brand. In his book *The Invisible Touch,* Harry Beckwith tells the story of a Texan who learned that lesson the hard way.

Two leather-skinned Texans find themselves side by side in a Houston bar. They begin to talk and learn they both own cattle ranches.

"So what's the name of your ranch?" the first rancher asks.

"The Circle K," the second says. "What about yours?"

"Mine's the Lazy L Bar T Circle Q Sleepy C Triangle D."

"Jeez, you must have a ton of cattle!" the second says. "About how many head do you have?"

The first winced. "To tell you the truth, not that many. Most of 'em don't survive the branding."[33]

The moral, says Beckwith, is to keep your brand name short.

Here is a list of what works and what doesn't work when it comes to brand names according to Frank Delano, author of *The Omnipowerful Brand.*[34]

What Works

- **Beginning and ending the brand name with the same letter**—Delano says that makes the name easy to remember. Examples include Nissan's **A**ltim**a** car, **O**rth**o** chemicals, and *Elle* women's magazine.
- **Adding a vowel to the end of a word, transforming a common word into a proprietary trademark**—An example is Lyric**a,** the name of a drug used to treat psychotropic conditions.
- **Ending a brand name with the letter "a"**—Delano says the letter "a" makes the name sound friendly, like Human**a.**
- **Ending a brand name with the syllable "va," particularly if the brand needs to have an international feel**—Delano says "va" means "to go forward" in Latin-based languages. Some examples include IBM's Apti**va** PC and Polaroid's Capti**va** instant camera. Delano cautions that you should be careful about the prefix or stem syllable that is linked with the "va" suffix. For example, Chevy No**va** means "no go" in some languages.
- **Starting a brand name with the letters "ch"**—Delano says brands beginning with the letters "ch" mirror such familiar words as church, charity, cheerfulness, and children, thus bringing to mind thoughts of joy, goodness, and fulfillment. An example is **Ch**eerios.
- **Ending the brand name with the vowel "o," particularly if you want the brand to appeal to men**—Words ending with the vowel "o" are more masculine sounding, according to Delano. One example is the name Terran**o** for Nissan' s 4 x 4 sport utility vehicle.
- **Beginning the brand name with the letters "Q" or "J"**—These letters are supposed to convey the image that the brand is something special, for example Infiniti's **Q**45 and **J**30 lines of cars.
- **Beginning the brand name with the letters "se," particularly if you want the brand to sound sexy**—Delano says the letters "se" carry a sensual overtone as in the examples of Gillette's **Se**nsor razor and **Se**cret deodorant.
- **Incorporating the letter "z" in the name**—Delano maintains that the letter "z" conveys the image of advanced technology, scientific

breakthrough, or superior performance. An example is Zantac, the antiulcer drug.

- **Using only one syllable and three or four letters**—Shorter names like Fab and Tide detergents are easier to remember. However, adds Delano, a name with multiple syllables and nine or more letters, such as Primerica or Microsoft, can convey stature and importance.
- **Combining two words**—For example, FedEx is a better name than Federal Express.
- **Using a name that sounds like the product's generic name**—Examples include Duracell for a battery cell and Ziploc for a plastic storage bag.

What Doesn't Work

- **Using a syllable in a brand name that can be spelled in more than one way**—For example, sym can be spelled sim, *cim,* or *cym.*
- **Ending the name with the letters "is"**—Delano notes that the names of most illnesses end with these letters. If you don't want your product associated with such things as syphilis, gingivitis, halitosis, and so on, then don't end the name with "is."
- **Names that sound like a curse word**—Delano notes that the makers of a brand of jams and jellies faced this problem head on with an inventive ad campaign that went, "With a name like Smucker's, it has to be good." However, it is preferable to avoid this problem if possible.
- **Names that try to be cute**—Examples include names like Cow Chip Cookies or Dog Poo Shampoo.
- **Overused words and symbols**—Delano notes that names of over 1,600 banks in the United States begin with the words "First National" and another 584 start with the word "Farmers."

In addition to keeping these recommendations in mind, Delano suggests that you ask yourself the following questions when selecting a brand name:[35]

1. Does the name capture the product's essence, uniqueness, and spirit?
2. Will the name capture the consumer's attention and inspire his/her imagination?
3. Is the sound of the name appropriate to the product's category?
4. Is the name simple?

5. Does the name create a visual image and sound that are recorded in the consumer's mind forever?
6. Does the name convey the correct sexual image?
7. Does the name make believable what you claim the product is delivering?

(See Exhibit 2.6 for some examples of names that Delano says are so good they are omnipowerful.)

Developing Rich Associations

Once you have picked a brand name your next task, say our gurus, is to establish positive associations with that name. For example, here are some the characteristics Philip Kotler says people associate with the brand name McDonald's:[36]

Big Mac	High calories	Golden Arches
Charity	Kids	Happy Meal
Consistency	Paper waste	Ronald McDonald
Fun	Quality	Value meal

EXHIBIT 2.6. Omnipowerful Brand Names

Frank Delano provides the following examples of what he says are brand names that catapulted their products to global marketing stardom:

- **Nissan's Pathfinder**—believable because the vehicle is built for off-road exploration.
- **Sony's Walkman**—simple and captures both the product's essence and consumer attention.
- **Planet Hollywood**—projects the image of an exciting dining experience inspired by the worlds of film and television.
- **Ford's Taurus**—the astrological sign Taurus suggests power, durability, and reliability.
- **Intel's Pentium**—captures the uniqueness of the product and consumer attention.
- **Absolut Vodka**—suggests the "ultimate" and captures the consumer's attention.
- **Procter & Gamble's Ivory Soap**—suggests the product's essence (clean smelling and white).
- **Volkswagen's Beetle**—unique, attention getting, and believable.

Source: Frank Delano, The Omnipowerful Brand: America's #1 Brand Specialist Shares His Secrets for Catapulting Your Brand to Marketing Stardom (New York: AMACOM, 1999), pp. 61–64.

Note that two of these associations, high calories and paper waste, are negative and suggest actions McDonald's might want to take such as reducing paper usage and introducing lower-calorie menu items.

Kotler maintains that you should consider five dimensions in building associations with your brand.

Attributes. A strong brand should trigger in the buyer's mind certain attributes. Thus, the Mercedes automobile triggers a picture of a well-engineered car that is durable, rugged, and expensive. If a car brand does not trigger any attributes, then it would be a weak brand.

Benefits. A strong brand should suggest benefits, not just features. Thus the Mercedes triggers the idea of a well-performing car that is enjoyable to drive and prestigious to own.

Company values. A strong brand should connote values that the company holds dear. Thus Mercedes is proud of its engineers and engineering innovations and is very organized and efficient in its operations. The fact that it is a German company adds more pictures in the buyer's mind about the character and culture of the brand.

Personality. A strong brand should exhibit some personality traits. Thus if Mercedes were a person, we would think of someone who is of middle age, serious, well organized, and somewhat authoritarian. If Mercedes were an animal, we might think of a lion and its implied personality.

Users. A strong brand should suggest the kinds of people who buy the brand. Thus we would expect Mercedes to draw buyers who are older, affluent, and professional.[37]

So how do you build these associations? Our gurus say you have basically four tools at your disposal—graphic representations (logos, trademarks, and "trade dress"), bylines, taglines, and brand stories. Let's look at each of these.

Graphic Representations

Graphic representations include trademarks, logos, and what is commonly known as "trade dress." There are two types of trademarks or logos—word marks such as

and device marks such as Weyerhaeuser's tree in a triangle icon.

Duane Knapp, author of *The Brand Mindset,* provides eight criteria that he says you should consider in selecting logos and trademarks:

Protectability: Consideration should be given to registering the mark as a trademark with the U.S. Patent and Trademark Office and in all other countries in which the brand will be marketed.

Acceptability: Colors and shapes should be carefully considered to effectively cross cultural boundaries.

Uniqueness: The mark should be designed to minimize preexisting associations, cut through complexity, and ensure easy recall. Market research, including focus groups, surveys, and interviews, is helpful to determine customer association of the mark with a product.

Compatibility: Graphic representations should work easily with other information likely to be in close proximity.

Flexibility: The mark should be able to translate into various media, including paper, fax, and Internet.

Recognizability: The mark should be recognizable in every language.

Timelessness: It should be timeless in style and not get caught in current trends.

Crispness: Graphic representation should be crisp across multiple mediums, that is, the Internet, packaging, print, television, and so forth.[38]

He notes that some of the most recognizable trademarks are a composite of a word mark shown in a distinctive graphic form. Starbucks' trademark is a good example.

"Trade dress" refers to all of the other features of packaging and presentation that give a brand its distinctive look and feel. This can include uniforms that employees wear, shapes of packages and containers, decor, and so on. Knapp notes that "individually, such ordinary features as waiter uniforms, menu look, artwork, plants, color, and architecture may not be very distinctive; however, in combination, they may represent a unique brand identity."[39] McDonald's Golden Arches, Altoids unique package, the distinctive shape of Coke's bottle, and the copper top on Duracell's batteries are all part of the trade dress and contribute to building the brand.

In *Emotional Branding,* Marc Gobé says that the trade dress of your brand should include sensory appeals. In addition to thinking about brand names, logos, and so on, Gobé says you should be answering the following kinds of questions:

> What music should we be playing in our stores to convey the emotional identity of our brand?
>
> How can we use color to set the appropriate emotional mood for our brand?
>
> What images can we put on our packaging, in our stores, and within our advertising that will help customers identify with our product?
>
> Can serving food to our customers affect their behavior?
>
> Can we use scent to create desirable associations with our brand?[40]

Bernd Schmitt and Alex Simonson discuss similar ideas in their 1997 book *Marketing Aesthetics.* In fact, Schmitt and Simonson argue that "aesthetics," that is, "attractive visual and other sensory markers and symbols," can actually serve as a differentiator, particularly if a company can develop a distinctive style.[41] See Exhibit 2.7 for a description of the primary elements that Schmitt and Simonson say comprise a distinctive style.

Byline

The byline typically accompanies the brand name and serves as descriptor of the brand. The words "Home Appliances" under the brand name "Whirlpool" describe the business. They instantly communicate to the potential customer the types of products Whirlpool sells.

Tagline

The tagline is the jingle or slogan that clarifies and dramatizes the emotional and functional benefits of the product or service.

Nikon—"We take the world's greatest pictures."

Brand Story

Knapp says all strong brands have a brand story. It captures the brand heritage and puts a human face on the brand. Typically the stories are about the founding of the company and/or creation of the product or service. They are usually filled with tales of hard work, sacrifice, persistence, and optimism. For example, as a junior at Yale, Fred Smith, the founder of Federal Ex-

---

EXHIBIT 2.7. **Primary Elements of Style**

Bernd Schmitt and Alex Simonson say that aesthetics can be used to create a *style,* that is, a distinctive quality or form or manner of expression for a company or brand. Among other things, say Schmitt and Simonson, this aesthetics-based *style* can help to create brand awareness, cause intellectual and emotional associations with the brand and/or company, differentiate the company's products and services, help consumers categorize a set of products and services as being related, and help subcategorize variations of products and services in a marketing mix. According to Schmitt and Simonson, the following are the primary elements of *style:*

Sight: Shape (product and packaging shapes such as Coca-Cola's distinctive bottle or the shape of Nike's logo), Color (logo colors, product colors, color of company uniforms; for example, IBM's blue, Mary Kay's pink, or Kodak's yellow), Typeface (Hyatt's distinctive bar stroke A, for example).

Sound: Loudness, Pitch, Meter (an example is United Airlines' use of George Gershwin's "Rhapsody in Blue").

Touch: Material, Texture (an example is the unique feel of the Oxo brand of kitchenware).

Scent: Taste, Smell (an example is Crabtree & Evelyn and the Body Shop's use of scents to provide unique identities for their products and retail spaces).

The key to style, say Schmitt and Simonson, is *synesthesia,* the stimulation of one sense by another.

Synesthesia creates an integration of primary elements such as colors, shapes, scents, and materials into "systems of attributes" that express a corporate or brand aesthetic style. Though identities are composed of the primary elements . . . [of sight, sound, touch, taste, and smell] . . . a holistic perception is the result.

Source: Bernd Schmitt and Alex Simonson, Marketing Aesthetics: The Strategic Management of Brands, Identity, and Image *(New York: Free Press, 1997), pp. 80–119.*

---

press, is said to have received a C on a term paper he wrote that analyzed the existing freight services and suggested that there might be a market for high-priority, time-sensitive delivery of goods and services such as medicines and electronic components. Brand stories are used in brochures, catalogs, and company histories to bring the brand to life.

Note: If you would like to read the stories of brands such as Amazon.com, Microsoft, Southwest Airlines, McDonald's, Staples, Starbucks, Wendy's, and many more, consult *The Guru Guide™ to Entrepreneurship* (John Wiley & Sons, 2000).

Managing Brand Contacts

Brand names, taglines, logos, and other associations are important to building a brand, but they are of little use if what the customer experiences isn't consistent with the brand image you are trying to convey. Therefore, say our gurus, the marketer's job doesn't end with building an image. He/she must make sure that the company actually behaves consistently with that image. Kotler writes:

> The brand manager needs to make sure that the *brand experience* matches the *brand image*. Much can go wrong. A fine brand of canned soup described in a full-page color ad may be found in a dented and dusty condition on the bottom shelf in a supermarket. The ad describing a gracious hotel chain may be belied by the behavior of a surly concierge. The well-honed image of a small appliance manufacturer is belied when the customer receives a damaged appliance because of careless packaging by the shipping clerk.
>
> Brand building therefore calls for more than brand image building. It calls for managing every *brand contact* that the customer might have with the brand. Since all company employees, distributors, and dealers can affect the brand experience, the brand challenge is to manage the quality of all brand contacts.[42]

So there you have it. The solution to marketing's **P** problems is simple. Develop a compelling value proposition for your product or service, select a brand name, develop rich associations with that brand name, and manage all contacts with your target customers to ensure that they are consistent with and support your brand positioning. Like magic you have solved your marketing **P** problems. Right? "Not quite," say some of the branding gurus. There is just a little bit more. "You see," they say, "a strong brand is good. But, a well-managed portfolio of brands is infinitely better." In the next chapter, we'll take a look at what these gurus have to say about managing multiple brands. For now, let's summarize the key ideas from this chapter.

KEY POINTS

- A brand is the internalized sum of all impressions received by the customers and consumers resulting in a distinctive position in their "mind's eye" based on perceived emotional and functional benefits.

- Seventy-two percent of customers say they will pay a 20 percent premium for their brand of choice; 40 percent will pay up to a 30 percent premium.

- Seventy percent of customers want to use a brand to guide their purchase decision.

- If you have a strong brand, you can:

  - Charge a premium price.

  - Launch new products more cheaply than your competitors.

  - Recoup your development costs earlier.

  - Cut your acquisition costs for new customers.

  - Have a higher profitability per customer.

  - Exercise more control over your distribution channels.

  - More readily seek out cobranding and licensing opportunities.

  - Leverage your brand across more target market segments.

- A strong brand is a brand with high brand equity.

- Brand equity consists of eight factors:

  - Brand permeation.

  - Brand distinctiveness.

  - Brand quality.

  - Brand value.

  - Brand personality.

  - Brand potential.

  - Competitive inoculation.

  - Brand behavior.

- The first step in developing a strong brand is to develop a value proposition (position or differentiation) for the brand. A brand's "position" or "differentiation" is the benefit you want consumers to think of when they think of your brand that is different from the benefit your competitor can offer. For example, Apple = Ease of use; Nordstrom = Highest level of retail service.

o—⟶ The eight primary ways for differentiating (or "positioning") a brand are:

- Be the first.

- Own an attribute.

- Be number one.

- Have a heritage.

- Be a specialist.

- Be preferred.

- Own a unique capability.

- Be the latest.

o—⟶ Brand names should:

- Capture the product's essence, uniqueness, and spirit.

- Capture the consumer's attention and inspire his/her imagination.

- Have a sound that is appropriate to the brand image.

- Be simple and easy to pronounce.

- Create a visual image and sound that will be recorded in the consumer's mind forever.

- Convey the correct sexual image.

- Make believable what you claim the product is delivering.

o—⟶ Logos, trademarks, "trade dress," bylines, taglines, and brand stories should be used to build rich associations that convey the brand's attributes, benefits, and company values; reflect the brand's personality; and suggest the kinds of people who buy the brand.

o—⟶ Brand building requires more than just brand image building. The brand manager must manage every brand contact that the customer might have with the brand to ensure that the company and its employees always behave consistent with the brand image.

EXHIBIT 2.8. **Brands/Companies Most People Associated with These Words**

Computer	Copier	Chocolate bar	Cola
IBM	*Xerox*	*Hershey's*	*Coca-Cola*

EXHIBIT 2.9. **Countries and Their Product Heritage**

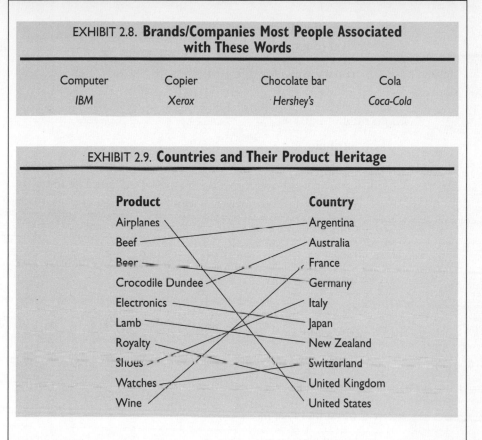

Product

Airplanes
Beef
Beer
Crocodile Dundee
Electronics
Lamb
Royalty
Shoes
Watches
Wine

Country

Argentina
Australia
France
Germany
Italy
Japan
New Zealand
Switzerland
United Kingdom
United States

David Aaker, coauthor of *Brand Leadership*

Sam Hill, coauthor of *The Infinite Asset*

Erich Joachimsthaler, coauthor of *Brand Leadership*

Chris Lederer, coauthor of *The Infinite Asset*

Al Ries, coauthor of *The 22 Immutable Laws of Branding*

Laura Ries, coauthor of *The 22 Immutable Laws of Branding*

3

All You Need Is Brand Management

I n the last chapter we discussed our gurus' recommendations for building a single strong brand. But suppose you have or want to have more than one brand? Suppose you are now or plan to be another GE with multiple products and product lines or another Marriott with a range of types of branded lodging? How do you make sense out of your portfolio of brands? In response to these and other questions, we will spend this chapter looking at the ideas of four gurus—David Aaker, Erich Joachimsthaler, Sam Hill, and Chris Lederer. We'll examine the ideas of Aaker and Joachimsthaler first and then turn to those of Hill and Lederer.

BRAND ARCHITECTURE—DAVID AAKER AND ERICH JOACHIMSTHALER

In *Brand Leadership,* David Aaker and Erich Joachimsthaler tell us that in order to generate clarity, synergy, and leverage across multiple brands, you need to develop a "brand architecture" to organize and clarify the relationship between your brands. Developing the brand architecture, say the gurus, involves (1) clarifying the relationships between your brands, and (2) constructing the brand architecture.

The Brand Relationship Spectrum

Aaker and Joachimsthaler discuss four basic strategies you can employ to structure the relationship between your brands—house of brands, endorser/endorsed brands, master/subbrands, and branded house. These four strategies represent points on a spectrum of possible relationships between endorsers or master brands (established brands/organizations that provide credibility; for example, Marriott) and subbrands (brands that are connected to the endorser and augment or modify the association the consumer has with the endorser; for example, Courtyard by Marriott.) House of brands and branded house represent opposite ends of the spectrum. The endorser/endorsed brands and master/subbrand strategies fall in between these two extremes.

House of Brands

In a house of brands strategy, subbrands are allowed to stand alone with little help from the endorser/master brand. For example, Procter & Gamble (P&G) has over 80 brands, but how many customers actually see the relationship between P&G subbrands such as Tide, Cascade, and Safeguard soap? Aaker and Joachimsthaler say there are four reasons why a house of brands strategy might be the best one:

1. You want to avoid an association with your endorser/master brand that would be incompatible with the subbrand offering. For example, if Budweiser wanted to launch a soft drink they might not want to call it "Budweiser Cola" since the association with the brand "Budweiser" might lead consumers to think that the new cola had a decidedly beer taste.
2. You want to signal to the consumer that your new brand is a genuine breakthrough or departure from the norm. That's why Toyota called its luxury car brand Lexus rather than "Toyota Deluxe."
3. You want to emphasize a key benefit of the subbrand. For example, your toothpaste makes teeth "Gleem" or your revolutionary new toothbrush has "Reach."
4. You want to minimize a possible channel conflict. For example, Head & Shoulders and Pantene are made by the same company but are sold through different channels.

Endorser/Endorsed

In this case, the subbrands are independent, but there is a clear endorsement of the subbrand by an endorser/master brand. For example, Courtyard by

Marriott and Fairfield Inn by Marriott are independent brands but there is a clear endorsement of them by the master brand Marriott.

Master/Subbrand

Here the link in the consumer's mind between the master brand and the subbrand is much closer than the link between the endorser brand and endorsed brand. Smucker's Simply Fruit brand is clearly linked to Smucker's and Gillette's Sensor razor is clearly linked to the Gillette master brand. In both cases, note Aaker and Joachimsthaler, the subbrand adds an additional and beneficial association to the master brand. For example, Smucker's Simply Fruit provides an added healthy/fresh/quality association in the mind of the consumer with the Smucker's master brand so that the master brand and subbrand both benefit.

Branded House

In this final strategy, the master brand becomes the dominant driver of the customer's association with the subbrand. For example, Virgin is the dominant driver of consumers' associations with Virgin Airlines, Virgin Records, Virgin Music, Virgin Rails, Virgin Cola, and so on. The Virgin names says service, quality, innovation, fun/entertainment, value, and so forth. The Virgin subbrands benefit from this association. Healthy Choice, Kraft, Sony, Disney, Levi's, and Nike all use a branded house strategy.

Aaker and Joachimsthaler note that your choice of brand relationship strategy should be driven by the extent to which your master brand will assist in building a positive and differentiated image for your subbrand. Sometimes your master brand will add credibility and value to the consumer's associations as in the example of the Sony brand and the Walkman subbrand. Sometimes, the master/subbrand relationship would be best left at a distance. Aaker's and Joachimsthaler's brand relationship spectrum gives you a range of choices.

Designing the Brand Architecture

Once you have decided upon the relationship that you want to convey between your master and subbrands, say Aaker and Joachimsthaler, you are then ready to design your brand architecture. You do so by completing five steps:

(1) identify the brands in your portfolio, (2) specify roles for each of your brands, (3) specify the product-market context of each of your brands, (4) develop your brand portfolio structure, and (5) design your portfolio graphics.

Step #1: Identify the Brands in Your Portfolio

Your brand portfolio, say our gurus, is all of the brands and subbrands you have in your product/service offerings, including those that you have co-branded with other firms. While the process of identifying your brands may seem simple, Aaker and Joachimsthaler caution that this may be a daunting task since you may have brands that are obscure or dormant. Nevertheless, your task here is to compile a complete list and to decide if you need to add some new brands to strengthen your portfolio.

Step #2: Specify the Role of Each of Your Brands

Aaker and Joachimsthaler tell us that each brand in a portfolio should be assigned one or more of the following roles:

Strategic Role—the brand is an important source of future profits.

Linchpin Role—the brand provides a key basis for customer loyalty. For example, Hilton Rewards is a linchpin brand for Hilton Hotels.

Silver Bullet—the brand positively influences the image of another brand. For example, IBM's Thinkpad brand boosted public perceptions of IBM.

Cash Cow—the brand has a significant customer base and does not require the level of investment of other brands, therefore it can be used to generate funds that can be invested in strategic, linchpin, and silver-bullet brands.

Step #3: Specify the Product-Market Context of Each of Your Brands

Aaker and Joachimsthaler note that a set of brands taken together comprise a product/service offering in a particular product-market context. For example, the Cadillac Seville and Northstar system brands work together in the following way:

> The Cadillac Seville with the Northstar system . . . is a particular offering for which Cadillac is the master brand with the primary driver role; Seville plays a subbrand role, and Northstar a branded component role.[1]

In this step, you identify endorser and subbrands (see our previous discussion), benefit brands (branded features, components, or services that augment the brand offering such as Ziploc's ColorLoc Zipper), and any co-brands in your offering. (Cobrands are arrangement you have to combine your brand with one or more brands from a different organization to create a unique offering. For example, Pillsbury cobranded with Nestlé to create Pillsbury's Brownies with Nestlé's chocolate.) Aaker and Joachimsthaler note that cobranding can be particularly powerful. For example, they cite a research study in which 20 percent of prospects said they would buy a fictional entertainment device if it carried the Kodak name, and 20 percent said they would buy it if it carried the Sony name. In contrast, fully 80 percent said they would buy the device if it carried both the Kodak and Sony name, that is, was a cobrand.[2]

Step #4: Develop Your Brand Portfolio Structure

The brand portfolio structure provides a way of grouping brands to clarify their logical relationships. For example, if you are a hotel chain, such as Marriott, you might group your various brands by segment (business vs. leisure travelers), product (overnight vs. extended stay), quality (luxury vs. economy), and so on. Alternatively, say Aaker and Joachimsthaler, you might find it helpful to clarify the relationships among your brands by drawing a "brand family tree" or hierarchical chart much like the organization chart in Figure 3.1.

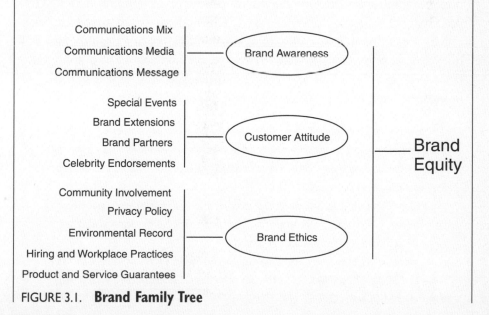

FIGURE 3.1. **Brand Family Tree**

Step #5: Design Your Portfolio Graphics

Finally, say Aaker and Joachimsthaler, you need to take a look at the visual representations that you use across your portfolio of brands, the logos, packaging, symbols, product design, layout of print advertisements, taglines—everything that has to do with the look and feel of the presentation of each of your brands. The key question here is, What kinds of signals are these visual representations sending about the relationships between the brands in your brand portfolio and are they the right signals? An illuminating exercise, say our gurus, is to take all of the graphic representations of your brands (logos and such) and put them on a large wall. Look at them together and ask yourself if they convey a consistent message and support your brand portfolio's structure.

BRAND MOLECULES—SAM HILL AND CHRIS LEDERER

Aaker and Joachimsthaler began their discussion of brand architecture with the assumption that you have or will want to have multiple brands and that you need an architecture to make sense of your individual brands and make sure that you are leveraging them to the greatest benefit. Hill and Lederer go further. They argue that there is a much more powerful reason today for understanding and managing the relationships between brands than just the search for consistency and leverage. The real power of branding, they argue, doesn't lie in how well you manage individual brands, although that does remain important. Instead, the real power and benefit of branding derives from how well you understand and manage your whole portfolio of brands. Hill and Lederer make their case this way:

> Time was brands succeeded or failed based on their own merits. . . . Not long ago, managing an individual brand successfully—understanding its market intricacies, engaging consumers, creating sustainable value, and increasing profitability—sufficed. . . .
>
> Today . . . the bar is higher. Yes, plenty of stand-alone brands are thriving out there. . . . But the most important brand work being done today is about much more than individual brands.
>
> Increasingly, companies are creating brand value by combining brands in new and compelling ways. . . . American Airlines, Citibank, and Visa jointly offer a credit card. . . .

In fact, the greatest brand value is now being created *in the intersections between individual brands.*[3]

Let's back up and repeat that last sentence.

In fact, the greatest brand value is now being created in the intersections between individual brands.

Kmart is a valuable brand, no doubt about it even if it is in a tad of trouble as we write this. And Martha Stewart—love her or hate her—is definitely a valuable brand also. There is no doubt about that either. But, say Hill and Lederer, when you put the Kmart brand together with the Martha Stewart brand, you really have something. And, having that something—leveraging the 2 + 2 = 200,000 value that comes from the synergy of two powerful brands working in tandem—is where the real power of branding is to be found today. The problem, they explain, is that traditional old brand portfolio management—the type Aaker and Joachimsthaler offer—is a good start but just doesn't hack it any longer. It's time, say Hill and Lederer, to update and rethink brand portfolios and how they work, and that's exactly what they say they have done.

Hill and Lederer's ideas about brand portfolio management differ in three fundamental ways from what has gone before. First, they don't restrict membership in a brand portfolio to brands owned by a single company.

Our brand portfolio, on the contrary, includes every brand that plays in the consumer's decision to buy. Intel drives Dell's new product strategy. Dell marketers should consider Intel part of Dell's brand portfolio. The price of a Hertz rental car depends on whether the customer flew United or American. Hertz marketers should consider the airlines part of the Hertz portfolio, since they clearly drive both choice and pricing. The National Basketball Association's (NBA) marketing plan depends on its contracts with Nike, NBC, TNT, and so forth.[4]

Additionally, say Hill and Lederer, not every brand the company owns should be in the portfolio. For example, they note that the buyer of a Kohler faucet probably doesn't care about Kohler's string of golf resorts, therefore Kohler's resorts and faucets should not be considered part of the same brand portfolio.

Second, Hill and Lederer say that traditional brand system mapping doesn't work for their brand portfolios.

Aaker says brand systems "fall into a natural hierarchy." For example, in a brand system hierarchy, Philip Morris naturally sits over its divisional brands—Miller, Kraft, Marlboro, et al. Kraft is over Maxwell House, Jell-O, Philadelphia Cream Cheese, and right on down the line. Traditional hierarchies neatly capture most of the brands in a given company on one page and reflect the brand organization—the reporting relationships of the brand managers—from the inside.

To manage our brand portfolios, on the other hand, we must consider the consumer's point of view as well. That is, we should know how important each brand is in the consumer's purchase decision. For a Marlboro purchaser, for example, the Philip Morris brand matters very little. And so, in a portfolio created for Marlboro, Philip Morris should go at the bottom of the page, not the top. Would the Philip Morris name always be at the bottom? Not necessarily. That's another difference with our brand portfolios: they're dynamic.[5]

Finally, Hill and Lederer say traditional brand organization doesn't work for their portfolios.

More traditional "brand systems" focus on managing a single brand. Even when a company employs category management, as Kevin Lane Keller says, "the duties of the individual brand managers, however, [are] essentially un-changed." That is, brand managers go all out to build their individual brands, and category managers coordinate their actions after the fact. We must man-age brands individually, to be sure; but to create new value, that's not enough. In our view, brand portfolio management is active, preemptive, and overarch-ing. Brand portfolio managers are strategic activists, who help set and over-see the brand agenda inside and beyond a firm's own brand system.[6]

In the future—perhaps in as little as five years—write Hill and Lederer, forward-looking companies will manage their brand portfolios the way they do their financial portfolios.

Brand portfolio strategists will search for the efficient frontier of the brand set, the boundary where brand managers can maximize their returns for any level of portfolio risk, much as savvy investors do today. Instead of the sales and shares of individual brands, they will discuss objectives like overall portfolio growth rate and minimizing risk by adding or removing new brands.[7]

So, what do you have to know to conduct a successful "search for the efficient frontier of the brand set"? (Don't you just love the way some of the gurus have of expressing themselves?) Hill and Lederer say you need two things:

1. You need a new way of visualizing or depicting your brands, their characteristics, and relationships both between each other and with the outside world.
2. You need a new set of tools with which to manage your portfolio.

The Brand Portfolio Molecule

You will recall that Aaker and Joachimsthaler's visual representation of the brand portfolio was a hierarchical chart showing endorser/master brands and subbrands and their horizontal and vertical relationships. Hill and Lederer argue that such a two-dimensional representation of the brand portfolio is outdated. They say we need a three-dimensional model that will allow us to see our brand portfolios from a number of different customer perspectives. They call this new representation the brand portfolio molecule. Figure 3.2 shows what a brand portfolio molecule might look like for Cadillac.

Hill and Lederer argue that their brand molecule has five distinctive advantages over alternative representations of brand portfolios.

1. The molecule allows you to visually depict all of the brands you should consider in making marketing decisions, including your own brands and linked brands, sometimes of other companies, that impact your marketing strategy.
2. Since each brand's relative contribution to the target market's purchasing decision is represented by the size of each brand's sphere in the module, you can easily see the relative value of different brands.
3. Further information about each brand's relative value in respect to influencing the purchasing decision is represented by color. Brands that make a positive contribution are black. Brands that have no impact are in gray and brands that have a negative impact are shown in white. Our gurus say you can use color also to represent value. They say that green, blue, and red work very well.
4. The molecule shows how the various brands in the portfolio are connected. For example, in the Cadillac molecule, the OnStar brand is

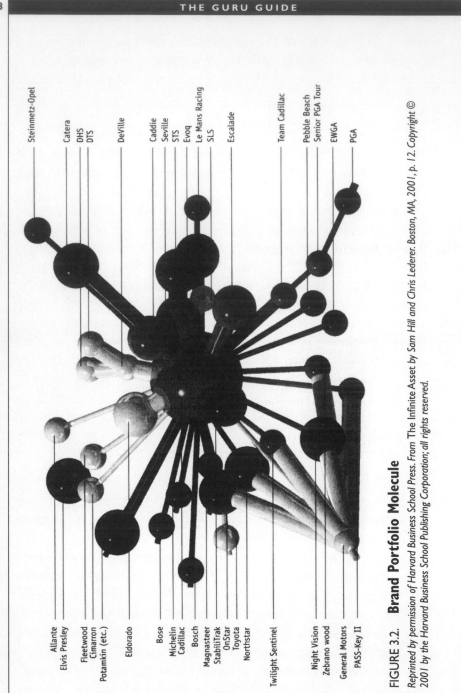

FIGURE 3.2.   **Brand Portfolio Molecule**

Reprinted by permission of Harvard Business School Press. From The Infinite Asset by Sam Hill and Chris Lederer. Boston, MA, 2001, p. 12. Copyright © 2001 by the Harvard Business School Publishing Corporation; all rights reserved.

shown as connected to GM and shared with other car companies such as Saab and Toyota. The thickness of the connection conveys the relationship. The connection with GM is thick and that with Cadillac is thin. The message, say our gurus, is that GM controls the OnStar brand and not Cadillac.

5. Finally, say our gurus, the positioning of the spheres in the brand molecule conveys additional information that allows marketers to differentiate the brands in question. For example, the DeVille sphere is positioned very close to the Cadillac sphere in the molecule while the Catera sphere is placed further away. Hill and Lederer note that this positioning reflects the long-standing marketing decision of GM to position DeVille very close to the Cadillac value proposition and loyal Cadillac market. On the other hand, Catera has been positioned further away from Cadillac, and it is seen as having a different value proposition and different market.

⊙ OUR VIEW

Okay, we agree that three dimensions always convey more relative information than two. So do four, five, and six dimensions. Hill and Lederer tell us that they have been able to extract a large volume of insight about Cadillac's marketing opportunities and problems by simply analyzing Cadillac's brand portfolio molecule. For example, they conclude from the Cadillac molecule that (1) the Catera brand that Cadillac hopes to use to woo younger customers is unlikely to do the trick, and (2) that it would be a risky play for Cadillac marketers to invest money in hyping the OnStar brand.[8] We won't go into their rationale for these conclusions here, but we will point out that (1) other marketers might have arrived at the same conclusions without the molecule, and (2) that most marketers if presented with our gurus' Cadillac molecule probably would not have come to the same conclusions. Undoubtedly, Hill and Lederer's molecule is more complex than Aaker and Joachimsthaler's chart, but it can be a little confusing at times.

The Brand Portfolio Toolkit

Let's assume for the moment that you have constructed your brand molecule in all three dimensions and in Technicolor. Let's also assume that you have derived some true insights from your molecule or hired consultants to come up with some. How do you use what you have learned to make things better? That, of course, takes us to the Hill and Lederer toolkit. Hill and Lederer offer eight tools that they say you can use to maximize your return on your portfolio of brands and minimize your risk, including (1) extension, (2) repositioning, (3) pruning, (4) overbranding, (5) cobranding, (6) amalgamation, (7) partitioning, and (8) scaling. Here is a summary of each.

Brand Portfolio Molecule Tool #1: Extension

Hill and Lederer note that brand extensions are the most common and oldest approach to boosting returns from brand portfolios. Proponents argue that brand extensions add new volume, increase the efficiency of advertising campaigns, are more successful than new products or services launched on their own, and require less overall investment to launch than products and services launched on their own. Opponents like Al and Laura Ries, authors of *The 22 Immutable Laws of Branding,* argue that brand extensions generally result in little or no net gain in market share and that often they can be dangerous to the core brand. For example, the Ries cite the experience of American Express, which went from few brands and a 27 percent market share in 1988 to 15 brands and an 18 percent market share in 2001. And Cadillac, say the Ries, did considerable damage to its core brand when it launched its ill-fated Cimarron subbrand (essentially an upscale Chevrolet Cavalier) as a brand extension designed to appeal to younger buyers.[9]

Hill and Lederer argue that proponents and opponents of brand extensions are both right in that extensions can create value but also bring risks to the core brand. The key to effectively utilizing brand extensions, say Hill and Lederer, is to recognize that there are two types of extensions—*interstitial* extensions and *boundary* extensions. Interstitial extensions "block competitors and lock in customers with a more compelling and specific offering."[10] For example, Colgate-Palmolive introduced Colgate Total as an antitartar extension to its line of toothpaste in 1998 as a way of attacking P&G Crest brand. In contrast, boundary extensions take the brand beyond the boundaries of the current brand portfolio. For example, P&G extended its Vicks brand into appliances such as humidifiers, vaporizers, and so on.

Hill and Lederer argue that interstitial extensions are often a good idea since they provide a way to fill in your brand portfolio and attack a market leader like Colgate-Palmolive used Colgate Total to attack P&G's Crest line. While they admit that too many extensions may indeed cannibalize your existing brands, most marketers would rather cannibalize their own brands than have them successfully attacked by a competitor.

In respect to boundary extensions, Hill and Lederer argue you should be careful never to extend your brand across consumer segments, distribution channels, or price points. As examples, they point to the experiences of the Virgin brand, which was highly successful with boundary extensions, and Holiday Inn, which wasn't. Virgin was successful, write the gurus, because it was "careful to keep every new offering within the overall brand portfolio positioning and personality, appealing to similar sets of customers with a similar youthful, cheeky message."[11] On the other hand, Holiday Inn was much less successful with its boundary extension Holiday Inn Express since it crossed price points. Consumers associated the Holiday Inn brand with a higher price point and wouldn't accept a brand carrying the Holiday Inn name as a low-priced hotel on the order of Microtel or Red Roof Inn. Holiday Inn would have been better off marketing their lower-priced offering under a different brand name as Hilton and Marriott have done. The lesson when it comes to boundary extensions, say Hill and Lederer, is to extend the brand across the technologies and products but never across consumer segments, distribution channels, or price points.

Brand Portfolio Molecule Tool #2: Repositioning

Next to brand extensions, repositioning is the most popular tool marketers use to improve their brand portfolio. It is also, according to Hill and Lederer, one of the highest risk tools since it requires you to first get consumers to "unlearn" what your brand no longer stands for before they relearn what you want it to stand for in the future. For example, think of the difficulty Oldsmobile had in convincing younger buyers that the "new" Oldsmobile was "not your father's Oldsmobile."

If you are going to use repositioning, say our gurus, don't depend upon advertising alone to do the trick and recognize that it may take years for the repositioning to stick in the minds of the consumers. Most importantly, don't try to reposition a single brand. Focus instead on repositioning the entire portfolio, like Harley-Davidson did in the early 1980s.

> Harley-Davidson repositioned its brand to be the "full-sized, classically styled motorcycle for people who see themselves as individuals." To do so, it targeted a new market (affluent baby boomers) and changed virtually

every component of the value proposition. It focused the core offering, by abandoning attempts to make smaller, high-tech bikes, improved its reputation for quality, and upgraded customer experience, by refitting dealerships and creating rallies and events. The only thing the company left alone was the portfolio's fundamental personality.[12]

As an alternative to risky repositioning, Hill and Lederer suggest that you simply return to your portfolio's roots to rejuvenate the old positioning. They cite Apple as one company that did this successfully.

Apple . . . [revisited] what had made it such a populist phenomenon in the first place, the small, aesthetically unique PC that didn't require a master's degree to set up and operate. That concept originated with the Macintosh in 1984, and though Apple lost its way in the interim, it managed to breathe new life into it in 1998 with the iMac. In a world of adobe-colored boxes, the egg-shaped, multicolored iMacs stood out like a beacon. And true to iMac's core brand promise, it offered the easiest setup and, most important for the new epoch, easiest online access of any machine on the market. The iMac launch campaign offered up simple print and TV ads, featuring the computers framed lovingly on white backgrounds, with no-nonsense copy addressing the computer's basic benefits. The ads did not have to recast Apple or Macintosh in any way. They merely reminded consumers of the key point of difference of the Macintosh brand all along, now boldly embodied in the sleek new machines. Indeed, the tag line for the iMac was "The Internet computer for the rest of us," a play on the old Macintosh slogan.[13]

Hill and Lederer recommend rejuvenation as a better alternative than repositioning if you have an older brand with well-entrenched levels of consumer awareness.

Brand Portfolio Molecule Tool #3: Pruning

Hill and Lederer note that marketers resist cutting brands from their portfolios for a number of reasons, including the reluctance to suffer the immediate loss in volume that cutting a brand is likely to engender and the fear that by cutting a brand they will leave a hole that competitors can exploit. Still, say our gurus, a little judicious pruning of the brand portfolio on a regular basis is important for the long-term success of the portfolio. They recommend that you let the brand portfolio molecule guide you in deciding which brands to cut and that you follow the following keys to success:

1. **Be decisive.** Cut; don't let brands simply atrophy.
2. **Choose the brands to be cut carefully.** Sure, size and growth-rate are important criteria, but even more important is the role of the brand in the overall system. Pepsi hung onto a relatively minor brand named Mountain Dew because it filled an important hole in the company's range. Today it is the hottest brand in the category.
3. **Cut cleanly.** Don't leave holdovers or connections to the existing portfolio that will create problems later. [14]

Brand Portfolio Molecule Tool #4: Overbranding

By overbranding, Hill and Lederer mean "using the brand of the division or company that owns the brand to help make the sale . . . [by] adding a brand on the package, in the advertisements, or on business cards *either in conjunction with or instead of a stand-alone brand.* . . . For example, GE has GE Aircraft Engines, GE Appliances, GE Capital, GE Lighting, GE Medical Systems . . . and so forth."[15] Hill and Lederer note that overbranding makes sense when you need to provide an additional trustmark on branded products in a category where existing brands are weak. For example, Disney used overbranding successfully to provide added trust to its cruise line brand. However, they warn that overbranding carries the same risks of boundary extensions and so you should use overbrands only when they will make sense to the consumer and you use it to tie together portfolios of similar customer bases, distribution channels, and price points.

Brand Portfolio Molecule Tool #5: Cobranding

Cobranding involves linking your portfolio to that of another company. Such links can provide you with access to new growth areas and reduce the risks of boundary extensions. However, warn our gurus, cobranding carries its own risk of failure and brand contamination; therefore it pays to be careful. The following are the keys to cobranding success, say Hill and Lederer:

1. **Effective matchmaking.** Specifically, brand portfolios should overlap but not occupy identical positionings, and there should be commonality of purpose as well. Cobranding will affect the positionings of both portfolios. Make sure that both portfolios have clearly stated objectives and guidelines and that the cobrand delivers.

2. **Keep the messaging simple.** The joint message should be clear and intuitively obvious. Look, for example, at "World-net from AT&T powered by Lycos," from the Internet service provider arena. It takes quite a bit deciphering to deduce exactly what the combined proposition is. Disney toys at McDonald's. Got it. Bacardi and Coke. Got it.

3. **Get what you pay for.** Cobranding increases risk. Make sure the return is worth it. The cobranding relationship should reflect the underlying business logic. Understand who is creating the value and share it appropriately.

4. **Manage risks proactively.** Remember, any time portfolios are linked, it creates a new set of risks. Sit down with the brand portfolio guidelines and brand molecules and really scrutinize every potential alliance. Put very careful and explicit guidelines in place about what is and is not OK ... [T]he better spelled-out the guidelines are, the better the results.[16]

Brand Portfolio Molecule Tool #6: Amalgamation

Amalgamation, the merging of two brand portfolios and elimination of one of the existing brand names, is one of the most powerful tools a marketer can use in managing his/her brand portfolio. But, say Hill and Lederer, it carries with it a high level of risk. It requires boldness and can result in volume loss and market share erosion if done poorly. Worse, once accomplished, amalgamation can be difficult to reverse. Therefore, it pays to do it right. They maintain that the secrets to success are to choose the amalgamated brand name wisely and to make sure that it is a more orderly and more manageable brand portfolio than the two it replaces.

Brand Portfolio Molecule Tool #7: Partitioning

Partitioning includes everything from selling off one or more brands to splitting the existing portfolio into two portfolios and giving the new portfolio its own unique name. Hill and Lederer note that partitioning is an excellent way to gain greater brand focus but that it is often underutilized because marketers fear losing market scale. While admitting that loss of scale is an issue, our gurus argue that when brand portfolios are ripe for partitioning they often don't have as much scale as is imagined. Hill and Lederer cite the split between the HP brand (printers, computer technology, Internet) and Agilent (technical, laboratory-oriented product lines). HP's market scale prior to the split was actually less than it seemed since in spite of its huge consumer advertising budget, it still had to advertise its technical and laboratory products in specialized publications and those products required their own product manager. Consequently the partitioning of HP (computer products) and Agilent (technical products) had little impact on marketing costs. The keys to making partitioning work, write Hill and Lederer, are as follow:

1. **Think like the consumer.** When the portfolio becomes confusing to the consumer, partitioning makes sense.
2. **Make sure that you split the portfolio in a way that creates two coherent new portfolios.** Don't just split the old portfolio in half.
3. **Establish some distance between the two new portfolios once they are created** so that there is no confusion about the identity of the two.

Brand Portfolio Molecule Tool #8: Scaling

Scaling involves "allowing the brand portfolio to follow its natural market, and then creating another portfolio to fill the upmarket or downmarket void."[17] For example, Gap originally catered to teens, but as its consumer base aged it upscaled to meet their more sophisticated tastes and to extend its offerings into GapKids, BabyGap, and so on. It then created Old Navy to backfill and hold onto teens.

THE CUSTOMER'S POINT OF VIEW

You will recall that Hill and Lederer say that an important difference between their approach to organizing the brand portfolio and the approach offered by Aaker and Joachimsthaler is that they take the customer's point of view. Indeed, in constructing their brand portfolio molecule and deploying their eight tools, Hill and Lederer caution us to consider the customers' viewpoints. A vocal group of marketing gurus would applaud their sensitivity to the customer; however, they would argue that Hill and Lederer don't go far enough in focusing on the customer rather than the product.

Do you hear that? We do. It's coming from our bookshelves and research notes. It's the voices of these marketing gurus. Listen. You can barely hear what they are saying.

Forget brand equity; it's customer relationships that matter.

They are getting louder.

Forget brand equity; it's customer relationships that matter.

And louder still.

Forget brand equity; it's customer relationships that matter.

We hear their voices and will give them their chance to make their case for the customer in the next chapter. For now, let's sum up the key ideas on brand management we've covered.

KEY POINTS

▪ A brand architecture specifies the relationships between brands in a brand portfolio. Four basic strategies are possible:

- **House of brands**—P&G with stand-alone subbrands Tide, Cascade, and Safeguard.

- **Endorser/endorsed**—Marriott with Courtyard by Marriott, Fairfield Inn by Marriott, and so on.

- **Master/subbrand**—Gillette with Gillette Sensor Razor.

- **Branded house**—Virgin with Virgin Airlines, Virgin Music, and others.

▪ A brand molecule can be used to provide a three-dimensional representation of the brand portfolio. It has the advantage of clarifying the relationships between not only the brands of a single company but also linked brands, sometimes of other companies, that impact marketing strategy.

○━━▼ Marketers have access to eight tools with which they can manage their brand portfolios: (1) extension, (2) repositioning, (3) pruning, (4) overbranding, (5) cobranding, (6) amalgamation, (7) positioning, and (8) scaling.

Steven Cristol, coauthor of *Simplicity Marketing*

Adam Curry, coauthor of *The Customer Marketing Method*

Jay Curry, coauthor of *The Customer Marketing Method*

Frank Davis Jr., coauthor of *Customer Responsive Management*

Seth Godin, author of *Permission Marketing*

Ian Gordon, coauthor of *Relationship Marketing*

Arthur Hughes, author of *The Complete Database Marketer*

Karl Manrodt, coauthor of *Customer Responsive Management*

Regis McKenna, coauthor of *Relationship Marketing* and author of *Real Time*

Frederick Newell, author of *Loyalty.com*

Don Peppers, coauthor of *The One-to-One Future*

Frederick Reichheld, coauthor of *The Loyalty Effect*

Martha Rogers, coauthor of *The One-to-One Future*

Don E. Schultz, author of *Integrated Marketing Communications*

Peter Sealey, coauthor of *Simplicity Marketing*

Patricia Seybold, author of *The Customer Revolution*

4

All You Need Is a Customer Relationship

O ur gurus agree that brands matter, but a vocal group of marketing pundits have been shouting for some time that

"Customer relationships matter more."

Customer relationship management (CRM) has been the favorite topic of scores of marketing consultants and academicians for over a decade. It has also been a major money maker in spite of the fact that there are at least two competing approaches to implementing CRM, one of which the majority of gurus would argue isn't much more than just an attempt at selling consulting time and computer hardware and software. In this chapter, we will show you how to distinguish between real CRM and a repackaged sales pitch. We will then deal with the following issues:

- What our gurus say is the key concept underlying CRM and its principal advantages over other approaches to marketing, such as branding.

- Why CRM is so important today.
- The four essential steps that our gurus say you must follow in implementing CRM.
- How our gurus say you must reorganize your marketing function and company in general to make CRM work.
- What key questions you should ask to determine if CRM is right for you and your company.

We'll begin with the basics: What is CRM? Or perhaps more importantly, how do you distinguish real CRM from traditional consulting and information systems technology that has been repackaged in CRM clothing?[1]

WHAT IS CUSTOMER RELATIONSHIP MANAGEMENT?

If you are going to give anyone credit for starting the CRM craze, it would have to be Don Peppers, with ample support from his partner and coauthor, Martha Rogers. Peppers's involvement with the concept, which Rogers and he call Marketing 1:1, dates from the summer of 1989. While working as a New York advertising-agency executive, Peppers received a last-minute assignment to give a speech at a meeting of the American Advertising Federation on the topic of "the future of media." With little time to prepare, Peppers cobbled together a presentation that made two essential points. First, said Peppers, the "new" media would be different from the "old" media in a number of ways, including the following:

1. **It would be individually addressable.** In other words, instead of yelling at potential customers in groups—one message to many—you would be able to speak softly to them, one at a time, and even custom-tailor your message.
2. **The media would be two way.** You could speak to your customer and your customer would be able to respond. In other words, instead of engaging in monologue, you could have a real dialogue.
3. **The new media would be cheap—very cheap.** In the past, if you wanted to address customers individually, about the only choice you had was the slow, cumbersome, and expensive postal system. And, if

you wanted to have a two-way conversation, the most you could afford probably was a few hundred people in inefficient focus groups.[2]

Peppers's second point was even more stunning. He said that the emergence of this inexpensive, two-way, and individually addressable media would produce a totally new kind of business competition in which companies would be forced to compete for customers *one at a time.* When that happened, he went on, mass marketing would be dead and the marketer's role would fundamentally change in a number of ways. According to Peppers:

> The mass marketer visualizes his task in terms of selling a single product to as many consumers as possible. This process includes advertising, sales promotion, publicity, and frequently a brand management system for organizing the efforts of the company's marketing department. The marketer's task has always been to make the product unique in a way that would appeal to the largest possible number of consumers, and then to publicize that uniqueness with one-way mass-media messages that are interesting, informative, and persuasive to the "audience" for the product.
>
> As a 1:1 marketer, however, you will not be trying to sell a single product to as many customers as possible. Instead, you'll be trying to sell a single customer as many products as possible—over a long period of time, and across different product lines.
>
> To do this, you will need to concentrate on building unique relationships with individual customers, on a 1:1 basis.[3]

The future of marketing, said Peppers, would be in customer relationships, and the future role of marketers would be to manage those relationships. The future would be about customer relationship management.

Peppers's speech received an explosive reaction. Over the next few years he followed it with other speeches refining the idea. In 1993, he formed a firm to preach the gospel of "one-to-one" marketing and then wrote a bestseller, *The One-to-One Future,* with Martha Rogers, an associate professor of marketing at Bowling State University. Peppers and Rogers became gurus and produced several more best-sellers. Other gurus and would-be gurus chimed in with their thoughts, and the doctrine of CRM grew. We summarize some of the key differences between CRM and traditional marketing in Exhibit 4.1.

EXHIBIT 4.1.   Customer Relationship Management versus Traditional Brand-Based Marketing

In addition to the work of Don Peppers and Martha Rogers, the comparisons in this exhibit are based upon the writings of the following gurus:

- **Frank W. Davis Jr.** and **Karl B. Manrodt**, coauthors of *Customer Responsive Management.*
- **Seth Godin,** author of *Permission Marketing.*
- **Ian Gordon,** author of *Relationship Marketing.*
- **Regis McKenna**, author of *Relationship Marketing* and *Real Time.*
- **Frederick Newell**, author of *Loyalty.com.*
- **Don Schultz**, author of *Communicating Globally: An Integrated Marketing Approach.*

TRADITIONAL BRAND-BASED MARKETING	CUSTOMER RELATIONSHIP MANAGEMENT
Approaches marketing and marketing communications as a military campaign in which the objective is to gain a competitive advantage, capture the attention and interests of consumers, and/or encourage dealer or distributor network support.	Approaches marketing and marketing communications as dating in which the objective is to form a long-term and mutually beneficial relationship. The marketer attempts to turn strangers into friends and friends into lifetime customers.
Sells one product at a time to as many customers as possible through product managers.	Sells as many products as possible to one customer at a time through customer managers.
Uses information about what customers have in common to sell to the widest range of customers and find the next most logical customer for a product.	Uses information about individual customers to find the next most logical product for that customer.
Differentiates products.	Differentiates customers.
Tries to acquire a constant stream of new customers.	Tries to get a constant stream of new business from existing customers.
Competes for market share.	Competes for share of customer.
Makes customers and marketers adversaries.	Makes customers and marketers collaborators.
Manages products.	Manages customer relationships.
Talks to customers—tell and sell.	Engages in a dialogue with customers—listen and learn.
Disseminates the same information to everyone in predigested form.	Allows individual consumers access to the information they want, where and when they want it, and in the form they want it.

(continued)

EXHIBIT 4.1. (continued)

TRADITIONAL BRAND-BASED MARKETING	CUSTOMER RELATIONSHIP MANAGEMENT
Takes customers to products.	Takes products to customers.
Focuses on satisfying customers.	Focuses on allowing customers to satisfy themselves through self-service.
Presents brand as a product differentiator created chiefly by advertisements broadcast by mass media.	Presents brand as an encapsulation of actual, experienced value, created through customer preferences expressed in dialogue with producers or service providers.
Bases the marketplace upon impersonal, arm's-length transactions during which buyers examine products and make selections based upon their individual needs.	Bases the marketplace upon relationships in which customers seek not only products but also advice and consistent care.
Views purchase events as independent of each other. Whether one customer buys a product or not is completely independent of whether another customer buys it. The rule of the marketer is to "line up" as many customers as possible who are satisfying a need the firm can fill. If necessary, the company must cut its price to whatever level is required to attract the last, most-marginal, least-interested customer.	Views purchase events as conditional on previous purchase events. The customer is presumed to remember the company from one purchase event to another. Thus, the company must ensure that the purchase events undertaken by any single customer remain linked together by the enterprise so that each successive purchase event becomes more convenient for that customer.
Creates an environment in which product and service providers compete on price.	Creates an environment in which product and service providers compete not just on economic price but also on the degree of hassle. Providers compete to see how effortlessly and completely they can meet customers' needs.
Is internally focused. Companies unilaterally anticipate future customer needs, define the ideal offering for the market, set up production, produce and distribute the offering, and try to sell the offering.	Is externally focused. Companies plan and build infrastructures that enable them to organize a network of services, communications, and processes so they can interact with customers, diagnose needs, develop customized delivery plans, and track results.
Depicts products as bundles of tangible and intangible benefits the company assembles in anticipation that customers will want them.	Depicts products as aggregations of individual benefits customers have participated in selecting and/or designing.

(continued)

EXHIBIT 4.1. **(continued)**

TRADITIONAL BRAND-BASED MARKETING	CUSTOMER RELATIONSHIP MANAGEMENT
Sells products and/or services.	Sells *prodices* (*products/services*)—things that look like products but act like services—in recognition of the fact that the consumers want *communication* and not phones; *meals* and not foodstuffs; *entertainment* and not CDs; *clean clothes* and not laundry products, and so on.
Emphasizes planning and stability to anticipate, define, produce, and distribute the optimum product in the optimum way for the marketplace.	Emphasizes flexibility to be responsive to customers and minimize wasted capacity.
Sets the price for a product and offers the product/price set in the marketplace, perhaps discounting the price in accordance with competitive and other marketplace considerations.	Sets the value of the product and therefore its price varies with the preferences and dictates of the customer. The price needed to reflect the choices made and value created is established through a process of collaboration.
Sees distribution as the channel that takes the product from the producer to the consumer.	Sees distribution as a process that allows the customer to choose where and from whom they will obtain the value they want.
Believes that customers must be treated equally.	Believes that customers must be treated individually.

Source: *This exhibit is based upon Don Peppers and Martha Rogers,* The One-to-One Future: Building Relationships One Customer at a Time *(New York: Currency/Doubleday, 1993); Don Peppers and Martha Rogers,* Enterprise One-to-One: Tools for Competing in the Interactive Age *(New York: Currency/Doubleday, 1997); Don Peppers and Martha Rogers (eds.),* The One-to-One Manager: Real-World Lessons in Customer Relationship Management *(New York: Doubleday, 1999); Frank W. Davis Jr. and Karl B. Manrodt,* Customer Responsive Management: The Flexible Advantage *(Cambridge, MA: Blackwell Business, 1996); Ian Gordon,* Relationship Marketing *(Etobicoke, Ontario Canada: John Wiley & Sons, 1998); Regis McKenna,* Real Time: Preparing for the Age of the Never Satisfied Customers *(Boston, MA: Harvard Business School Press, 1997); Frederick Newell,* Loyalty.com: Customer Relationship Management in the New Era of Internet Marketing *(New York: McGraw-Hill, 2000).*

WHY CRM IS IMPORTANT NOW

As we said, CRM has been a hot topic in marketing for over a decade. Rather than cooling off, some gurus think CRM will only become a hotter topic in the years ahead. These gurus say we are experiencing nothing less than a customer revolution that is shifting power in the buyer/seller relationship away from companies and toward customers. No one describes this customer revolution better than Patricia Seybold, the author of the 2001 book—yes, you guessed the title—*The Customer Revolution*.

Seybold begins her argument with a series of warnings.

> Fasten your seatbelts! The turbulence you've been experiencing in the stock market isn't over yet. In fact, it's probably going to get worse.
>
> Why? Because we're in the midst of a profound revolution. And it's bigger than an Internet revolution or a mobile wireless revolution. It's a *customer revolution*.
>
> Customers have taken control of our companies' destinies. Customers are transforming our industries. And customers' loyalty—or lack thereof—has become increasingly important. . . . Customers are . . . changing the face of business as we know it. And your company's value is in their hands. Your customer franchise has suddenly become the scarcest and the most crucial resource for your business.
>
> What's more, your company is probably at risk. . . .
>
> You are no longer in control of your company's destiny. Your customers are. . . . They're demanding that we change our pricing structures, our distribution channels, and the way we design and deliver our products and services to them. They won't be denied. They have the power and they know it. Companies that don't "get it" will be out of business soon.[4]

Is this just consultant hyperbole designed to shock and sell books? Of course it is—but only in part. Then again, Seybold and fellow devotees of the *customer relationship* mantra are serious. They really do see a revolution in process. The fact that the existence of such a revolution would make their expertise more valuable is beside the point.

So, what evidence can Seybold cite to support her and her fellow gurus' contention that a customer revolution is actually underway? She offers the following "quick litany" of ways she says customers have taken control and are reshaping business/consumer relationships.

- **In the past . . .** providers of intangible goods—information, software, music, entertainment, services—could reap high profit margins due to low cost of goods sold (after the creation of the first instance).

- ☐ **Today** . . . customers demand to freely share and reuse digital goods, paying once (or not at all) and then altering, distributing, and repurposing the original material.
- ■ **In the past** . . . banks, brokerages, and insurance companies counted on customers' inertia. The switching costs were high to move accounts from one firm to another,
  - ☐ **Today** . . . customers can easily move their financial records and their relationships.
- ■ **In the past** . . . pricing for products and services could vary dramatically from one country to another, and pricing was so complex (particularly in the business-to-business realm) that it was difficult to compare the real costs of doing business with one firm over another.
  - ☐ **Today** . . . pricing is much more transparent; customers are demanding equal prices around the globe, and they now have much more information at their fingertips to allow them to compare prices. In many industries, customers are already dictating prices to their suppliers.
- ■ **In the past** . . . manufacturers could give lip service to designing and configuring products for customers.
  - ☐ **Today** . . . manufacturers have the tools to make custom-manufacturing cost-effective and practical. Customers are voting with their feet and flocking to suppliers that offer them customized products and services.
- ■ **In the past** . . . one could only imagine on-line marketplaces where buyers and sellers could efficiently find one another and transact business.
  - ☐ **Today** . . . those e-markets exist with customers' building projects, medical records, systems configurations, and/or inventory at their core. Customers' projects, processes, and supply needs are now the magnets that draw suppliers to compete and cooperate in dynamic e-market spaces.[5]

These kinds of changes in customer relationships, says Seybold, are not going unnoticed by the stock market. "In today's extremely volatile stock market," she writes, "there are only two things that investors can count on: the breadth and depth of your relationship with your customers and your commitment to sustaining and growing those relationships for as long as possible."[6] In the future your customer capital, the sum of the value of all of your customer relationships, will determine the value of your company. She goes on to predict that your investors are going to start expecting to be told not just about your company's return on equity (ROE) and return on assets

(ROA) but also data on the value of your customers such as your average profit per customer, customer retention rate, changes in profits per customer from year to year, and so on.

It is clear, says Seybold, that your customers are in the driver's seat today. They are directing the course of your business and they determine its value. In short, customer relationships count. They count in a big way. It's no wonder then, writes Seybold, that old line product-centric companies are scrambling to become more customer focused. Everyone, it seems, already has or is racing to implement some kind of comprehensive customer relationship management system. Therein lies a problem. Well intentioned or not, say our gurus, some people are getting CRM all wrong.

MISCONCEPTIONS ABOUT CRM

As we noted earlier, CRM has been a hot topic among consulting organizations and assorted business circles for some time. Like most management concepts that become management fads, CRM has suffered from its share of misinterpretation and, in some cases, outright misrepresentation. Our gurus say that there are at least two important misconceptions about customer relationship management.

Misconception #1: CRM Is a Technology-Driven Solution to Sales and Marketing Management

Don Schultz, author of *Integrated Marketing Communications,* says that over the last six or seven years two decidedly different approaches to CRM have evolved in the United States and in Northern Europe:

> [T]he North American version . . . grew out of the technology arena, including data aggregation and consolidation, datamarts, data handling and salesforce automation. In short, the U.S. version is a technology driven solution to sales and marketing management. It focuses primarily on managing the information flow between the buyer and seller, such as lead management and telemarketing support, seeking efficiencies in sales-force costs.

For the most part, it focuses on new customer acquisition, for it assumes the marketer will have to generate the relationship and manage it through various forms of contact.

The other version of CRM was developed primarily in Scandinavia and Northern Europe out of services marketing—that is, how an organization develops and maintains relationships with customers over time. The Nordic School focuses much more on aligning the organization's resources in such a way that ongoing relationships are formed and maintained. Thus, the primary focus is on building customer loyalty and retention.

Interestingly, the North American approach to CRM is generally developed, implemented and managed by the information technology group. Sales and marketing people provide the input, but IT manages the system. In the Nordic School of CRM, however, the sales and marketing people manage the process. While technology is a key ingredient in the Scandinavian approach, it's the drive for customer-understanding that differentiates the methodology employed. While data is important, it's important not just in terms of how the system can be managed, but also what type of learning can be gained and solutions provided to customers on an ongoing basis. In short, it's a customer retention approach rather than a customer acquisition approach.[7]

In short, the U.S. version is technology heavy, sales focused, and lead driven. The goal is still largely customer acquisition rather than customer retention. In contrast, the European version is directed toward building long-term relationships with a selected group of customers, knowing and understanding them, and aligning the organization to meet their needs. Most of our gurus would argue that Schultz's European version is much closer to the real CRM than his U.S. version.

 **OUR VIEW**

If you encounter a consultant whose CRM pitch focuses primarily on such things as databases, datamarts, date integration, and assorted plug-in technology that is guaranteed to produce marketing miracle cures, understand that what he/she is selling has more to do with hardware, software, and consulting than it has to do with CRM.

Misconception #2: CRM Is about Loyalty Programs

All of our gurus agree that customer loyalty is a key concept of CRM. Therefore, it would seem natural that loyalty programs such as frequent buyer or frequent shopper programs would be an important feature of CRM efforts. They aren't, say our gurus, and for good reason. Most loyalty programs, as they are normally implemented, don't produce much customer loyalty. Frederick Newell reported on the dismal statistics in his book, *Loyalty.com:*

> In the nineties marketers began to develop their customer information files, and they rushed to all kinds of customer bribes under the guise of loyalty programs. While marketers hoped these points programs, rebate schemes, and other rewards would build customer loyalty, the original purpose of most programs was to capture customer data.
>
> That was particularly true in the retail field. If the retailer could persuade customers to carry a "club" card and show it or swipe it on every purchase occasion, it was easy for point-of-sale technology to capture transaction data and add that to customer records in the database. Still many believed the club rewards would build loyalty.
>
> But that has not happened. Despite all of the loyalty program efforts, customers are still switching stores at a great rate. The Food Marketing Institute, which asked customers if they had switched their most-used self-service store during the past year, found that Switzerland had the smallest percentage of customers switching stores (7 percent), followed by Germany (10 percent) and Spain (11 percent). This compared with 24 percent in the United Kingdom and 26 percent in France.
>
> Interestingly, low-switching Switzerland had the lowest participation in loyalty schemes (15 percent), as opposed to the high-switching United Kingdom which had the highest number of customers participating in loyalty programs—83 percent of customers.
>
> The study also revealed that 52 percent of UK customers admit to participating in two or three loyalty programs, and another 40 percent do not consider such schemes "worthwhile." Even though most loyalty card programs are discounted, 30 to 50 percent of customers in existing programs are not participating.[8]

So why don't loyalty programs work? The answer is simple, say our gurus—there are so many loyalty programs today that consumers no longer see them as unique or personal, and treating customers in a personal and unique way is a key feature of CRM.

THE KEY CRM CONCEPT

If you had to pick one concept or principal that constitutes the foundation of customer relationship management, that principal would almost certainly be this: *Retaining the loyalty of the right customers is the key to long-term profits in just about any company.*

While all of our CRM gurus preach the gospel of customer loyalty, none does it better or more authoritatively than Frederick Reichheld, director of the strategy consulting firm Bain & Company and author of *The Loyalty Effect.* Reichheld argues the following:

> By raising customer retention rates by as little as five percentage points, companies can increase the lifetime value of their average customer by 25 to 100 percent, depending upon industry.[9]

In other words, if an advertising agency can retain just 5 percent more clients—for example, increase its retention rate from 90 to 95 percent— then it can be expected to increase its total lifetime profits from a typical client by an average of 75 percent. An insurance company would see a 90 percent increase from the same improvement in retention rates, and a branch bank could be expected to see an 85 percent increase. Similar gains have been found across industries. (See Exhibit 4.2 for examples.)

Reichheld says two factors are at work here. First, customer loyalty has a substantial impact on the growth of customer inventory. Think of your customer base as water in a bucket, says Reichheld. If you have a hole in the bottom of your bucket—losing customers—then you have to keep pouring water in to the top of the bucket—keep adding new customers—just to keep your volume the same.

> Say you steadily add new customers to the top of your inventory, but old customers are steadily vanishing from the bottom. If you could slow the de-

EXHIBIT 4.2. **Impact of a 5-Percent Increase in Retention Rate on Total Lifetime Profits from a Typical Customer**

Industry	Increase in Profits
Advertising agency	95%
Life insurance company	90%
Branch bank deposits	85%
Publishing	85%
Auto service	81%
Auto/home insurance	80%
Credit card	75%
Industrial brokerage	50%
Industrial distribution	45%
Industrial laundry	45%
Office building management	40%

Source: Frederick Reichheld and Thomas Teal, The Loyalty Effect (Boston, MA: Harvard Business School Press, 1996), p. 36.

fection rate, the new customers you gained would increase the total at a much faster rate. It's like a leaky bucket. The bigger the leak in your bucket of customers, the harder you have to work to fill it up and keep it full.

Imagine two companies, one with a customer retention rate of 95 percent, the other with a rate of 90 percent. The leak in the first firm's customer bucket is 5 percent per year, and the second firm's leak is twice as large, 10 percent per year. If both companies acquire new customers at the rate of 10 percent per year, the first will have a 5 percent net growth in customer inventory per year, while the other will have none. Over fourteen years, the first firm will double in size, but the second will have no real growth at all. Other things being equal, a 5-percentage-point advantage in customer retention translates into a growth advantage equal to a doubling of customer inventory every fourteen years. An advantage of ten percentage points accelerates the doubling to seven years. [10]

Second, says Reichheld, customer retention is critical for profits in most industries, because customers almost always become more profitable over time. Retain your customers, he adds, and four really nice things will begin to happen:

1. Your per-customer revenue will increase—One of the nicest things about keeping customers long term is that they tend to spend more over time. For example, the customer who initially comes into an auto service center for an oil change is likely to return for more expensive services such as tune-ups. Reichheld cites research that shows that the typical auto service center customer triples his or her spending between the first and fifth year of doing business with the center. The same pattern of increased spending over time occurs in many other industries. Insurance is another good example:

> In personal insurance, the average premiums of loyal customers grow at a rate of 8 percent a year. A typical family's increasing affluence accounts for part of this increase. Insurance on the new Lexus costs more than it did on the old Toyota. An addition to the house means more coverage, and so does the vacation home. Another part of the 8 percent average derives from the fact that long-term customers also tend to consolidate their insurance policies, so that a single long-term agent or company picks up auto, home, and life. At Northwestern Mutual, 55 percent of new sales come from existing policyholders.[11]

2. Your operating costs will decline—Another nice thing about keeping customers long term, writes Reichheld, is that they are usually easier to serve. Not only have these loyal customers learned about your business and what services they can and cannot expect from you, but your business has learned about them.

> In financial planning, for instance, planners log about five times as many hours on a first-year client as they do on a repeat customer. Much of this is simply the time it takes to understand a new client's balance sheet, tax status, income profile, and risk preference. Meanwhile, the client is learning to communicate with the planner and the company. Over time, this collaborative learning between client and planner can create enormous productivity advantages that translate directly into lower costs.[12]

3. You get more personal referrals—In addition to spending more over time and costing less to service, loyal customers are an excellent source of referrals. That's important because personal referrals are a major source of new customers for many businesses. For example, insurance agents and home builders get the majority of their new clients from personal referrals and, says Reichheld, there is another benefit of personal referrals—research shows that "customers who show up on the strength of a personal recommendation tend to be of higher quality—that is, to be more profitable and stay with the business longer—than customers who respond to conquest advertising, sales pitches, or price promotions."[13] Reichheld notes that there are good reasons referral customers are better customers:

> Veteran customers paint a more accurate picture of a business's strengths and weaknesses than advertisements or commissioned salespeople. In addition, since people tend to associate with people like themselves, chances are good that referred customers will fit well with the products and services the company offers. Though businesses are quick to give the credit for good growth to sexy advertising, brilliant marketing campaigns, or skilled salespeople, the chances are their profitable growth is driven by referrals.[14]

Reichheld adds that the more customers you retain long term, the more referrals you are likely to receive.

4. You will be able to charge a price premium—Finally, long-term customers generate more profits because they often pay more for the same products or services than new customers. This may occur because established customers aren't eligible for special introductory offers or because established customers are usually less price sensitive. They are acquainted with the company's procedures, employees, and product line, and therefore get greater value from the relationship. Unfortunately, writes Reichheld, few companies capture and give long-term customers credit for this price premium.

> Even companies that have customer profitability systems generally miss the full impact [of the price premium for long-term customers], because most such systems merely reshuffle information originally gathered to measure product-line profitability. That is, they tote up profits product by product, then calculate the profit from a particular customer or group of customers on the basis of the products customers buy. This approach ends up averaging coupons and other price discounts across all customers, irrespective of the price actually paid. As a result, firms overvalue transactions and undervalue relationships.[15]

It is clear from the research, writes Reichheld, that loyal customers are extremely valuable, yet most companies don't know the cash value of their customers. Worse, they draw the wrong conclusions from data in their sales figures and average customer tenure. The fault, he says, lies in the basic language of business accounting:

> Accountants have developed sophisticated techniques for appraising capital assets and their depreciation; they have learned how to monitor the constantly changing value of work-in-progress; but they have not yet devised a way to track the value of a company's customer inventory. They make no distinction between sales revenue from brand-new customers and sales revenue from long-term, loyal customers, because they do not know or care that it costs much more to serve a new customer than an old one. Worse, in most businesses, accountants treat investment in customer acquisition as one more current expense, instead of assigning it to specific customer accounts and amortizing it over the life of the customer relationship. The result is that generally accepted accounting principles actually hide the value of a loyal customer, an impressive feat of concealment given what loyalty can do for the great majority of companies.[16]

Therefore, you shouldn't look to your accountants for help with figuring out the value of your long-term, loyal customers. If you want that information, you will have to calculate it yourself, and the figure you should be looking for, say our gurus, is *the lifetime value of your average customer.*

> Today knowing the lifetime value of your current customers is no longer an esoteric marketing exercise. It's a crucial management tool.
>
> *Patricia Seybold[17]*

The Lifetime Value of the Average Customer

Most of our CRM gurus provide some information on how to calculate the lifetime value of the average customer; however, Arthur Hughes provides one of the best explanations in his book *The Complete Database Marketer.*

Hughes defines the lifetime value of the average customer as "the net present value of the profit that you will realize on the average new customer during a given number of years."[18]

Hughes illustrates the calculation of customer lifetime value using the example of a chain of children's clothing stores he calls Mary Anne's Closet.[19] For purposes of the exercise, Hughes assumes that Mary Anne's Closet has approximately 100,000 customers, with sales of about $12 million per year and profits of about $3.6 million per year. For the last two years, the store has offered its customers a loyalty program. Participating customers were given an identification card and offered a 5 percent discount on their purchases if they showed the card each time they shopped. Through the loyalty program, Mary Anne's Closet has assembled two years' data on the names, addresses, and purchase history of 10,000 customers who started shopping with the store two years ago. Hughes calculates the average lifetime value of Mary Anne's Closet's customers as summarized in Exhibit 4.3 and discussed in detail following.

EXHIBIT 4.3.   **Steps in Calculating Average Lifetime Value of a Customer**

Step #1: Determine customer retention rate.
Step #2: Determine the spending rate and total revenue.
Step #3: Determine gross profits.
Step #4: Determine net present value profits and cumulative net present value profits.
Step #5: Determine the average customer lifetime value for each year.
Step #6: Determine the average customer lifetime value for future years.

Step #1: Determine Mary Anne's Closet's Customer Retention Rate

Examining data on purchases made by the 10,000 customers in the loyalty program database, Hughes discovers that only 3,000 of the customers made a purchase in the second year. Thus, the store's retention rate is 30 percent.

$$\text{Retention Rate} = \frac{3,000 \text{ customers in the second year}}{10,000 \text{ in the first year}} = 30\%$$

Your calculations so far look like this (see Chart 4.1):

CHART 4.1. Step #1: Average Customer Lifetime Value

Mary Anne's Closet	YEAR 1	YEAR 2
Number of Customers	10,000	3,000
Retention Rate	N/A	30%

(We provide a summary of all calculations in Chart 4.6.)

Step #2: Determine the Spending Rate and Total Revenue.

Based upon sales figures in the database, Hughes determines that the average customer spent $120 in a year. The store's total revenue for these 10,000 customers was thus $1,200,000 for the first year and $360,000 for the 3,000 customers retained the second year.

$$\underline{Total\ Revenue\ (first\ year) = 10,000\ customers \times \$120 = \$1,200,000}$$
$$Total\ Revenue\ (second\ year) = 3,000\ customers \times \$120 = \$360,000$$

Your calculations so far look like this (see Chart 4.2):

CHART 4.2. Step #2: Average Customer Lifetime Value

Mary Anne's Closet	YEAR 1	YEAR 2
Number of Customers	10,000	3,000
Retention Rate	N/A	30%
Spending Rate	$ 120	$ 120
Total Revenue	$1,200,000	$360,000

Step #3: Determine Gross Profits

Next Hughes calculates the store's gross profits by subtracting the store's total variable costs from total revenues. Variable costs are those costs that vary with the level of sales, such as the cost of merchandise sold and other variable costs like expenses for customer service, debt collection, deliveries, returns, and credits. (Note: Hughes says you should not include fixed costs such as the cost of buildings, overhead, debt service, and so on because these cost will not increase with increased sales.)

In the case of Mary Anne's Closet, Hughes figures the cost of merchandise at 50 percent of revenues and other variable costs at 20 percent of sales. Mary Anne's Closet's variable costs are therefore $840,000 in the first year ($1,200,000 × .70) and $252,000 in the second year ($360,000 × .70). Hughes calculates the store's gross profits for the two years as follows:

Gross Profit (year 1) = $360,000
(Total Revenues [$1,200,000] − Variable Costs [$840,000] = $360,000)

Gross Profit (year 2) = $108,000
(Total Revenues [$360,000] − Variable Costs [$252,000] = $108,000)

Your calculations so far look like this (see Chart 4.3):

CHART 4.3.   **Step #3: Average Customer Lifetime Value**

Mary Anne's Closet	YEAR 1	YEAR 2
Number of Customers	10,000	3,000
Retention Rate	N/A	30%
Spending Rate	$ 120	$ 120
Total Revenue	$1,200,000	$360,000
Variable Costs	$ 840,000	$252,000
Gross Profits	$ 360,000	$108,000

Step #4: Determine Net Present Value Profits and Cumulative Net Present Value Profits

Since future profits are not worth as much as today's profits, Hughes uses a discount rate to express future profits in today's dollars. The discount rate is calculated as:

Discount Rate $= (1 + i)^n$ where:

i = the interest rate and
n = the number of years you have to wait to get the money.

The current interest rate is 8 percent, but since Mary Anne's Closet has a lot of competition from department stores, Wal-Mart, and catalogs, Hughes doubles the interest rate to account for the risk that Mary Anne's Closet might not be around in two or three years to collect the profits.

Therefore, the discount rate for Mary Anne's Closet in year 1 is:

$$\text{Discount Rate (year 1)} = 1 \text{ or no discount}$$
$$\text{Discount Rate (year 2)} = (1 + .16)^1 = 1.16$$

Hughes divides the discount rate for each year by the gross profits for each year to arrive at net present value profit as follows:

$$\text{Net Present Value Profits (year 1)} =$$
$$\text{Gross Profits (\$360,000) / Discount Rate (1)} = \$360,000$$

$$\text{Net Present Value Profits (year 2)} =$$
$$\text{Gross Profits (\$108,000) / Discount Rate (1.16)} = \$93,103$$

Cumulative net present value profits for year 1 are equal to the net present value profits of year 1 or $360,000. Cumulative net present value profits for year 2 are the sum of net present value profits of year 1 and year 2 or $453,103.

Your calculations so far look like this (see Chart 4.4):

CHART 4.4. **Step #4: Average Customer Lifetime Value**		
Mary Anne's Closet	**YEAR 1**	**YEAR 2**
Number of Customers	10,000	3,000
Retention Rate	N/A	30%
Spending Rate	$ 120	$ 120
Total Revenue	$1,200,000	$360,000
Variable Costs	$ 840,000	$252,000
Gross Profits	$ 360,000	$108,000
Discount Rate	1.0	1.16
Net Present Value Profits	$ 360,000	$ 93,103
Cumulative Net Present Value Profits	$ 360,000	$453,103

Step #5: Determine the Average Customer Lifetime Value for Each Year

To arrive at the average customer lifetime value, Hughes simply divides the cumulative net present value profits for each year by the original 10,000 customers.

Average Customer Lifetime Value (year 1) = Cumulative Net Present Value Profit (year 1) $360,000 / 10,000 = $36.00

Average Customer Lifetime Value (year 2) = Cumulative Net Present Value Profit (year 2) $453,103 / 10,000 = $45.31

(Note: Hughes explains that he divides the cumulative net present value profit for year 2 by 10,000 instead of 3,000 [the number of customers retained in year two] because he is interested in obtaining the average customer lifetime value of all of the customers who walk into the store.)

Your calculations so far look like this (see Chart 4.5):

CHART 4.5. **Step #5: Average Customer Lifetime Value**

Mary Anne's Closet	Year 1	Year 2
Number of Customers	10,000	3,000
Retention Rate	N/A	30%
Spending Rate	$ 120	$ 120
Total Revenue	$1,200,000	$360,000
Variable Costs	$ 840,000	$252,000
Gross Profits	$ 360,000	$108,000
Discount Rate	1.0	1.16
Net Present Value Profits	$ 360,000	$ 93,103
Cumulative Net Present Value Profits	$ 360,000	$453,103
Average Customer Lifetime Value	$ 36.00	$ 45.31

Step #6: Determine the Average Customer Lifetime Value for Future Years

Next Hughes uses the calculations he has performed for years 1 and 2 to make some projections about what the average customer lifetime value might be like in future years assuming that things do not change. He comes up with the following:

Customers (year 3) = Customers (year 2) × Retention Rate (.30) = 900
Total Revenue (year 3) = Spending Rate ($120) × Customers (year 3)
(900) = $108,000

Variable Costs (year 3) = Total Revenues (year 3) ($108,000) × Variable Cost
Percent (.70) = $75,000
Gross Profits (year 3) = Total Revenues (year 3) ($108,000) − Variable Costs
($75,000) = $32,400
Discount Rate (year 3) = $(1 + .16)^2$ = 1.35
Net Present Value Profits (year 3) = Gross Profit ($32,400) / Discount
Rate (1.35) = $24,000
Cumulative Net Present Value Profits (year 3) = Cumulative Net Present Value Profits
(year 2) ($453,103) + Net Present Value Profits (year 3) ($24,000) = $477,103
Average Customer Lifetime Value (year 3) = Cumulative Net Present Value Profits
(year 3) / 10,000 customers = $47.71

Therefore, Hughes calculates the *average lifetime value* of any new customer to be $36.00 in the first year, $45.31 in the second, and $47.71 in the third. Your calculations so far look like this (see Chart 4.6):

CHART 4.6. **Average Customer Lifetime Value**
(Assuming a *30 percent retention rate* and a *$120 spending rate*)

Mary Anne's Closet	YEAR 1	YEAR 2	YEAR 3
Number of Customers	10,000	3,000	900
Retention Rate	N/A	30%	30%
Spending Rate	$ 120	$ 120	$ 120
Total Revenue	$1,200,000	$360,000	$108,000
Variable Costs	$ 840,000	$252,000	$ 75,600
Gross Profits	$360,000	$108,000	$ 32,400
Discount Rate	1.0	1.16	1.35
Net Present Value Profits	$ 360,000	$ 93,103	$ 24,000
Cumulative Net Present Value Profits	$ 360,000	$453,103	$477,103
Average Customer Lifetime Value	$ 36.00	$ 45.31	$ 47.71

So, what are the benefits of all of these calculations? Why go to so much trouble? First, says Hughes, if you are the manager or owner of Mary

Anne's Closet, the average customer lifetime value that you have calculated gives you a much better picture of the value of retaining customers. Second and perhaps more importantly, you can determine with some degree of precision just what impact an improvement in your customer retention rate would have on your long-term profits. For example, let's say that you decide to implement CRM and by doing so you expect to be able to improve your retention rate from 30 percent to 50 percent. What difference would that degree of improvement have on your profits and the average lifetime value of your customers? All you have to do, says Hughes, is plug in the numbers. Here is what happens (see Chart 4.7):

CHART 4.7. **Average Customer Lifetime Value**
(Assuming a *50 percent retention rate* and a *$120 spending rate*)

Mary Anne's Closet	YEAR 1	YEAR 2	YEAR 3
Number of Customers	10,000	5,000	2,500
Retention Rate	N/A	50%	50%
Spending Rate	$ 120	$120	$ 120
Total Revenue	$1,200,000	$600,000	$300,000
Variable Costs	$ 840,000	$420,000	$210,000
Gross Profits	$ 360,000	$180,000	$ 90,000
Discount Rate	1.0	1.16	1.35
Net Present Value Profits	$ 360,000	$155,172	$ 66,667
Cumulative Net Present Value Profits	$ 360,000	$515,172	$581,839
Average Customer Lifetime Value	$ 36.00	$ 51.52	$ 58.18

Your average customer lifetime value in the third year goes from $47.71 to $58.18, an increase of nearly 22 percent. That's a pretty useful number to have. And there's more, says Hughes. Let's assume that you are the manager of Mary Anne's Closet and you actually do implement CRM, plus you make a major effort to get better-satisfied customers to join the loyalty program so you can collect data on their purchases. Let's say you get half of your customers to join. You are now collecting data on 50,000 customers instead of 10,000. After three years, you plug in the numbers, including the changes in your variable costs that resulted from hiring all of our gurus to help you implement CRM. As your previous calculations suggested your average customer lifetime value goes up to $58.18 in year 3. You perform some calculations to see just what that means to your bottom line, and you discover that your CRM program, even after deducting expenses for hiring all of those high-priced consultants, has netted you an increase in profits of over one-half million dollars. That's better than a 14 percent gain in profits, and your actual gain might be even higher. Remember that Reichheld said customers who stay with you longer spend more. Therefore, it is likely that your improvement in customer retention would be accompanied by an increase in spending rate, which would make your total gain in average lifetime value and profits from those 50,000 customers even higher. In fact, Hughes does a calculation for Mary Anne's Closet using a 50 percent retention rate and a spending rate of $150 instead of $120. The $30 increase in spending rate results in a customer lifetime value in the third year of $62.45, or a net gain in profits of $737,000, which is about 20 percent. Hughes notes that such results from a marketing program can give a real boost to a marketer's career. We imagine they would. (See Chart 4.8.)

CHART 4.8. **Change in Average Customer Lifetime Value (Assuming a _50 percent retention rate_ and a _$150 spending rate_)**

Mary Anne's Closet	
Customer Lifetime Value After CRM	$58.18
Customer Lifetime Value Before CRM	−$47.71
Change	$10.47
Total Increase in Profits (Change in Lifetime Value × 50,000 customers)	=$523,500

THE ESSENTIAL STEPS TO CRM

Let's assume for the moment that you buy into Reichheld's argument that your company's best path to long-term profits is through customer retention. Let's further assume that you have calculated the lifetime value of your customers and determined that you could substantially increase your profits and your own career by improving your customer retention rate. Consequently, you have decided to implement CRM—the real CRM and not techno-wizardry or frequent-buyer programs. How should you go about it? As you might expect all of our gurus have their own four-step, five-step, or six-step process to help you out. However, most of them, in one way or another, cover the following four basic steps suggested originally by Don Peppers and Martha Rogers: (1) identify your customers; (2) differentiate your customers according to their value to your firm; (3) interact with your customers to learn their needs, interests, and expectations; and (4) customize some aspect of your products or services. Let's look at each of these steps in more detail.

Step #1: Identify Your Customers

Your first step, according to Peppers and Rogers, is simply to identify as many of your customers as you can by asking yourself the following questions:

- IIow many customers does your firm actually *know*, individually?
- Do you have a customer database with identifying information on all your customers, or any portion of them? (" 'Customer identifying information' is any information you can use to separate one particular customer from another, track your transactions and interactions with the customer over time, or get in touch with the customer individually. Name, rank, serial number. Other examples include postal address, phone number, e-mail address, position description or title, account number."[20])
- How current and accurate is that database?
- How much information about each customer does it contain?
- Does each different business unit within your company have its own database?
- Are there other sources of customer-identifying information?
- Are there any simple ways to increase the amount of customer data available to your firm?

Peppers and Rogers predict that one problem you are likely to encounter as you attempt to answer these questions is arriving at a definition of "customer." "Is your customer simply the next step down in your distribution channel? Or is your customer better defined as the end user of your product?"[21] There is no correct answer but, warn our gurus, the way you answer this question will significantly impact how you implement CRM. For example, take a manufacturer of building materials such as Owens Corning. Is its customer the end user of the building materials, the chain retailer, or the wholesale distributor? If Owens Corning identifies the "first buyer" (the wholesale distributor) as its customer, it has a lot fewer customers than if it identifies its customer as one of the millions of end users of its products.

Once you have defined your customer, Peppers and Rogers instruct you to do three things:

1. Take an inventory of all customer data already available in an electronic format.
2. Locate customer-identifying information that is currently "on file" but not in an electronic format.
3. Devise strategies for collecting more information. This latter step may entail going to third-party database firms that sell individual customer information.[22]

> The competitive position of a company and its relative profitability is likely tied directly to the cumulative volume of data it maintains on its customers, relative to its competitors.
>
> *Ian Gordon[23]*

Your goal at this stage, say our gurus, is to identify and bring together all of the information you can find for each and every customer, or at least for those customers who are most valuable to your firm. (See our later discussion of the customer pyramid.) For a list of the types of information one of our gurus thinks you should include in your customer database, see Exhibit 4.4 if your customers are individuals and Exhibit 4.5 if your customers are businesses.

EXHIBIT 4.4. **Customer Information—Individual**

The following is a partial list of types of information for a business customer information file as suggested by Ian Gordon in his book *Relationship Marketing*.

Identification:
- Account or identification number.
- Name.
- Telephone number.

Customer rating:
- Position in customer pyramid.
- Pyramid target.
- Permission level.
- Permission target.

Background:
- Household size.
- Family structure.
- Spouse.
- Children.
- Age.
- Date of birth.
- Home address.
- Business address.
- Shipping address.
- Salary income or range.
- Asset or wealth estimate or range.
- Highest level of education achieved.
- Educational institutions attended.
- Memberships of professional associations.
- Memberships of other organizations: leisure, community, religious, or other.
- Height.
- Weight.
- Consumption habits or preferences.
- Color preferences evident in items of fashion, nonfashion.
- Purchase locations (where are purchases made).
- Timing of spending (e.g., any noticeable skews by time of day, day, week, month, year).
- Lifestyle categorization.
- Psychographic segment.
- Leisure pursuits.

(continued)

EXHIBIT 4.4. (continued)

Presale Communication:

- Number of "touches" or contacts prior to purchases.
- Types of information sought.
- Channels of communication initiated by customer (telephone, Internet).
- Type of information sought.
- Offers and promotional material sent directly, by date.
- Sensitivity to different media.
- Medium that contributed to first purchase (telemarketing, Internet, etc.).

Purchase Behavior:

- Specific items by categorization code, such as SKU number.
- Date of customer's first purchase.
- Date of all subsequent purchases.
- Date of last purchase.
- Frequency with which purchases are made (per day, week, month, year).
- Amount spent on customer's first purchase.
- Amount spent on all subsequent purchases.
- Amount spent on last purchase.
- Margin derived from customer's first purchase.
- Margin derived from all subsequent purchases.
- Margin derived from last purchase.
- Average expenditures.
- Average margin on expenditures.
- For first purchase and all subsequent purchases: method of payment for goods or services bought— cash, credit card, store card.

Postpurchase Behavior:

- Items returned.
- Condition in which returned.
- Purchase amounts of returned product.
- Tone and manner of return, customer.
- Customer complaint frequency, recency.
- Customer satisfaction with issue resolution.
- Elapsed time between product purchase and return.

Predicted Behavior:

- Product or service expected to be bought next.
- Purchase location where product may be bought.
- Media of primary influence.
- Level of expenditure or price range of product.
- Ancillary services that customer may purchase together with the product.

(continued)

EXHIBIT 4.4.   (continued)

Creditworthiness:

- Bad debt history.
- Balance on account.
- Default on minimum payments on account.
- Credit scoring and rating.

Attitudes and Perceptions:

- Key selection and patronage criteria, company overall.
- Key selection and patronage criteria, specific departments or product lines.
- Perceptions of the company in respect of criteria.
- Perceptions of competitors in respect of criteria.
- Opportunities to improve positioning, by major area of purchase.
- Opportunities to improve positioning, overall.

Adapted from Ian Gordon, Relationship Marketing: New Strategies, Techniques and Technologies to Win the Customers You Want and Keep Them Forever *(Etobicoke, Ontario, Canada: John Wiley & Sons, 1998), pp. 206–209.*

EXHIBIT 4.5.   **Customer Information—Business Customer**

The following is a partial list of types of information for a business customer information file as suggested by Ian Gordon in his book *Relationship Marketing*.

Identification:

- Account or identification number.
- Company name.
- Main telephone number.

Customer Rating:

- Position in customer pyramid.
- Pyramid target.
- Permission level.
- Permission target.

Background:

- Industry classification code (SIC).
- Employment levels.
- Date first incorporated.
- Date first started making relevant products.
- Corporate affiliations and interownerships.

(continued)

EXHIBIT 4.5.   (continued)

- Head office location.
- Regional offices.
- Manufacturing locations.
- Size—total sales.
- Growth rate—total.
- Size—relevant products.
- Growth rate—relevant products.
- Profitability—overall.
- Profitability—relevant products.
- Cash flow, overall.
- Financial position—relevant ratios, from financial statements. Could include:
  - Return on investment.
  - Operating profit on net sales.
  - Asset turnover: sales/assets.
  - Current ratio: current assets/current liabilities.
  - Stability ratios, such as debt/assets.
  - Overhead: general, selling, and administration/net sales.
  - Coverage: times interest earned.
  - Growth: sales growth/asset growth.
- Market size for customer's products.
- Market segment participation.
- Market share.
- Customer's major customers.
- Major suppliers to this company.
- Duration of relationships with major suppliers.

Presale:

- Number of "touches" or contacts prior to purchases.
- Types of information sought.
- Channels of communication initiated by customer (telephone, Internet, etc.).
- Contact history—nonpersonal.
- Offers and promotional material sent directly, by date.
- Sensitivity to different media.
- Medium that contributed to first purchase, such as telemarketing, Internet, etc.
- Call history—personal sales calls, by date, by audience.
- Call reports.

Purchases:

- Specific items or services bought by categorization code, such as SKU number.
- Date of customer's first purchase.
- Date of all subsequent purchases.

(continued)

EXHIBIT 4.5. **(continued)**

- Date of last purchase.
- Frequency with which purchases are made (per day, week, month, year).
- Amount spent on customer's first purchase.
- Amount spent on all subsequent purchases.
- Amount spent on last purchase.
- Margin derived from customer's first purchase.
- Margin derived from all subsequent purchases.
- Margin derived from last purchase.
- Average expenditures.
- Average margin on expenditures.
- Financing—for first purchase and all subsequent purchases: method of payment.

Decision Makers:

- Names.
- Titles.
- Our staff who have relationships with these people.
- Scoring of quality of relationships we enjoy.
- Relationship scoring we plan to achieve, by person.

Decision Making:

- Process.
- Decision initiators.
- Decision influencers.
- Decision makers.
- Decision confirmers.
- Executors of decision.
- Purchase cycle.
- Time required to make decision, by type of decision: new buy, rebuy.
- Month when decisions are initiated, by type of product.
- Month when decisions are final.
- Criteria and positioning.
- Vendor selection criteria.
- Product selection criteria.
- Key selection and patronage criteria, overall company.
- Key selection and patronage criteria, specific departments or product lines.
- Perceptions of our company in respect of criteria.
- Perceptions of competitors in respect of criteria.
- Opportunities to improve positioning, by major area of purchase.
- Opportunities to improve positioning, overall.

(continued)

EXHIBIT 4.5. **(continued)**

Influences:

- Factors influencing level of business contracted.
- Business cycle.
- Derived demand dependencies.

Postpurchase Behavior:

- Services required.
- Items returned.
- Condition in which returned.
- Purchase amounts of returned product.
- Tone and manner of return, customer.
- Customer complaint frequency, recency.
- Customer satisfaction with issue resolution.
- Elapsed time between product purchase and return.

Channels:

- Intermediaries used for product, type and name.
- Intermediaries used for service, type and name.
- Customer satisfaction with channel intermediaries.
- Opportunities to enhance aspects of intermediary performance.

Pricing:

- Pricing history.
- Pricing expectations.
- Win/loss assessments: prices of winning vendors.
- Pricing structures preferred.

Predicted Behavior:

- Product or service expected to be bought next.
- Decision maker for next purchase.
- Value of purchase.
- Decision maker's expectations of supplier preceding purchase.
- Media of primary influence.
- Ancillary services that customer may purchase together with the product.
- Vendor preference, if any.
- Current incumbent, if any.

Creditworthiness:

- Debt history.
- Receivables on account.
- Payment schedule.
- Credit scoring and rating.

(continued)

> ## EXHIBIT 4.5. **(continued)**
>
> **Selected Relevant Information:**
> - Customer's customers.
> - Business strategies.
> - Key initiatives.
> - Account planning.
>
> *Adapted from Ian Gordon,* Relationship Marketing: New Strategies, Techniques and Technologies to Win the Customers You Want and Keep Them Forever *(Etobicoke, Ontario, Canada: John Wiley & Sons, 1998), pp. 209–213.*

 **OUR VIEW**

Yes, we know, we said earlier that databases, data integration, datamarts, and all the technology stuff wasn't true CRM. And yes, now we are saying that step one has a lot to do with building and maintaining such databases and therefore purchasing and installing a lot of the techno-wizardry that is promoted as CRM. What gives? The point is that the techno stuff isn't enough. If you just get the technology—just do step one—and don't do the remaining steps, you haven't done CRM and you won't reap its benefits.

Step #2: Differentiate Your Customers

Once you have identified your customers and the information you have about them, your next step, say Peppers and Rogers, is to differentiate them by their value to your company. The key point our CRM gurus are making in this step is that when it comes to their contribution to your company's long-term profitability, all customers are not created equal. Sure, your CRM goal is to retain customers, but not just any customers. You want to retain your most valuable customers. But how do you determine which customers are most valuable? One of the best explanations of this aspect of CRM can be found in the book *The Customer Marketing Method* by Jay Curry and Adam Curry.

Curry says that the best way to start understanding how customers vary in their impact on your revenue and profits is to construct a "customer pyramid" like that shown in Figure 4.1.

FIGURE 4.1. **Customer Pyramid.**

Here is how Curry suggests you construct your customer pyramid:.

1. **Identify the top 1 percent of your customers in terms of sales.**
   They go at the top of the pyramid—these are your top customers. (For example, if you have 1,000 active customers, the 10 customers who bought the most from you last year are your top customers.) (Note: Curry says that as an alternative you may find it more practical and useful to categorize your customers by something other than sales. Banks and insurance companies sometimes group customers by the number of products or product clusters each customer has purchased—one account or type of policy, two, three, and so on. Retail organizations might use number of visits per month or year customers make to stores as the major factor. Auto dealers might use consecutive purchases. For example, customers who had purchased four or more automobiles in the past would be top customers.)
2. **Identify the next 4 percent of your customers,** again in terms of sales revenues. These are your big customers. They go next on the pyramid.
3. **Identify your medium customers.** These are the next 15 percent of your active customers.
4. **Identify the remaining 80 percent of your customers.** These are your small customers.
5. **Identify your inactive customers.** These are customers who have done business with your company in the past but who haven't made a

purchase recently; for example, in the last six months or year. They go next on the pyramid.

6. **Identify your active prospects.** These are people or companies with whom your sales department has established some kind of relationship but that have not purchased from you yet. They may be people who responded to a mailing, people who have requested information about your company, sales leads from trade shows, and so on. Ask your sales department for input.

7. **Identify your suspects.** These are people or companies that might need your products or services but with whom you have yet to establish a relationship. Check with your marketing department.

8. **At the bottom of the pyramid, lump everyone else in the world.** These are companies and people who have no need for your products or services. Curry says that "while you will never make any money with this group, it is important to visualize them to dramatize how much marketing time and money you spend trying to communicate with people and companies with whom you will never do any business!"[24]

Now that you have your customers and prospects properly categorized, you are ready to do some analysis. Here are some of the questions the Currys suggest that you ask about your customer pyramid and some of the lessons they say you might learn.

Question #1: Which Customers in Your Customer Pyramid Deliver Most of the Revenues?

Find out what percentage of your total revenues come from your top, big, medium, and small customers and how much revenue each of these categories of customers generate per customer (see Chart 4.9).

A Lesson You May Learn

If your company is like most, says Curry, you will probably be surprised to discover just how few of your customers are responsible for the bulk of your revenues. In the example shown here, the top 20 percent of customers are responsible for over 75 percent of total revenues. Additionally, over 90 percent of revenues come from existing customers, which demonstrates how important an established base of customers is for the success of a business.

CHART 4.9. Percentage of Total Revenues by Customer Category

Customer Category	Percent of Customers	Percent of Total Revenues	Revenue per Customer
Top	1%	22%	$129,774
Big	4%	26%	$ 37,187
Medium	15%	29%	$ 11,082
Small	70%	16%	$ 1,201
Inactives	10%	7%	$ 983

Source: Based on Jay Curry and Adam Curry, The Customer Marketing Method: How to Implement and Profit from Customer Relationship Management (New York: Free Press, 2000), pp. 18–27.

Question #2: Which Customers Generate the Most Profits?

Now, determine the percentage of your company's profit and profit per customer for each of your customer groups—top, big, medium, and small. To do this you will have to allocate direct, sales, marketing, and other costs to the various groups and then deduct those from revenues generated by each group. Curry notes that arriving at the proper allocations can involve some interesting discussions. For example, how should you allocate overhead—by revenues or by number of customers? Curry suggests 50 percent by revenues and 50 percent by number of customers. How do you allocate marketing and sales costs? For example, where do your salespeople spend their time? Discuss the issues and reach a consensus with your top team on how these costs should be allocated. Curry says you shouldn't be concerned that the resulting numbers lack precision. You are not preparing a report for shareholders, the Securities Exchange Commission, or the IRS. You are just trying to get a good understanding of what kinds of customers are profitable and which are not. Once you have performed your calculations, you will probably come up with results that look something like the following (see Chart 4.10).

Some Lessons You May Learn

If your company is like most, says Curry, you will probably be surprised to discover that the top 20 percent of your customers not only deliver most of your revenues but actually over 100 percent of your profits. The costs associated with marketing, selling, invoicing, collecting revenues, and otherwise servicing your small customers and inactives eats up all of the margin

CHART 4.10. **Percentage of Total Profits by Customer Category**

CUSTOMER CATEGORY	PERCENT OF CUSTOMERS	PERCENT OF TOTAL PROFITS	PROFIT PER CUSTOMER
Top	1%	49%	$34,015
Big	4%	23%	$ 8,620
Medium	15%	40%	$ 2,649
Small	70%	(12)%	$ (993)
Inactives	10%	(8)%	$ (489)

Source: Based on Jay Curry and Adam Curry, The Customer Marketing Method: How to Implement and Profit from Customer Relationship Management (New York: Free Press, 2000), pp. 18–27.

for these customers. In other words, you are losing money on 80 percent of your customers!

Question #3: Where Do You Spend the Bulk of Your Marketing Budget?

Next, examine how you are spending your marketing dollars. Your results may look something like this (see Chart 4.11):

CHART 4.11. **Percentage of Marketing Budget by Customer Category**

CUSTOMER CATEGORY	PERCENT OF MARKETING BUDGET	PERCENT OF REVENUES	PERCENT OF PROFITS
Top	1%	22%	49%
Big	3%	26%	23%
Medium	8%	29%	40%
Small	15%	16%	(12)%
Inactives	3%	7%	(8)%
Prospects	25%	N/A	N/A
Suspects	35%	N/A	N/A
Rest of World	10%	N/A	N/A

Source: Based on Jay Curry and Adam Curry, The Customer Marketing Method: How to Implement and Profit from Customer Relationship Management (New York: Free Press, 2000), pp. 18–27

Some Lessons You May Learn

According to Curry, if your company is like most you will probably find that most of your marketing budget (60 to 80 percent) is spent on communicating

CHART 4.12.   **Effect of Upward Migration of Six Customers on Revenues and Profits**

	Top	Big	Medium	Small	I/P/S	Totals
1999						
# Customers	4	18	68	360	N/A	450
Revenues	$566,115	$462,561	$550,633	$447,674	N/A	$2,026,983
Profit	$161,586	$ 95,322	$ 76,605	$(96,113)	$(145,900)	$ 91,499
2000						
# Customers	5	20	71	354	N/A	450
Revenues	$707,643	$513,957	$574,926	$440,213	N/A	$2,236,739
Profit	$201,982	$105,913	$ 79,985	$(94,511)	$(145,900)	$ 147,469
Difference						
# Customers	+1	+2	+3	–6	N/A	0
Revenues	$141,529	$51,396	$24,293	$(7,461)	N/A	$209,756
Profit	$ 40,396	$10,591	$ 3,380	$ 1,602	N/A	$ 55,969
% Change Revenues	25%	11%	4%	(2)%	0%	10%
% Change Profits	25%	11%	4%	(2)%	0%	61%

Source: Based on Jay Curry and Adam Curry, The Customer Marketing Method: How to Implement and Profit from Customer Relationship Management (New York: Free Press, 2000), Figure 11.16, p. 122.

with noncustomers. While that may not be too surprising, since it takes time, effort, and money to turn noncustomers into customers, you may be surprised at how much you are spending to communicate with people who are not even suspects. A great deal of money is often spent, says Curry, on communicating with people in the "rest of the world" category—people who have no need for or interest in your products or services and who never will.

Question #4: What Would Be the Impact on Your Revenue and Profits of Moving a Small Number of Customers Up the Pyramid?

Curry suggests you perform some what-if calculations, such as what would happen to your revenues and profits if you were able to move just a few small customers up the pyramid. See Chart 4.12 for an example.

Some Lessons You May Learn
You very likely will find that a small movement of customers up the pyramid can yield significant gains in revenues and substantial grains in profits. In the example in Chart 4.12, the movement of just six small customers—one to top, two to big, and three to medium—resulted in a 10 percent increase in revenues and an astounding 61 percent increase in profits. Curry notes that many small customers have the potential of becoming medium, big, or even top customers if given some attention. In fact, you may find that a small customer in your pyramid is actually a top customer in your competitor's. These customers are small in your pyramid because your "share of customer" is low. (Note: "share of customer" refers to the proportion of a customer's potential business you are getting. For example, if you are Office Depot and a customer buys his printer from you but buys his paper, toner, and ink cartridges from someone else, you are missing some share of customer.)

Question #5: What Would Be the Impact on Your Revenue and Profits of Losing a Small Number of Your Top or Big Customers?

Now, says Curry, you should run some calculations to see what would happen if you lost a few of your top customers. See Chart 4.13 for an example.

Some Lessons You May Learn
You very likely will find that the loss of just a few key customers can do significant damage to your revenues and profits. In the example in Chart 4.13,

CHART 4.13. **Effect of Losing Two Customers on Revenues and Profits**

	Top	Big	Medium	Small	I/P/S	Totals
1999						
# Customers	4	18	68	360	N/A	450
Revenues	$566,115	$462,561	$550,633	$447,674	N/A	$2,026,983
Profit	$161,586	$ 95,322	$76,605	$(96,113)	$(145,900)	$ 91,499
2000						
# Customers	3	17	68	360	N/A	448
Revenues	$424,586	$436,863	$550,633	$447,674	N/A	$1,859,757
Profit	$121,189	$ 90,026	$ 76,605	$ (96,113)	$(145,900)	$ 45,807
Difference						
# Customers	–1	–1	0	0	N/A	-2
Revenues	$(141,529)	$(25,698)	$0	$0	N/A	$(167,226)
Profit	$ (40,396)	$ (5,296)	$0	$0	N/A	$ (45,692)
% Change Revenues	(25)%	(6)%	0%	0%	0%	(8)%
% Change Profits	(25)%	(6)%	0%	0%	0%	(50)%

Source: Based upon Jay Curry and Adam Curry, The Customer Marketing Method: How to Implement and Profit from Customer Relationship Management (New York: The Free Press, 2000), Figure 11.15, p. 121

just two customers defected—one top and one big. Their loss resulted in an 8 percent decline in revenues and a whopping 50 percent fall in profits. As Curry says, the lesson to be learned is that "if you can't manage your relationship with your key customers, you are going to be in serious trouble."[25]

Question # 6: Where Do You Want Your Customers to End Up in Your Customer Pyramid Next Year?

Curry says your path to riches, power, and fame is simple. Get new customers into your pyramid. Move your existing customers higher in your pyramid, and keep customers from leaving your pyramid. To accomplish those goals, you need to gather information about each and every customer and do some planning. Among other things, you need the following types of information:

Customer / Prospect Data

Basic Information: Name, address, phone, and so on.

Total Spend: This is the total amount this customer will spend on your category of products/services in a year. For example, if you are a grocer, the total spend for the Smith family would be the total amount they would spend for food in a year. If you are a travel agent, the total spend for company A would be the total amount that company would spend on business travel in a year. Curry suggests three possible sources for information about total spend. First, do market research. For example, if you know the number of people in a family, their ages, and their zip code you can obtain fairly reliable estimates on the amount of money the family will spend on food and clothing in a year. Second, you can interview the customer and ask them. Finally, if interviews are not possible or you don't have time to conduct them, you can ask your sales people for their best guesstimates.

Revenues: What did each customer spend with you last year? Curry suggests you break this down by type of product/service.

Customer Share: This is the proportion of a customer's total spend that your company received last year. For example, if customer A's total spend was $1,000,000 and you sold that customer $100,000 of products last year, your customer share for customer A last year was 10 percent.

CHART 4.14. Customer Goals

	STRUCKMAN	GREEN	SENTINEL	BATES	BRISTOL	BOWDOIN
Last Year:						
Total Spent	$592,700	$34,800	$151,800	$18,900	$58,000	$3,900
Revenues	$296,337	$31,010	$13,659	$1,717	$0	$0
Customer Share	50%	89%	9%	9%	0%	0%
Costs	$ 16,251	$ 5,066	$ 2,232	$ 828	$ 375	$1,722
Profit	$102,285	$ 7,337	$ 3,368	$ (55)	$ (375)	$(1,722)
M&S ROI	2,170%	348%	241%	(13)%	(192)%	(139)%
Pyramid	Top	Big	Medium	Small	Inactive	Prospect
Plan:						
Total Spent	$616,408	$36,192	$156,354	$19,467	$59,740	$4,017
Revenue Target	$354,419	$32,250	$28,138	$3,537	$ 8,961	$0
% Change	20%	4%	106%	106%		
Cust. Share Goal	57%	89%	18%	18%	15%	
Customer Goal	Keep	Keep	Upgrade	Keep	Reactivate	Keep
Target Pyramid	Top	Big	Big	Small	Medium	Prospect

Source: Jay Curry and Adam Curry, The Customer Marketing Method: How to Implement and Profit from Customer Relationship Management (New York: Free Press, 2000), Figure 11.14 and Figure 11.42, pp. 120, 163.

Costs: Marketing, sales, and other costs that can be allocated to this customer

Profit: Revenues - Costs

M&S ROI: Profit as % of marketing and sales costs.

Location in Pyramid: Top, big, medium, small, inactive, or prospect.

Once you have assembled this data you then construct a table that looks something like Chart 4.14.

OUR VIEW

Like us, you may be looking a little askance at these tables. It looks like a lot of work and you may be somewhat skeptical about mixing guesstimates with hard numbers. Still, as Curry argues, this approach is intended to help you visualize the movement of customers in, up, down, and out of your pyramid and plan for your relationships with customers and prospects. The numbers are working tools and need only to be as precise and accurate as your comfort level dictates. The *real* test is whether they help you get new customers into your pyramid, get a larger share of the business of your existing customers, and avoid losing those who are most profitable. In other words, will the analysis Curry recommends help you manage your customer relationships? At least Curry thinks it will.

Step #3: Interact with Your Customers

Once you have identified your customers and differentiated them by their value to your company, your next step, say Peppers and Rogers, is to interact with your customers to learn more about their needs, interests, and priorities. Your major objective in this step is to initiate an ongoing dialogue with your customers through all communication channels available to you including

- Promotional offers.
- Collections/invoices.
- Web-site contacts.
- Complaint handling.

- Orders/purchases.
- Customer inquiries.
- Direct sales calls.
- E-mail.
- Faxes.
- Telephone calls (inbound and outbound).

> The secret of CRM is to listen and learn, not tell and sell. CRM is about empowering and delighting and letting the customer feel as though their interaction with us is within their control.
>
> *Frederick Newell[26]*

In respect to these and other opportunities you might have to interact with your customer, Peppers and Rogers say you should ask yourself whether your employees are taking advantage of these exchanges to learn more about the customer and his/her particular needs, engage the customer in a dialogue, and use the experience and understanding acquired from the exchanges to develop a stronger and more long-lasting relationship with the customer. They add that during all of these exchanges, you should keep three things in mind:[27]

1. The interaction should be accomplished in a way that minimizes the customer's inconvenience.
2. The exchange should result in some outcome that has real benefit to the customer.
3. The results of the exchange should influence your company's specific behavior toward that customer in the future.

Seth Godin adds that you should seek the customer's permission before attempting to start such a dialogue. In the past, says Godin, when mass marketers communicated with customers or potential customers, they engaged in what could be called "interruption marketing." They *interrupted* what the customer was doing—"Now a word from our sponsor"—and asked them to take some action—"Buy Super-Duper Dog Food." In contrast, CRM insists that you stop interrupting and start asking permission. Godin uses an analogy of getting married to explain the difference:

The Interruption Marketer buys an extremely expensive suit. New shoes. Fashionable accessories. Then, working with the best database and marketing strategists, selects the demographically ideal singles bar.

Walking into the singles bar, the Interruption Marketer marches up to the nearest person and proposes marriage. If turned down, the Interruption Marketer repeats this process on every person in the bar.

If the Interruption Marketer comes up empty-handed after spending the entire evening proposing, it is obvious that the blame should be placed on the suit and the shoes. The tailor is fired. The strategy expert who picked the bar is fired. And the Interruption Marketer tries again at a different singles bar.

If this sounds familiar, it should. It's the way most large marketers look at the world. They hire an agency They build fancy ads. They "research" the ideal place to run the ads. They interrupt people and hope that one in a hundred will go ahead and buy something. Then, when they fail, they fire their agency! The other way to get married is a lot more fun, a lot more rational, and a lot more successful. It's called dating.

A Permission Marketer goes on a date. If it goes well, the two of them go on another date. And then another. Until, after ten or twelve dates, both sides can really communicate with each other about their needs and desires. After twenty dates they meet each other's families. Finally, after three or four months of dating, the Permission Marketer proposes marriage.

Permission Marketing is just like dating. It turns strangers into friends and friends into lifetime customers. Many of the rules of dating apply, and so do many of the benefits.[28]

Step #4: Customize Some Aspects of Your Enterprise's Behavior toward the Customer

Your final step in implementing CRM, say Peppers and Rogers, is to take what you have learned from identifying and differentiating your customers and engaging them in dialogue to tailor your company's offerings to fit the specific needs, desires, and preferences of individual customers. They note that while most people call this process "mass customization," very little is really customized.

What really happens is that "mass customizers" design their products around modular components. These modules are premanufactured and then configured in hundreds or even thousands of unique ways to create "customized" products to meet individual customer requirements. For example, a jean manufacturer might combine a relatively small number of waist/hip sizes and leg sizes to produce thousands of versions of "customized" jeans. A publisher might draw upon hundreds or even thousands of individual articles to produce "customized" newsletters designed to provide content geared to the needs and interests of individual readers.

In addition to customizing products, companies have a number of ways to tailor offerings to customers including, write Peppers and Rogers, any or all of the following:[29]

Bundling: Selling two or more related products together. For example, Amazon.com as of this writing is offering *The Guru Guide*™ and *The Guru Guide*™ *to Entrepreneurship* at substantial discounts if you purchase both books.

Configuration: Dell Computer preinstalls specialized and proprietary software for some corporate customers.

Packaging: You provide smaller and lighter packages with instructions in large type for seniors.

Delivery: You offer overnight, two-day, Saturday delivery, and so on.

Ancillary services: The new car you buy comes with quarterly detailing, biweekly wash-and-wax, and pickup and delivery service for routine maintenance.

Service enhancements: You offer customers guaranteed next-day on-site repair services on your PCs or even guaranteed overnight repairs.

Invoicing: You agree to invoice the customer in his/her desired format at a time of the month that is convenient to the customer.

Payment terms: You provide a wide range of payment terms to meet individual needs and preferences.

In short, say Peppers and Rogers, there are many ways you can say to your customers, "Have it your way." Just keep in mind, say some of our other gurus, that there is such a thing as providing your customers with too many options.

Steven Cristol and Peter Sealey, authors of *Simplicity Marketing,* point out that extensive marketing research has demonstrated that most consumers have difficulty evaluating more than a single pair of product features at a time. For example, when faced with the option of choosing a treadmill in the same price range with a heart rate monitor and loud motor or one with no heart rate monitor but a quieter motor, most consumers would find it relatively easy to make a choice. However, if asked to weigh the relative importance of the loudness of the motor, availability of a heart rate monitor, price, type of digital display, running/walking surface, and storage options, the consumer would have much more difficulty. Indeed, as the number of options increases, the consumer's stress level increases also. Anyone who has had to make a choice among the shows on 200+ cable or satellite channels knows what the authors mean.

What consumers want, say Cristol and Sealey, is a level of mass customization that provides them with *optimum choice*—the ability to select just among the features and benefits most important to them—rather than maximum choice. It's the marketer's job, say the gurus, to use the information he/she can glean from customer dialogues and through other marketing research to fine-tune the customization options to provide *optimum choice* in each product and service category, not maximum choice.

Note that Patricia Seybold says that a key component of the *optimum* choice that customers are seeking today is a "seamless customer experience." She writes:

Today's customers are increasingly demanding that companies offer them convenience and freedom of choice. Customers want the freedom to decide whether it's more convenient to call on the phone or to drop into a branch or store. And today's customers have absolutely no patience for the "seams" that occur between most companies' disparate customer support groups. Why should a customer call a different phone number for Web support than for phone support? If a customer walks into a bricks-and-mortar store, he expects to see the items that are featured on the company's Web site. If he shops on the Web, he expects to be able to go into a retail outlet and touch and feel the merchandise, or test drive the car before he makes a final decision. In short, today's demanding customers want a seamless customer experience, and a good one, no matter how they choose to interact with us.[30]

IS CRM THE RIGHT SOLUTION?

So there you have it, say our CRM gurus. Identify your customers, differentiate them by value, interact with them, and customize your offering to provide your customers with optimum choice including a "seamless customer experience." Do that and you'll retain customers for the long term. And long term they will reward your carefully crafted relationship with purchases and profits. What's more, all of those pesky **P** problems from Chapter 1 will seem like nothing more than minor annoyances.

Is that really true? Not exactly, say another herd of gurus. Branding is good and retention is nice, but neither alone is enough. Branding may build "brand equity." CRM may build "retention equity." But, what you really need, say this other group of marketing gurus, is something more than branding or CRM. Call it "customer equity," and it's the subject of our next chapter. But first, let's recap with a summary of the key ideas we covered in this chapter.

KEY POINTS

- Customer relationship management is *not* a technology driven solution to sales and marketing management. Technology is part of CRM, but only part.

- CRM is *not* about creating loyalty programs. Loyalty programs may be employed as part of CRM but by themselves they are not CRM.

- CRM is primarily about establishing and maintaining long-term and mutually beneficial relationships with customers.

- The key concept is that retaining the loyalty of the right customers is the key to long-term profits in just about any company.

- By raising the customer retention rate by as little as five percentage points, companies can increase the lifetime value of their average customer by 25 to 100 percent, depending upon industry.

- Customer loyalty has a substantial impact on the growth of customer inventory. A company with a five-percentage-point advantage in customer retention over its competitor will double in size in 14 years while the competitor has no growth at all.

- Customer retention is critical for profits in most industries because (a) customers spend more over time, (b) it costs less to service long-term customers than new customers, (c) long-term customers are an important source of personal referrals, and (d) long-term customers are usually willing to pay a price premium to do business with a company they know.

○━┳ The lifetime value of the average customer is a key statistic for understanding the importance of and managing customer retention.

○━┳ The four essential steps for implementing CRM are

- Identify your customers and build a database of key information about their individual purchasing behavior.

- Differentiate your customers according to their value to your company.

- Interact with your customers to learn more about their needs, interests, and priorities.

- Customize at least some aspects of your enterprise's behavior to each customer.

Robert Blattberg, coauthor of *Customer Equity*

Kevin Clancy, coauthor of *Counterintuitive Marketing*

Laura Day, author of *Practical Intuition for Success*

Gary Getz, coauthor of *Customer Equity*

Peter Krieg, coauthor of *Counterintuitive Marketing*

Katherine Lemon, coauthor of *Driving Customer Equity*

Roland Rust, coauthor of *Driving Customer Equity*

Jacquelyn Thomas, coauthor of *Customer Equity*

Valarie Zeithaml, coauthor of *Driving Customer Equity*

5

All You Need Is Customer Equity

In the late 1990s and early 2000s, several groups of marketing gurus looked at the remedies proposed for marketing's **P** problems, particularly the passion for brands and customer relationships, and announced that they were displeased. None of these remedies, said these gurus, offered a real cure for marketing's ills. They had a better potion and a catchy name for their elixir. The answer to marketing's problems, they said, was customer equity, which they defined as the sum of the lifetime value of all of a company's customers. A company's customers were real financial assets and should be managed as such. The long-term goal of a company should be to maximize customer profitability, not product profitability. In fact, they said, "a slavish devotion to product profitability [as advocated by brand management gurus] can be hazardous to a company's health!"[1] In their book, *Driving Customer Equity,* marketing professors Roland Rust, Valarie Zeithaml, and Katherine Lemon call this hazard the *"product profitability death spiral."*

PRODUCT PROFITABILITY DEATH SPIRAL

Rust, as we will refer to Rust, Zeithaml, and Lemon, notes that companies that concentrate on branding and other product-centric marketing strategies often fall into a cycle of destructive behavior. They measure the profitability of their products; determine the minimum level of profitability that they find acceptable and eliminate from their product lines any product that isn't minimally profitable; and then they repeat the process. The logic behind this *product profitability paradigm,* says Rust, is simple:

> If the unprofitable products are winnowed out, then they will cease to be a drain on the profitability of the firm. Only profitable products will remain, so the firm's resources will be focused where they yield the best return. Over time, the average profitability of the firm's products will become higher and higher, along with the overall profitability of the company. All of the major financial indicators of the firm (e.g., return on equity, return on assets, net profit, etc.) should increase as the company becomes increasingly successful.[2]

Rust admits that it is hard to argue with such logic. After all, how can a company be successful selling unprofitable products? Yet, say our gurus, there is something wrong with the logic. In fact, the logic of the product profitability paradigm is bad both for companies and for customers. Rust illustrates this conclusion with a story about a small but once profitable grocery chain called "Schmidt Groceries".[3]

The fictitious Schmidt Groceries was once the dominant grocery store in the Hillvue neighborhood of Music City, Tennessee. In the late 1970s, like many grocery chains, Schmidt began installing scanner technology that, among other things, would let it track product sales and fine-tune its inventory to winnow out slow-selling and unprofitable products. By doing so, Schmidt was confident that it could not only increase its profits but also ensure that it was stocking the items its customers most desired. Store personnel at the Hillvue store, like those at other Schmidt stores, were trained to analyze scanner data on a regular basis and eliminate less-profitable items.

One of the first things Schmidt's personnel at the Hillvue store noticed was that certain gourmet items such as freshly squeezed orange juice and fresh pâté didn't sell as well at the Hillvue store as they did at Schmidt's store in the more upscale Emerald Heights section of the city. Hillvue management moved quickly to eliminate these unprofitable items. As they expected, some customers complained, even threatening to drive across town to the upscale grocer Andre's if necessary to get these items. Schmidt's store management just explained that the orange juice and pâté were unprofitable and had to be discontinued. Of course, they lost a few upscale customers, but they weren't too concerned. They were confident that most of Schmidt's customers wouldn't drive the extra distance to Andre's. Anyway, they reasoned, most of Schmidt's customers didn't buy the fresh orange juice or the pâté. That's why these items were unprofitable. Schmidt's management remained unconcerned when Andre's opened a store a few blocks away, even though Schmidt's lost a few more customers. After all, Andre's prices were considerably higher than Schmidt's and management was sure that most Schmidt customers would never pay the price premium. Of course, the scanner data was beginning to show that most gourmet items that Schmidt offered were now no longer profitable. Schmidt's management did the only logical thing. They eliminated the remaining gourmet items.

Over the next few months, things seemed to be going well. Sales were down somewhat, but thanks to the ongoing analysis of the scanner data, Schmidt's management was able to identify a number of unprofitable items in its health foods section that they could eliminate, so short-term profits actually went up. Management remained unconcerned when the higher-priced Whole Earth Market opened a bulk and natural foods store in Hillvue. Schmidt's lost a few more customers, but management was again able to boost profits in the short term by finding unprofitable items to eliminate, such as the rest of the health foods section.

Everything seemed fine for a while, but it soon became evident that Schmidt's overall sales were noticeably down. Schmidt's management continued to look for unprofitable items to eliminate. Additionally, they decided to increase prices overall to compensate for the lost customers. This latter strategy soon drew the attention of executives at Dixie Discount Grocers, who recognized an opportunity to compete with Schmidt's on price and opened a store in the Hillvue neighborhood. Shortly after the Dixie Discount store opened Schmidt's sales plummeted. Schmidt's management fought back for a while with promotions, triple coupons, and deep discounts but eventually their efforts were to no avail. Schmidt's remaining profitable products were simply not profitable enough to support the store, which was soon closed.

What happened to Schmidt Groceries? Rust explains that the story of Schmidt's demise is a classic example of the death spiral brought on by overzealous adherence to the profitable product paradigm.

> Schmidt viewed its business as being made up of products. Some products make money and some don't, so if they get rid of the ones that don't, they will make bigger profits. That strategy would work well if it were not for the existence of customers who shop for more than one item at a time.

The problem is that some "unprofitable" items are considered important by some customers. Suppose, for example, that breakfast cereal was profitable but that milk wasn't. Eliminating milk would alienate cereal eaters, because they go to the store not to buy an item individually, but rather to buy an assortment of items. Discontinuing milk would probably guarantee that cereal eaters would stop buying at that store, which then would make cereal unprofitable also.

Of course, once a market segment is alienated, a market opportunity naturally arises. New entrants can enter the market successfully because the original store is vulnerable to losing the disaffected segment. Thus a large, general competitor may set itself up for attack from niche competitors. More and more niche competitors may enter the market until there is not much general market left, and the original market leader goes out of business. There is a spiral because the more customers the store loses, the more items become unprofitable. As more items become unprofitable, more are discontinued, and, thus, more customers are alienated. The more customers are alienated, the more potential there is for niche competition, which reduces the original store's number of customers and continues the downward spiral.[4]

Okay, you say, that's a good lesson for managers of grocery stores, but I don't run a grocery store. It doesn't matter, say our gurus, the profitable product death spiral can be found in just about any industry. Airlines eliminate unprofitable routes, which allows niche carriers to enter, which results in more unprofitable routes for the big carrier who cuts more routes until there is little left. Service businesses cut their workforce to boost profits, but the reduced workforce leads to less service and lost customers, which leads to more staff cuts, which leads to more lost customers and so on. In industry after industry, marketers make the same mistake. They focus on product profitability and building strong brands, eliminating unprofitable products and weak brands. The built-in assumption is that profits come from products. Wrong—dead wrong—say our gurus. Profits come from customers. More specifically, profits come from the lifetime value of customers.

Now, you are probably saying to yourself,

Haven't we heard that someplace before, like maybe back in the last chapter? Isn't this customer lifetime value stuff what the customer relationship management people were preaching? If so, how are these customer equity gurus saying anything different? We've heard it all before. Customer relationships are more important than products. Customer retention is more important than customer acquisition. And, so on and so on. Isn't this just the same old stuff Peppers and Rogers and all the other CRM gurus have been selling for a decade?

Yes and no, say the customer equity gurus. The CRM folks got part of it right. Customer retention is important, but there are some myths about customer retention.

MYTHS ABOUT CUSTOMER RETENTION

Our customer equity gurus don't disagree that customer retention is critical to a firm's success; but they do argue that retention is no magical solution to marketing's **P** problems. Robert Blattberg, Gary Getz, and Jacquelyn Thomas write in their book *Customer Equity* that there are two myths about customer retention: (1) that companies should strive always for 100 percent customer retention, and (2) that maximizing customer retention is synonymous with maximizing profits. Let's look at what our gurus say is wrong with each of these assumptions.

Myth #1: Companies Should Strive for 100 Percent Customer Retention

It may be counterintuitive, given the benefits that have been documented for high levels of customer retention, says Blattberg, but it makes more sense to treat some types of customers as "transaction" customers rather than customers with which you seek to form a long-term relationship. Blattberg and his coauthors use the airline industry as an example:

It makes sense that airlines strive for 100 percent retention among their top customers. These customers have exceptionally high lifetime value. However, aiming for similar retention rates among very price conscious college students would be foolish. Airlines use yield management pricing techniques to put these customers on the plane for as little as 10 percent of the prices they charge their best, frequent-flying customers. But airlines recognize that college students are not loyal—they seek the lowest fares— and generally do not have high retention rates because after college many move to other markets with different hub airlines.

So, should the airlines avoid adding these low-valued, price-sensitive fliers who are incrementally profitable? Obviously not. If an airline concentrated on and compensated its managers on overall retention rate alone, it would not serve this customer segment. By accepting a retention rate of less than 100 percent, the airline can gain customer classes who have lower inherent retention rates but add incremental profit.[5]

Myth #2: Maximizing Customer Retention Is Synonymous with Maximizing Profits

A second myth about retention, say our gurus, is that incremental increases in customer retention levels translate into similar increases in profits. In fact, they argue, in some cases after a point further increases in retention levels can actually represent a drain on profits. Blattberg again uses an example from the airline industry:

You might guess that it is optimal for an airline to retain 100 percent of its best, frequent-flying customers. This would be true if maximum attainable retention ensured maximum profits. But it does not, and here's why. An easy way to increase retention rates is to offer lower prices to the best customers. If an airline charges this group too little, it leaves money on the table. It is better off losing some high-valued customers at the expense of its retention rate, because the profits gained by charging higher prices to the majority who are retained exceed the profits lost from the defectors. The result is an optimal retention rate among high-valued customers of less than 100 percent. This optimal rate depends on the price sensitivity of the best customers and their inherent retention rate.[6]

Kevin Clancy and Peter Krieg make a similar point in their book *Counterintuitive Marketing.*[7] They cite the example of executives at Compaq, the computer manufacturer, who asked them to develop a strategy to increase the retention rate of Compaq's customers from 86 percent to 100 percent. Clancy and Krieg say they gave the matter some thought and came up with a simple but highly effective idea. They told the executives that Compaq should give all of their defecting customers a car. The executives were incredulous. What do you mean, Give them a car? they asked. Clancy and Krieg explained, "If you give each of your defecting owners an automobile—you know, give them a new Mazda Miata—they'd stay on for at least another year."[8] Of course, the gurus admit they were joking. It would be ridiculous to give people a $20,000 car to get $800 worth of repeat business. Yet an unbridled devotion to 100 percent customer retention would lead you to just such an absurd conclusion.

What too many advocates of customer retention fail to recognize, say the customer equity gurus, is that the relationship between customer retention and profits is curvilinear. Profits do rise as customer retention improves, but only *up to a point*. Thereafter, further improvements in retention levels not only do no good, they do considerable damage. (See Figure 5.1.)

The fact that the relationship between retention and profits is curvilinear means that you have to know when to stop trying to retain more customers. That's another problem our customer equity gurus have with current approaches to marketing, such as branding and CRM. They say these other

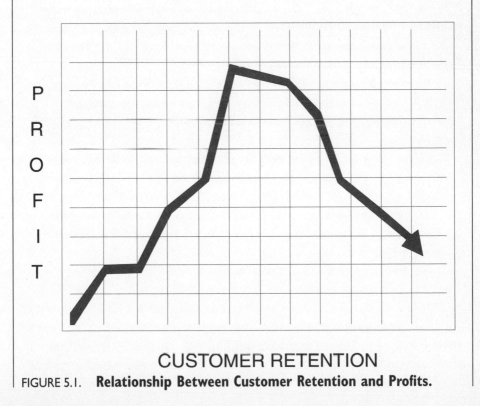

CUSTOMER RETENTION

FIGURE 5.1.   **Relationship Between Customer Retention and Profits.**

approaches offer no true basis for rational thought. Instead of rational thought, say our gurus, marketing is dominated by what Clancy and Krieg call "testosterone decision-making," or to put it another way, "the manly way to screw up."[9]

TESTOSTERONE DECISION MAKING

Clancy and Krieg's first exposure to testosterone decision making was in the late 1970s. There was a gas crisis and the Japanese were beginning to have some success selling small cars to Americans who, in turn, were beginning to question whether their devotion to gas guzzling land yachts was such a good thing. The gurus met with a group of General Motors executives to share the results of their most recent market research. Clancy and Krieg describe the meeting this way:

> We are working with the late Florence Skelly, one of the intellectual giants in marketing research, and General Motors is a client. The executives are all middle-aged men, all living in Detroit, and all employed by General Motors for a long time. They drink Manhattans at lunch while they eat big steaks with potatoes. It might still have been the 1950s.
>
> After one long, heavy lunch, we go up to the office in the GM Building, temple to the automobile, and Florence says, "Small cars. You gotta get ready." GM is paying us to be visionaries, so we predict, "Small cars are coming."
>
> The senior marketing executive climbs out of his chair, looks out the window, and says, "I don't know what you're talking about. I don't see any small cars."
>
> We say, "You don't see any small cars because we're in the General Motors Building in Detroit, Michigan, in the Midwest. People out here are all driving big iron."
>
> He gives us a scornful look. "I don't believe it. I don't see any small cars."[10]

That was more than 20 years ago, but our customer equity gurus say that little has changed. Too many marketing decisions, such as how much of the market budget to invest in brand building and customer acquisition and how much to spend on customer retention, are still made based on a modicum of research and large doses of intuition. It is, say Clancy and Krieg, a "male thing." "Testosterone-driven decision-makers are the guys who assemble complex toys on Christmas Eve without reading the directions, cook without a recipe, [and] make business decisions without research."[11]

> Why does it take a million sperm to fertilize a single egg? Because they won't ask directions.
>
> Kevin Clancy and Peter Krieg[12]

People joke about it, but men, in particular, still do it. Testosterone-driven decision makers do what "feels right" and often end up doing what is wrong. Our customer equity gurus argue that such ineffective, testosterone-driven marketing decision making must end. They argue that marketers can avoid both the product profitability death spiral and the excesses of customer retention if they will only allow customer equity to be their guide. Rust and his coauthors frame the argument this way:

In many firms, the marketing function is inefficient, unaccountable, and imprecise. Too often there are no solid numbers to show which marketing initiatives will be successful and which will fail. When return on investment cannot be calculated, all investments look the same. To be safe, firms too often cover all of their bases equally—increasing the value customers perceive, building brands, and trying to retain customers through loyalty programs. Some of those expenditures turn out to be poor investments because they miss their targets.

The era of the inefficient, unaccountable marketing function must end. Marketing research information and databases that gather and store information about customer choice and customer profitability are paving the way for a new, focused marketing function. In this new environment, expenditures can finally be concentrated where they will have the greatest impact.

We need to cut back on ineffective marketing expenditures while boosting the performance of our most effective marketing strategies. The key to this powerful combination is having a valid measure to evaluate all marketing expenditures on the same basis. Customer lifetime value offers such a metric at the individual customer level. Customer equity—the combined lifetime values of the collective customer base—provides the basis for comparing strategic marketing alternatives. Evaluating how much the return from an investment exceeds the cost of capital can make marketing more exacting because it helps firms choose intelligently among options, cutting out the alternatives that yield an unacceptable return. Quantifying the projected financial return for each marketing expenditure makes marketing more accountable. The result is a new, surgically precise approach that identifies strategic initiatives with the greatest impact on the long-term profitability of the firm's customer base, thereby escalating the firm's value.[13]

Of course, to achieve such surgical precision, you have to know more about customer equity than the fact that it is the sum of the lifetime value of all of your company's customers. At a minimum, you need to know what drives customer equity, how you calculate it, and how you determine if your efforts to improve customer equity are having a positive impact on your bottom line. Our gurus answer these questions, but there is a problem. They give different answers.

(Note: For a counterargument to our customer equity gurus' contention that intuition-based testosterone-driven marketing decision making is always bad and logic, analysis, and rationality is always the way to go, see Exhibit 5.1)

EXHIBIT 5.1. The Drawbacks of Logic and Analysis

In the late 1990s, a number of books came out by gurus who praised intuitive decision making and argued that pure rationality, logic, and analysis were not always the best path to marketing or any other success. Prominent among these were Barrie Dolnick's *The Executive Mystic,* Sandra Weintraub's *The Hidden Intelligence,* and Laura Day's *Practical Intuition* and *Practical Intuition for Success.* Here are the drawbacks to logic and analysis, according to Day:

- **There's too much information today to handle.** We're suffering from information overload. It has become impossible to gather all the relevant information for even the most simple decisions, and to sort the good information from the bad. What's worse, we become less decisive, paralyzed under the weight of all our information.
- **The world has become too complex.** It's fairly well agreed upon that the world has become increasingly chaotic, with paradox and change the norm rather than the exception. My brother studied physics at Harvard, and the whole situation of business executives today reminds me of the revolution created in physics a century ago by quantum mechanics and the theory of relativity. The assumptions of classical physics worked up to a point, and then broke down completely. Business executives today use twentieth-century technology and analytical techniques but base their thinking on nineteenth-century assumptions about the way the world works.
- **Gathering "all the available" information takes too long.** Someone once said that doing market research was like driving by watching your rearview mirror. By the time

(continued)

EXHIBIT 5.1. (continued)

---

we've analyzed all the data we've spent so much time gathering, the world has changed. In today's turbulent times, you simply can't afford to wait "until all the research is in" before acting. By the time you've satisfied your logical, rational mind that there are valid reasons to act, it's often too late.

- **Our analysis is only as good as premises and reasoning.** In today's complex world, many of our old assumptions no longer apply. . . . The problem is that we don't know which assumptions are still valid and which aren't. A big problem with analysis is that if you start from a faulty premise, the rigorous application of cold logic will lead you unavoidably to an absurd conclusion.
- **Our analysis is only as good as our information.** Even flawless reasoning can produce absurd results if the information it relies on is faulty or incomplete. Remember that information today becomes obsolete at an accelerating pace. Computer programmers use the acronym GIGO—Garbage In, Garbage Out—to describe how a computer produces bad results when "fed" bad information.

Day argues that rather than relying upon analysis alone or intuition alone, you should use some of both. Intuition, she says, should get the nod in situations such as the following:

- When information is sketchy.
- When you are trying to predict what might happen far in the future.
- When you want to check the logic of someone's "logical" analysis.
- When you need to understand the "big picture."
- When your decision has to do with perceiving the needs, beliefs, or values of others.
- When you need to make a decision fast.
- When you have too many options to choose from or too much information.

Source: Laura Day, Practical Intuition for Success: A Step-by-Step Program to Increase Wealth Today (New York: HarperCollins Publishers, Inc., 1997), pp. 105–106, 147–149.

CUSTOMER EQUITY—COMPETING APPROACHES

As of this writing, there are two competing approaches to the topic of customer equity. While both approaches emphasize treating customers as financial assets and maximizing customer profitability over product profitability, they differ in what their advocates say are the drivers of customer equity and how customer equity should be calculated. The first approach, which we will refer to as the Rust approach, is described by Rust, Zeithaml, and Lemon in their book, *Driving Customer Equity: How Customer Lifetime Value is Reshaping Corporate Strategy.* The second, which we will refer to as the Blattberg approach, is described by Blattberg, Getz, and Thomas in their book, *Customer Equity: Building and Managing Relationships as Valuable Assets.*

We will outline the key features of each of these approaches in the remainder of this chapter, starting with the Rust approach.

(Note: In the remainder of this chapter we will continue using the name Rust to refer to gurus Rust, Zeithaml, and Lemon, and we will use the name Blattberg to refer to gurus Blattberg, Getz, and Thomas.)

Customer Equity—The Rust Approach

Rust, Zeithaml, and Lemon are marketing professors at the University of Maryland, the University of North Carolina, and Boston College, respectively. They say that customer equity can be decomposed into three constituent parts—value equity, brand equity, and retention equity—which they define as follows:

Value Equity

For all customers, choice is influenced by perceptions of value, which are formed primarily by perceptions of quality, price, and convenience. These perceptions tend to be relatively cognitive, objective, and rational (for example, there may be little argument about a product's price, or its objective attributes). . . .

Brand Equity

Customers may also have perceptions of a brand that are not explained by a firm's objective attributes . . . For example, a car may be considered sexy, or exciting, or classic. These perceptions tend to be relatively emotional, subjective, and irrational. . . .

Retention Equity

Customer Equity comes from customers choosing to do business with the company. Some of the firm's business comes from customers who chose the company in their most recent purchase occasion and this time choose it again, and some of the firm's business comes from customers who did not choose the firm last time or are new to the market. For repeat customers, retention programs and relationship-building activities can increase the odds that the customer will continue to choose the firm.[14]

Each of these drivers of customer equity represents a reason customers conduct business with a company. Rust says companies can grow their customer equity by (1) growing value equity, (2) growing brand equity,

(3) growing retention equity, or (4) doing all of the above. We will take a look at each of these approaches.

Growing Value Equity

Rust says value equity derives from the customer's objective assessment of the value of the brand in respect to quality, price, and convenience. Companies grow value equity in one of two ways. First, they can grow value equity by giving customers more of what they want compared to the offerings of a competing firm or brand. For example, the firm can provide objectively better quality, lower prices, or more convenient buying experiences. Alternatively, companies can increase value equity by reducing what customers have to give up to do business with the firm. Rust notes that typically we think of price as the primary thing customers have to give up to do business with a company, but there are other sacrifices such as those involving time, risk, search costs, and so on that a company can reduce. For example, instead of offering lower prices, a firm could seek to build value equity by offering time-conscious customers savings in the time required to acquire or use the product or service, such as shorter waiting lines for service or faster checkout. Grocery stores do this when they offer fast, self-service checkouts. Restaurants do the same when they offer customers beepers so they don't have to wait but can go about other business and be called when their table is ready. Notice that in the latter instance, the actual waiting time might not change at all, but the perception the customer has of the waiting time does. Rust maintains that it is the customer's perception about quality, price, or convenience that matters.

See Exhibit 5.2 for a summary of these value equity connections, some questions to ask to assess value equity, and a list of situations in which Rust says value equity matters most.

Growing Brand Equity

Rust defines brand equity as "that portion of Customer Equity attributable to the customer's perceptions of the brand. More specifically, brand equity represents the *customer's subjective and intangible assessment of the brand, above and beyond its objectively perceived value.*"[15] Rust says brand equity has three roles: (1) it is a magnet that attracts new customers to the firm, (2) it acts as a "Hallmark card" to remind customers about the firm's products and services, and (3) it provides customers an emotional tie

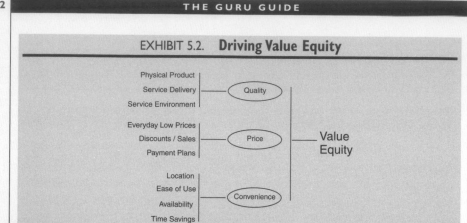

EXHIBIT 5.2. **Driving Value Equity**

Situations in which value equity matters most:

- When there are differences between competing products so one company can exploit patent protection, different capabilities, unique resources, special labor practices, or its company culture.
- When customers are making purchases that are complex and/or expensive so that the customer is carefully weighing competing offerings.
- Business-to-business purchases that are large and involve the expenditure of a great deal of money.
- Purchases of innovative new products or services where the customer is trying to decide whether the new product or service meets his/her needs and will deliver the value promised.
- Where a firm is attempting to recycle or reposition an existing and mature product.

Key questions to ask to assess how much your customers care about value equity:

- Do customers perceive discernable differences between brands? Do they focus on the objective aspects of the brand?
- Do you primarily market in a business-to-business environment?
- Is the purchase-decision process complex in your industry?
- Is innovation a key to continued success in your industry?
- Do you revitalize mature products with new features and benefits?

Key questions to ask to assess how well you are doing with value equity:

- Are you the industry leader in overall quality? Do you have initiatives in place to continuously improve quality?
- Do your customers perceive that the quality they receive is worth the price they paid?
- Do you consistently have the lowest prices in your industry?
- Do you lead the industry in distribution of your products and services?
- Do you make it most convenient for your customers to do business with you?

Source: Roland T. Rust, Valarie A. Zeithaml, and Katherine N. Lemon, Driving Customer Equity: How Lifetime Customer Value Is Reshaping Corporate Strategy *(New York: Free Press, 2000), pp. 72–74, and Katherine N. Lemon, "What Drives Customer Equity?" Marketing Management, Spring 2001, p. 21.*

to the firm. He identifies three specific drivers of brand equity, including brand awareness, brand attitude, and brand ethics.

Brand Awareness

Brand awareness includes efforts by the firm to communicate with the customer or potential customer to send a seamless and consistent message about the brand. The firm does this through its selection of marketing mix (advertising, sales promotion, publicity), choice of media (TV, radio, the web, direct mail, e-mail), and construction of message (what the firm hopes to convey).

Brand Attitude

Brand attitude involves efforts by the firm to use sponsorship of special events, brand extensions, brand partners, product placement, celebrity endorsements, and so on to create a positive image in the heart and mind of the customer.

Brand Ethics

Brand ethics are efforts by the firm to convey to the customer or potential customer that the values of the brand and firm are consistent with the customer's values. Firms establish brand ethics through community involvement (disaster relief, volunteer work), developing and maintaining a privacy policy, maintaining a good environmental record, workforce diversity, work/life friendly workplaces, and customer friendly product/service guarantees.

See Exhibit 5.3 for a summary of these brand equity connections, some questions to ask to assess brand equity, and a list of situations in which Rust says brand equity matters most.

Growing Retention Equity

Rust defines retention equity as the *"customer's tendency to stick with the brand, above and beyond objective and subjective assessments of the brand."*[16] Unlike value equity or brand equity, retention equity is derived from the actual experiences that customers have doing business with a company and the company's efforts to (1) increase the likelihood that a customer returns for future purchases, (2) maximize the size of those future purchases, and (3) minimize the likelihood that a customer will purchase from a competitor. Customers build retention equity, says Rust, by providing benefits to customers that make it more costly for them to switch to a competitor (e.g., Amazon already has my billing and shipping information

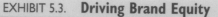

EXHIBIT 5.3.   **Driving Brand Equity**

Situations in which brand equity matters most:

- When the consumer is making a routine purchase of packaged goods and the purchase decision is simple.
- When customers are making purchases of products that are highly visible to others, such as the purchase of clothing that makes a fashion statement.
- When experiences associated with a brand can be passed down from one generation to another. For example, "I use Tide detergent because that's what my mother always used."
- When it is difficult for the consumer to evaluate the quality of the product or service before purchasing it. For example, "I've never stayed in a hotel in this city before but I always trust Marriott."

Key questions to ask to assess the importance of brand equity to the customer:

- Are the emotional and experiential aspects of the purchase important? Is consumption of your product highly visible to others?
- Are most of your products frequently purchased consumer goods?
- Is the purchase-decision process relatively simple?
- Is it difficult to evaluate the quality of your products or services prior to consumption or use?
- Is advertising the primary form of communication to your customer?

Key questions to ask to assess how you are doing with brand equity:

- Are you the industry leader in brand awareness?
- Do customers pay attention to and remember your advertising and the information you send them?
- Are you known as a good corporate citizen? Are you active in community events?
- Do you lead your industry in the development and maintenance of ethical standards?
- Do customers feel a strong emotional connection to your brand?

Source: Roland T. Rust, Valarie A. Zeithaml, and Katherine N. Lemon, Driving Customer Equity: How Lifetime Customer Value Is Reshaping Corporate Strategy *(New York: Free Press, 2000), pp. 80–94, and Katherine N. Lemon, "What Drives Customer Equity?" Marketing Management, Spring 2001, p. 21–22.*

whereas I would have to provide that information to a competitor), rewarding repeat purchases (e.g., loyalty programs), and sponsoring programs that build an emotional attachment to the firm (e.g., I'm a member of the Harley-Davidson Owners Group [H.O.G.]).

See Exhibit 5.4 for a summary of these retention equity connections, some questions to ask to assess retention equity, and a list of situations in which Rust says retention equity matters most.

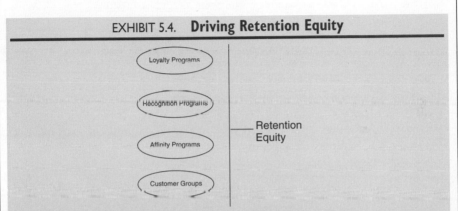

EXHIBIT 5.4. **Driving Retention Equity**

Situations in which retention equity matters most:

- When the benefits the customer associates with the loyalty program are significantly greater than the monetary value of the program. For example, my increasing frequent flyer points mean that I am getting closer to my vacation to Paris.
- When the community associated with the product or service is as important as the product or service itself. For example, membership in the Harley-Davidson Owners Group is as important to me as owning a Harley.
- When the learning relationship between the customer and the firm creates a significant bond. For example, I stay with XYZ Investment Services because their financial advisors understand my investment priorities.
- When action is required to discontinue the service. For example, I have to quit the boo club.

Key questions to ask to assess the importance of retention equity to your customers:

- Are loyalty programs a necessity in your industry?
- Do customers feel like "members" in your community?
- Do your customers talk about their commitment to your brand?
- Is it possible to learn about your customers over time and customize your interactions with them? Do your customers perceive high switching costs?
- Are continuing relationships with customers important?

(continued)

EXHIBIT 5.4. **(continued)**

Key questions to ask to assess how you are doing with retention equity:

- Do customers perceive that you have the best loyalty program in your industry?
- Do you lead the industry in programs to provide special benefits and services to your best customers?
- To what extent do your customers know and understand how to do business with you?
- Do customers perceive you as the leader in providing a sense of community?
- Do you encourage dialogue with your customers?

Source: Roland T. Rust, Valarie A. Zeithaml, and Katherine N. Lemon, Driving Customer Equity: How Lifetime Customer Value Is Reshaping Corporate Strategy (New York: Free Press, 2000), pp. 95–111, and Katherine N. Lemon, "What Drives Customer Equity?" Marketing Management, Spring 2001, p. 23.

Measuring Customer Equity—The Rust Approach

Of course, the ultimate goal of growing value equity, brand equity, and/or retention equity is to increase customer equity. Consequently, you have to have a measure of customer equity in order to know if it has increased. As we noted earlier, our customer equity gurus use as their measure of customer equity customer lifetime value. Each has their own formula for calculating customer lifetime value. See Exhibit 5.5 for the formula proposed by Rust.

Beyond offering a refinement of the formula for calculating customer lifetime value, one of the real contributions that Rust makes is to point out some of the difficulties marketers face at arriving at the true lifetime value of customers. The three most important of these are (1) the impact of "switching" on estimates of customer retention rates, (2) the impact of the planning horizon on the level and accuracy of the lifetime value calculation, and (3) the impact of new entrants and competitive reaction. Let's look at each of these.

The Impact of "Switching"

Rust notes that in the typical calculation of customer lifetime value, such as we covered in the last chapter, customer retention rates are assumed to be the same from period to period. You will recall that in the example of Mary Anne's Closet from the last chapter, out of the 10,000 customers in the first year, the store retained 3,000 or 30 percent in the second year and 900 (or 30 percent × 3,000 = 9 percent) in the third year. The assumption was that once Mary Anne's Closet lost a customer, that customer was gone for good. But Rust questions the validity of that assumption. He cites research that suggests that rather than being 100 percent loyal customers or 100 percent disloyal, in real-

---

EXHIBIT 5.5. **Formula for Calculating Lifetime Value**

Lifetime value of a customer $= (1-d)^{-t} \times F_t \times S_t \times A_t$

Where:

d = discount rate

t = time period

F = frequency of customer purchases

S = the expected share of the customer's wallet

A = the average contribution from a purchase by the individual in time t

---

Note: For more detailed information on the Rust formula for calculating customer equity, see their technical paper "Driving Customer Equity: Linking Customer Lifetime Value to Strategic Marketing Decisions," Working Paper, Report No. 01–108. (Cambridge, MA: Marketing Science Institute, 2001). The paper can be ordered from the Marketing Science Institute at 1000 Massachusetts Avenue, Cambridge, MA 02138; telephone 617.491.2060; Internet site www.msi.org.

Source: Roland T. Rust, Valarie A. Zeithaml, and Katherine N. Lemon, Driving Customer Equity: How Lifetime Customer Value Is Reshaping Corporate Strategy (New York: Free Press, 2000), p. 265.

ity many customers are "polygamous." They divide their loyalty among several different brands.[17] For example, they may purchase brand A 70 percent of the time, brand B 20 percent of the time and brand C 10 percent of the time. If they are business customers, they may decide to spread out their purchases among a number of different suppliers in order to give them some leverage in price negotiations and to avoid being dependent on a single vendor.

Since customers are often polygamous, Rust maintains that you will underestimate the value of your customers if you make the simplistic assumption that the retention rate is constant and that once customers leave they are gone for good. In order to correct for this problem and get a more accurate picture of customer lifetime value, our gurus say you have to derive from your research not only the probability that a customer who purchases from you in time period A will purchase from you in time period B, but also the probability that a customer who switches from you to a competitor in time period B will switch back to you in time period C. In short, to arrive at a true lifetime value for your customers you have to develop projections of the "share of wallet,"[18] or share of each customer's business, you are likely to receive for each period (month, year, etc.).

The Impact of Planning Horizon

Estimates of the lifetime value of a customer or group of customers are calculated for a given time period or, if you prefer, "planning horizon." For example, in the previous chapter, we showed a sample calculation for Mary Anne's Closet that covered three years (a planning horizon of three years). Obviously, say our gurus, the longer your planning horizon, the greater the lifetime value since as the number of years increases, the customer's lifetime value increases. Therefore, you get a better sense of the true lifetime value by having a long planning horizon. Unfortunately, says Rust, the further in the future you plan, the more the discount rate impacts your calculation. In an inflationary economy, sales far into the future may have little or no value because the discount rate will be so high. In a low-inflation economy, the discount rate will be low and future sales can have a substantial impact on lifetime value. Your problem is figuring out what is likely to happen to the economy more than a few months in advance.

OUR VIEW

And, if you think any of us is good at predicting the future, just think about the bets we all were making on the U.S. economy in the late 1990s.

The Impact of Competition

Most calculations of lifetime value assume static competition. The competitors of tomorrow are assumed to be the same as the competitors of today. Such an assumption, writes Rust, is not without merit since sometimes the best guess you can make about the future is that it will be much like the past. But you should keep in mind, say our gurus, that such an assumption can trip you up and turn your lifetime value calculations into so much trash. New competitors can enter your markets. For example, let's assume that you run an airline, and you wake up one day to discover that Southwest Airlines has decided to fly some of your same routes. To make matters worse, you learn that your competitors have figured out what you are doing to grow customer equity and are now doing the same thing. They go out and hire their own customer equity gurus and start building value, brand, and/or retention equity themselves.

Understanding and Acting upon the Drivers of Customer Equity

Rust admits that value equity, brand equity, and retention equity are important to all firms. However, he argues, they are not equally important. In some firms and industries, value equity has the greatest impact on customer equity. In other firms and industries, brand equity is most important. In still others, retention equity carries the greatest leverage. If you are to maximize customer profitability, that is, maximize customer equity, then you need to know where to invest your marketing dollars. Rust offers a four-step process he says you should follow to make those decisions.

Step #1: Understand Your Customers' Connections to Your Firm

Your first step is to conduct surveys, hold focus group sessions, and consult with industry experts and your employees to determine the relative importance of value, brand, and retention equity to your customers. You will want to ask questions such as those we listed in Exhibits 5.2, 5.3, and 5.4. Based upon your findings, you should be investing relatively more of your marketing dollars in the equity area that has the most influence on your total customer equity.

Rust notes that different equity drivers are important in different industries. For example, in the airline industry brand equity is most important, followed by retention equity and value equity. In the rental car business, retention equity is most important, followed by value equity and brand equity. In fact, value equity is about four times more important in the rental car industry than it is in the airline industry.

Step #2: Determine What Is Most Important to Your Customers in Each of the Equity Areas

In this step, you should identify the specific actions you can take to strengthen value, brand, and retention equity. Rust suggests that you ask yourself, "What drives Value Equity? What actions does the firm take (or not take) that affect the customer's perceived value of its goods and services? What actions can be taken to improve? What drives Brand Equity? What enhances the customer's association with the brand? What drives Retention Equity? What programs are currently in place to strengthen the customers' connections to the firm? How do the firm's best customers perceive these programs? What else would deepen these customers' commitment to the firm?"[19] In each case, you are looking for answers to these questions that suggest specific actions you can take to improve value, brand, and/or retention equity.

Step #3: Benchmark Your Firm's Performance Relative to Your Key Competitors

It's not enough, says Rust, just to know how your firm stacks up on value, brand, and retention equity; you must know how well your competitors are doing. If you can identify the firm with the best value, brand, and/or retention equity in your industry, then you can compare your firm's performance to that of the best firm and determine not only how much you have to improve but the financial benefits of improving. You determine the latter by subtracting your firm's customer equity from the customer equity of the company with the best value, brand, or retention equity. For example, if value equity was the most important driver of customer equity for your firm, you might look at this calculation of the financial benefit for improving value equity to the industry-best level:

Financial Benefit = Customer Equity given the best Value Equity in the industry
– Current Customer Equity[20]

The result of the calculation, says Rust, is the dollar value of not being the best in value equity (or brand or retention). You know where to focus your effort (in this case value equity), how much you need to improve (the difference between the value equity of the best in the industry and your firm's), and how much you can afford to invest (the financial value of being the best).

Step #4: Invest in the Equity Areas That Promise the Highest Payback to Your Firm in Terms of Customer Equity

Having done your research in steps one through three, you are now prepared to make a non-testosterone-driven decision concerning where to invest your limited marketing dollars. "The key idea," writes Rust, "is that not all investments—in the brand, in the product or service, or in the customer—are created equal. Understanding what drives customers to do business with the firm, now and in the future, should drive decisions of where to invest. By following this approach, the firm can optimally allocate strategic resources to maximize Customer Equity."[21]

Are Rust, Zeithaml, and Lemon right in their approach to customer equity? Partially, say our other customer equity gurus Blattberg, Getz, and Thomas. Focusing on customer equity is right and so is the attention to research and financial calculations, but say the Blattberg/Getz/Thomas team, the Rust group gets the drivers wrong.

Customer Equity—The Blattberg Approach

Blattberg and Thomas are marketing professors at Northwestern's Kellogg Graduate School of Management and Emory's Goizueta School of Business, respectively. Getz is a director at the consulting firm Integral, Inc., specializing in marketing and customer strategy. They say that the central question marketers should be asking is not, How much should we invest in value, brand, and retention equity? but, How much should we be investing in the acquisition of new customers, the retention of existing customers, and increasing sales through add-on selling? The marketer's ultimate goal, says Blattberg, should be to achieve an optimal level of spending in each of those marketing areas in order to maximize the total lifetime value of the firm's customers. (Again, we use the name Blattberg to refer to Blattberg, Getz, and Thomas.) He writes:

> Customer equity management is built around three core strategies: acquisition, retention, and add-on selling. From the moment a company decides to target customer prospects to the time these customers make their final purchases, these strategies provide a framework for all marketing decisions. Every marketing activity affects an acquisition, retention, or add-on selling effort, or a combination of them.
>
> These three strategies are not new to marketing, but the way in which customer equity management combines them is. Most companies apply them in isolation. They embark on acquisition drives with special promotions. They develop new customer service initiatives to improve retention. They come up with new product lines to increase revenues through add-on selling. But rarely do they investigate the links between these strategies or conduct the rigorous financial analyses necessary to show which strategy deserves the most investment at any particular time. A firm that uses customer equity management, on the other hand, understands each strategy in terms of both its effects on the other strategies and its contribution to total customer value over time.[22]

The marketer's job, then, is to manage (1) a mix of customer acquisition, (2) customer retention, and (3) add-on selling activities in such a way as to maximize customer equity. Blattberg provides the following guidance for each of these activities.

Managing Customer Acquisition

Blattberg defines customer acquisition as the interactions that occur between the firm and the customer from the time of first contact up until the time that the customer makes a repeat purchase. He notes that this "process" perspective differs from the traditional "transactional" perspective that says acquisition ends with the customer's first purchase.

> The process perspective is better because it includes the initial bonding and development stage of the customer-firm relationship. This is a very important time, during which the customer forms attitudes about the firm's product and ancillary services. It includes interactions such as customer service encounters that affect the customer's decision whether to purchase again. Managers, for their part, face many difficult business decisions at this stage, such as how much to invest in courting prospects and what service levels to offer them. Throughout the acquisition process, companies incur significant nonproduct costs. For instance, financial planners often meet with clients several times prior to first purchases, and direct marketers may send numerous mailings before prospects respond. Then, once a first purchase is made, a customer may request service or other activities that impose further costs. All this is part of customer acquisition. The retention phase of the relationship begins once the customer decides to make the first repeat purchase.[23]

In fact, says Blattberg, the acquisition process can be thought of as occurring in the following five stages, which correspond to the phases a customer goes through in making a purchasing decision. Each of these stages must be managed.

Stage #1: Need Recognition and Product Awareness

The first stage of the customer decision-making process begins when the buyer realizes a difference between his current state of being and his desired state of being. Various internal and external stimuli trigger this realization. Hunger and thirst, for example, are internal stimuli. In contrast, external stimuli, such as advertising, can be managed by marketers.

Stage #2: Information Search

The customer's search for information on how to satisfy his or her need characterizes the second stage of the purchase-decision process. Customers may use several sources for their information. Personal sources might include friends and family. When a customer uses these sources, it is more difficult for the firm to manage perceptions and expectations. Firms can more directly influence the information gathered if the customer relies on commercial sources (e.g., advertising, salespeople, product packaging), public sources (e.g., mass media) or experiential sources (e.g., product handling and examining). The marketer has the greatest influence on commercial sources of information.

Stage #3: Evaluation of Alternatives

Once the information is gathered, the customer can evaluate the alternatives. During this stage, the larger set of purchase options of which the customer is aware generally narrows to a smaller choice set. The customer will select a product for purchase from this choice set after additional searching. Thus the customer uses a two-phase decision process. In phase one, the customer creates a broad set of alternatives. In phase two, the customer uses a set of rules or heuristics to create a smaller group of choices, which the customer then evaluates in more detail.

Stage #4: The Purchase Decision

The customer purchases a product.

Stage #5: Postpurchase Behavior

The customer decision-making process does not end with the product purchase. During the postpurchase stage, the customer is still forming attitudes and assessing satisfaction levels. Customer service at this stage can be and often is crucial.[24]

Of course, the need to acquire customers and manage the five-stage acquisition process is obvious. After all, how can you have a business without customers? Beyond the obvious, says Blattberg, there are other important reasons to manage customer acquisition well. First, even companies with extraordinarily high customer retention rates lose customers. You can't keep them all. Therefore every company, regardless of how good it is at keeping customers, must find at least some replacements. Second, companies that are good at customer acquisition have the advantage of a large pool of customers from which they can reap the rewards of retention and add-on selling. Finally, says Blattberg, it is important to manage customer acquisition well because the customer relationships that are formed at that stage have a significant impact on the firm's retention rate and success with add-on selling. He writes:

Much depends on the kinds of customers a firm acquires and on the expectations that these customers have. Many firms behave as if the strategic elements of customer equity—acquisition, retention, and add-on selling—function independently. For example, firms often analyze data about existing customers without considering response and interaction data about nonacquired prospects. This results in misleading conclusions and missed opportunities because it gives no insight into what prevented the nonacquired prospects from becoming customers. Failing to link customer acquisition to retention also leads to other errors, including inaccurate forecasts about how long customers stay, the profitability of customers, and the impact of marketing efforts. The usual result: a myopic, acquisition-fixated marketing strategy that leaves substantial customer equity on the table.[25]

How big of an investment should companies make in customer acquisition? Blattberg provides two rules.

Rule #1: The Greater Your Profits from Retention, the Greater Your Investment in Acquisition Should Be

While this rule might sound counterintuitive—why would you need to invest more in acquisition if you lose fewer customers?—the logic behind this rule is simple, writes Blattberg. "If future profits from a customer are high, then the firm can afford to lose more on its initial investment to acquire the customer."[26] You can afford to invest more because you have confidence that the return on your investment will be high.

Rule #2: The Higher the Percentage of the Initial Acquisition Investment That Your Firm Recovers in the First Year, the Greater Its Investment in Acquisition Should Be

In short, you can afford to invest more if you know you can expect a fast payoff from your investment.

If you put these two rules together, says Blattberg, you come up with four model acquisition strategies:

- **Full Throttle:** High retention-profit potential combined with short-term investment recovery makes new customer acquisition a major opportunity. The firm invests as much as possible in acquisition until the NPV [net present value] of the marginal customer is negative. The risk of this strategy is low, and its return is high.
- **Slingshot:** High retention-profit potential combined with a long investment recovery time calls for a slingshot strategy, so named because the more invested in acquisition, the greater the future payout. The long time until payout—initial investment is very high relative to first-year returns—makes the investment risky. The firm must bet on a high NPV

driven by high retention profits. A slingshot strategy is typical of the customer-investment environment among Internet companies. Many e-tailers invested heavily in acquisition spending without recognizing the risk associated with lower-than-expected retention profits.

- **Pay As You Go:** This strategy is most appropriate when retention-profit potential is low and acquisition-investment recovery time is short. (Most of the investment recovery occurs during the first period.) The firm invests as though all profits will accrue in the current period. Short-term profit goals drive the firm's investment.

- **Divest/Restructure:** In this situation, a firm must restructure its marketing system. Customer acquisition will not pay out because the initial payback is low and retention and add-on sales are low. The firm will not be profitable in the long run, and it will have very low customer equity.[27]

Managing Customer Retention

On the surface, the phrase "customer retention" appears to be easily defined. Most of us would say a customer is retained if he or she purchases the product or service repeatedly over a specified period of time. However, notes Blattberg, there are two significant problems with such a simple definition. First, some high-valued products have a low frequency of purchase. The customer may go a year or more without making his/her next purchase. For example, the customer who purchased a car from your auto dealership may not return to buy another car for two, three, four, or more years. Therefore, at what point do we say that the customer has defected? To remedy this problem, Blattberg proposes that for products with a purchase cycle longer than a year, the definition of a retained customer should be any customer who indicates the intention to purchase the product or service at the next purchasing occasion. Of course, admits Blattberg, even that definition has a problem. There is such a thing as silent attrition. The customer has decided not to purchase from your firm again but has not revealed his/her intention to defect to you. You treat the customer as retained. Actually he/she has already gone.

A second problem with retention, says Blattberg, is that people often confuse it with loyalty. In reality loyalty and retention are not the same thing. You can retain customers who are not loyal. Blattberg gives the example of the customer who regularly invests some money through a traditional brokerage and other money through an Internet brokerage. The customer isn't loyal to the traditional brokerage or Internet brokerage but he/she is retained by both.

In short, says Blattberg, one of the first problems you will have in managing customer retention is figuring out just which customers you have retained. Assuming you can do that with some reasonable precision, your next task is to find actions you can take to increase retention. Here, says Blattberg, your options fall in seven areas that he calls the "determinants of customer retention." You manage retention by taking action to influence these determinants.

Determinant #1: Customer Expectations versus Delivered Quality

Customers do not evaluate your product or service on its own merits. They evaluate it relative to their expectations and they begin developing these expectations during the acquisition process. If the expectations the customer has developed exceed what the product or service delivers, then the customer will defect. The quandary for the marketer is that he or she must raise expectations to generate trial but avoid raising expectations so high that the product/service falls short of the promise.

Determinant #2: Value

Blattberg defines value as quality divided by price. Firms increase value by either offering higher quality at the same price as a competitor or by offering the same quality at a lower price. Your problem in managing value is that quality is in the mind of the consumer and therefore is hard to define and measure.

Determinant #3: Product Uniqueness and Suitability

The more difficult it is for the customer to find a suitable substitute for your product or service the more likely you are to retain the customer.

Determinant #4: Loyalty Mechanisms

Blattberg argues that loyalty mechanisms such as frequent flyer/buyer programs can generate high retention rates even when the competing products or services are almost identical. (Note: Some gurus disagree. Recall our discussion of loyalty programs in the chapter on customer relationship management.)

Determinant #5: Ease of Purchase

If your product or service is hard to find or difficult to buy then you are going to have a difficult time retaining customers.

Determinant #6: Customer Service

Blattberg notes that some studies have suggested that customer service may be the most important factor in customer retention. It is also one of the most difficult determinants of retention for a marketer to manage. The reason, says Blattberg, is that many parts of the organization provide it. "Accounting provides customer service when it solves a customer's billing problems, logistics handles customer service when the product is not delivered, and engineering provides customer service when it shows a customer how to utilize the equipment more efficiently."[28] All of these components of customer service have to be managed and a breakdown in any one can result in a defection.

Determinant #7: Ease of Exit

If they can't leave, they won't.

Managing Add-On Selling

Finally, says Blattberg, companies can increase customer equity through add-on selling, which he distinguishes from cross-selling

> Most managers confuse add-on selling with cross-selling. However, add-on selling is broader than cross-selling: It includes cross-selling, but is not limited to it. Cross-selling depends on specific interactions or relationships between products. Add-on selling does not. Selling printers with personal computers is an example of cross-selling. Add-on selling is closer to the concept of installed-base selling, which IBM used so effectively in the 1950s and 1960s when it required its sales force to sell additional products to its customer base. Add-on selling is the activity associated with selling any additional products and services to current customers.[29]

Add-on selling is important for a number of reasons. First and most obviously, it directly increases profits per customer. As a result, greater emphasis can be placed on customer acquisition. (Recall the earlier rule that said the greater your profits from retention, the greater your investment in acquisition should be.)There is one other beneficial effect of add-on selling. Blattberg reports research that shows that add-on selling, specifically "cross-buying (buying from multiple product categories) increases retention **and** lifetime value for all customers but particularly for recent, less-frequent and low volume customers."[30]

While add-on selling benefits all firms, Blattberg says that the actual value that a firm will derive from add-on selling depends upon a number of factors including the following:[31]

- **Number of offers**—Among other things, the number of offers a firm can make to its existing customers depends upon the types of products and services it offers and its research and development capabilities. A crucial decision companies have to make about add-on selling is whether to go outside the firm to acquire additional products and services for its offers. See Exhibit 5.6 for some factors Blattberg says you should consider in making the make-or-buy decision for add-on offers.
- **Response rate**—Response rate affects the cost of add-on selling. Obviously, the higher the response rate, the lower your cost per customer. Blattberg identifies five factors that he says determine response rate,

---

EXHIBIT 5.6. Considerations When Making Make-or-Buy Decisions

Blattberg, Getz, and Thomas say you should consider the following factors when making the decision whether to make or buy products for add-on selling:

- **The level and uncertainty of demand for products or services:** Acquiring a product from third parties reduces the risk posed by possible low demand. The following rule works well: Outsource the add-on product or service if expected demand is low or the risk relative to expected demand is high.
- **The firm's expertise in manufacturing products or providing services:** Many firms have limited expertise in manufacturing products that are not core to their production systems or operations. Unfortunately, many firms are bound by their production expertise and want to exploit it. As a result, they miss significant opportunities to enhance customer equity.
- **The firm's ability to manage outsourcing:** Some firms recognize the need to outsource. They create procurement teams responsible for identifying products, evaluating them, and then monitoring their quality. If a firm is weak in this area, it likely will fail to provide customers with quality, cost-effective products and services and as a result will lower its customer equity.
- **The quality of outsourced products or services:** If the outsourced product or service falls below required standards, the firm will face serious backlash from its customers and a consequent loss of customer equity. Firms can solve this problem through sophisticated quality control system requirements similar to the requirements that many original equipment manufacturers (OEMs) have placed on their suppliers.

(continued)

EXHIBIT 5.6. **(continued)**

- **The risks of outsourcing:** Risks of outsourcing include supplier's bankruptcy; supplier's change of ownership, resulting in changes in costs or, more likely, changes in quality control; varying quality; rising costs if there are few suppliers in the market; and product liability. By assigning a team of managers from different functional areas (e.g., finance, legal, production, marketing) to oversee the outsourcing agreement, a firm can reduce the risks of outsourcing.

- **The cost structure for internal production or service provision versus the cost of acquiring products or services:** Assessing the costs of outsourcing requires a comprehensive understanding of incremental, semi-incremental, and fixed costs. Many firms look at their in-house production costs on a fully loaded basis, but their true costs are significantly lower. On the flip side, many do not take into account hidden administrative and management expenses when evaluating outside production costs. The flexibility of outside production also affects costs. If a firm contracts for production on a variable-cost basis and demand declines or is below expectations, then the producer accepts the risk. Also, because in many situations outside producers view the production as additional incremental volume, they might be more willing to offer low prices that cover incremental costs and provide some profit margin. These lower costs can be difficult for internal production teams to meet if they do not identify costs as incremental, semivariable, or fixed.

Source: Robert Blattberg, Gary Getz, and Jacquelyn S. Thomas, Customer Equity: Building and Managing Relationships as Valuable Assets *(Boston: Harvard Business School Press, 2001), pp. 116–117.*

(1) the value of the product or service to the customer, (2) how well the add-on product fits with the other products the customer is already buying from the firm, (3) the affinity the customer has with the firm, (4) how expensive the products are, and (5) how targeted and positioned the marketing communications are.

- **Sales quantity per offer**—If the offering is a low-priced item, the revenue generated by the product offering might not be significant even with a high response rate. Blattberg notes that firms must balance the price of the item (high price means fewer add-on sales) with the potential sales volume (low priced items generate fewer sales dollars).

- **Marketing costs per offer**—Blattberg notes that companies that don't have solid customer databases may find add-on selling to be prohibitively expensive since they will be forced to use highly inefficient mass marketing techniques to reach customers.

- **Margin**—Margin is determined by the type of product or service offered and the cost of manufacturing it. Blattberg says marketers must make a trade-off between offering a smaller number of high-margin products (usually high margin because they are manufactured in-house) and offering a larger number of low-margin products many of which are sourced from the outside.

Calculating Customer Equity—The Blattberg Formula

Like Rust, Blattberg provides a formula for calculating customer equity. In fact, he provides a range of formulas for calculating acquisition equity, retention equity, add-on selling equity, and ultimately customer equity. Most of these formulas are much too complicated for us to cover here, so we refer you to Blattberg's Web site at http://www.customerequity.com for the details. See http://www.customerequity.com/ce_in_depth/ce_calculations/corr_ce_calc.htm for the fundamental equation that corrects an error in the equation Blattberg provides in his book.

Blattberg's basic formula for calculating customer equity goes like this:

$$\text{customer equity} = \text{acquisition equity} + \text{retention equity} + \text{add-on selling equity}$$

Here are the calculations using data from a fictitious company Blattberg refers to as firm A (see Charts 5.1, 5.2, and 5.3).

Calculation of Customer Equity

$$\text{Customer Equity} = \text{Acquisition Equity} + \text{Retention Equity} + \text{Add-On Selling Equity}$$
$$\text{Customer Equity} = (\$592.50) + \$2,548 + \$1,750.19 = \$3,705.69$$

Optimizing Customer Equity—The Blattberg Formula

Blattberg writes that in theory a company's best strategy would be to maximize acquisition, retention, and add-on selling equities. From a practical standpoint, he admits, such a strategy is rarely possible since all firms have limited resources. The trick, then, becomes one of balancing your allocation of funds to the three areas (acquisition, retention, and add-on selling) in order to drive customer equity to the highest level. The advantage of the acquisition equity, retention equity, and add-on selling equity calculations, says Blattberg, is that they reveal the drivers of total customer equity. Understand the calculations and you will know just where to invest your marketing dollars for maximum impact.

CHART 5.1. **Calculation of Acquisition Equity for Firm A**

A	Number of prospects contacted	10,000
B	Number of sales calls over "life" of prospects	20,000
C	Cost per sales call	$50
D	Total cost of sales calls (B x C)	$1,000,000
E	Direct marketing materials cost per prospect	$0.50
F	Direct marketing costs (A x E)	$5,000
G	Incremental administrative expenses	$200,000
H	Total acquisition costs (D + F + G)	$1,205,000
I	Number of prospects who became customers	1,000
J	Acquisition response rate (A / I)	10%
K	Average customer purchase	$1,750
L	Gross margin	35%
M	Net profit on first purchases (K x L)	$612.50
N	Total net profit (I x M)	$612,500
O	Total acquisition equity (N - H)	($592,000)
P	Acquisition equity per customer (O / I)	($592.50)

Source: http://www.customerequity.com/ce_in_depth/ce_calculations/aquisition_equity.html, November 12, 2001.

CHART 5.2. **Calculation of Retention Equity for Firm A**

A	Retention rate year 1	70%
B	Retention rate year 2	71%
C	Retention rate year 3	72%
D	Retention rate year 4	71%
E	Average retention rate ((A + B + C + D) / 4)	71%
F	Average expected relationship duration (1 / (1 - E)) or (1 / (1 - .71))	3.45 years
G	Average margin over 4 year period	$999
H	Average costs over 4 year period	$260
I	Net margin (G - H)	$739
J	Expected retention equity per customer (I x F)	$2,548

Source: http://www.customerequity.com/ce_in_depth/retention/rmc_calc.htm, November 12, 2001.

CHART 5.3. **Calculation of Add-On Selling Equity for Firm A**

A	Expected relationship duration from calculation of retention equity	3.45 years
B	Average margin for add-on purchase	$200
C	Average expenditures to generate an add-on purchase	$10
D	Net margin per add-on purchase (B - C)	$190
E	Average response rate to add-on purchase promotions	2.67%
	Six promotions over four years with response rates of 2%, 3%, 2.4%, 3.1%, 2.6%, and 2.9% yields average response rate of 2.67%	
F	Add-on selling equity (D $\times$ A $\times$ E) or $190 $\times$ 3.45 years $\times$ 2.67	$1,750.19

Source: http://www.customerequity.com/ce_in_depth/add_on_selling/calculation_resp_rates.htm, November 12, 2001.

Does it work? Well, yes and no. For example, Blattberg says that in order to arrive at its customer equity, the fictitious firm A had to have a unique identifier (preferred customer card, credit card, or other tracking mechanism) for its customers. It had to capture at least 80 percent of a customer's purchases.[32] It had to track marketing communications, special promotions, pricing, customer service, and returns. It also needed good data on the costs of goods, warehousing, distribution, and other costs. And it had to track sales calls and marketing activities to prospects and be able to extract sales to new customers from data on all customer sales. Blattberg admits that many companies simply don't have customer data that is reliable enough and/or detailed enough to support the calculations he proposes, although he reassures us that customer equity management firms do collect such data.

OUR VIEW

Who can argue with Blattberg's and Rust's contention that marketers should seek a better foundation for their decisions than gut instinct and intuition alone? And, balancing value/brand/retention or acquisition/retention/add-on selling makes sense. Still, you have to wonder about all those calculations the gurus serve up.

Mathematical formulas are very intriguing. There is nothing so comforting to the besieged decision maker or pontificating guru as adding up the positives, subtracting out the negatives, raising the unknown to a power, and multiplying the result by a given to yield an unmistakable conclusion. Unfortunately the world makes the positives less certain, the negatives unknowable, the unknown power mysterious, and the given somewhat less than a present. All of the precise calculations end up too often being the result of bad data, flawed assumptions, and fuzzy estimates. We might wish that we could reduce the world to a set of formulas, but we can't. Reality is much too real for that. Even physicists end up with probabilities. So, what are we to do? Some gurus say we should abandon our spreadsheets and just get out on the streets and do some good old-fashioned marketing. The cure for marketing's **P** problems isn't more elaborate formulas, branding, or relationships, they argue. It's just more "buzz." Their wisdom will be the topic of our next chapter. But first, here are the key ideas we have covered in this one.

KEY POINTS

- A slavish devotion to product profitability can be hazardous to a company's health.

- It makes more sense to treat some types of customers as transaction customers rather than customers with whom you seek to form a long-term relationship. Companies should not necessarily strive for 100 percent retention of customers.

- Incremental increases in customer retention levels do not necessarily translate into similar increases in profits. The relationship between customer retention and profits is curvilinear. Profits rise with customer retention to a point, but only to a point.

- Too many marketing decisions, such as how much of the marketing budget to invest in brand building and customer acquisition and how much to spend on customer retention, are still made based on a modicum of research and large doses of intuition.

- There are two competing approaches to customer equity. One emphasizes growing value equity, brand equity, and retention equity. The other emphasizes achieving an optimal balance between investments in customer acquisition, customer retention, and add-on selling.

- Quality, price, and convenience are the key drivers of value equity.

☛ Companies can grow value equity in two ways: (1) by offering customers greater value (quality or convenience) at the same price as the competition, or (2) by offering the same value as the competition at a lower price.

☛ Brand equity represents the customer's subjective and intangible assessment of the brand, above and beyond its objectively perceived value.

☛ Brand equity has three roles: (1) it is a magnet that attracts new customers to the firm, (2) it acts as a "Hallmark card" to remind customers about the firm's products and services, and (3) it provides customers with an emotional tie to the firm.

☛ Retention equity is the customer's tendency to stick with the brand, above and beyond objective and subjective assessments of the brand.

☛ Retention equity is derived from the actual experiences customers have while doing business with the firm and the company's efforts to (1) increase the likelihood that a customer returns for future purchases, (2) maximize the size of those future purchases, and (3) minimize the likelihood that a customer will purchase from a competitor.

☛ Firms build retention equity by providing benefits to customers that make it more costly for them to switch to a competitor, rewarding repeat purchases, and sponsoring programs that build an emotional attachment to the firm.

☛ Customer equity can be measured by calculating the lifetime value of the average customer.

☛ The true lifetime value of customers is impacted by (1) switching—the tendency of customers to purchase from more than one vendor at a time and/or to defect and then return, (2) the planning horizon—longer planning horizons yield higher customer values but are also less accurate due to the need to estimate future inflation, and (3) new entrants entering the market and existing competitors adopting new strategies.

☛ Customer acquisition encompasses all interactions the firm has with customers from first contact through first purchase and up to first repeat purchase.

- Customer relationships formed during the acquisition stage have a significant impact on the firm's retention rate and success with add-on selling.

- The greater a firm's profits from retention, the greater the firm's investment in acquisition should be since the return on the acquisition investment will be high.

- The higher the percentage of the initial acquisition investment that a firm can recover in the first year or accounting period, the greater the firm's investment in acquisition should be since it can expect a fast payoff for the investment.

- Customer retention refers not only to customers who repurchase products during a specified period of time but also customers who express an intention to purchase from the firm again at some time in the future.

- You can retain customers who are not loyal.

- Customer retention is determined by the following: (1) the customer's expectations versus delivered quality, (2) delivered value, (3) the effectiveness of loyalty mechanisms such as frequent buyer clubs, (4) ease of purchase, (5) customer service, and (6) how easy it is for the customer to leave.

- Add-on selling is the activity associated with selling any additional products or services to current customers.

- Add-on selling is important because it (1) increases profits per customer, (2) makes it possible for a firm to invest more in acquisition, and (3) has been shown to increase both customer retention and customer lifetime value.

- Customer equity is the sum of acquisition equity, retention equity, and add-on selling equity.

- The marketer's goal should be to maximize customer equity by optimizing investments in acquisition equity, retention equity, and add-on selling equity.

THE BUZZ GURUS

Darren Bridger, coauthor of *The Soul of the New Consumer*
Malcolm Gladwell, author of *The Tipping Point*
Seth Godin, author of *Unleashing the Ideavirus*
Guy Kawasaki, author of *Rules for Revolutionaries*
David Lewis, coauthor of *The Soul of the New Consumer*
Emanuel Rosen, author of *The Anatomy of Buzz*

6

All You Need Is Buzz

In the mid-1990s, a strange thing happened to the company Hush Puppies. Sales of the classic shoes were down—way down. In fact, sales were so bad that Wolverine, the company that made Hush Puppies, was seriously considering dumping the line altogether. Then something happened that was nothing less than marketing magic. The dog of a shoe suddenly became a fashion hound. Malcolm Gladwell, author of *The Tipping Point,* describes the events of late 1994 and early 1995 this way:

> At a fashion shoot, two Hush Puppies executives—Owen Baxter and Geoffrey Lewis—ran into a stylist from New York who told them that the classic Hush Puppies had suddenly become hip in the clubs and bars of downtown Manhattan. "We were being told," Baxter recalls, "that there were resale shops in the Village, in Soho, where the shoes were being sold. People were going to the Ma and Pa stores, the little stores that still carried them, and buying them up." Baxter and Lewis were baffled at first. It made no sense to them that shoes that were so obviously out of fashion could make a comeback. "We were told that [the designer and lifestyle television and Internet personality] Isaac Mizrahi was wearing the shoes himself," Lewis says. "I think it's fair to say that at the time we had no idea who Isaac Mizrahi was."
>
> By the fall of 1995, things began to happen in a rush. First the designer John Bartlett called. He wanted to use Hush Puppies in his spring collection. Then another Manhattan designer, Anna Sui, called, wanting shoes for her show as well. In Los Angeles, the designer Joel Fitzgerald put a twenty-five-foot inflatable basset hound—the symbol of the Hush Puppies brand—

on the roof of his Hollywood store and gutted an adjoining art gallery to turn it into a Hush Puppies boutique. While he was still painting and putting up shelves, the actor Pee-wee Herman walked in and asked for a couple of pairs."[1]

What had happened to Hush Puppies? Simple, say our gurus. The lucky company had just taken a ride on the "buzz" train. The train left the station, recalls Gladwell, when kids in the East Village and Soho started wearing Hush Puppies simply because no one else would wear them. It was an anti-establishment protest kind of thing—the kind of thing kids do. Fashion designers noted what the kids were doing, and, wanting to make it clear that they were in on the latest trends, started to use the shoes in their shows. As a result, the buzz train picked up steam. People who followed what the designers were doing started noticing the shoes on the fashion models and decided Hush Puppies must be in fashion. Soon, says Gladwell, everything "tipped." The slow-moving Hush Puppies buzz train seemingly became overnight a decidedly cool, high-speed, luxury express, and the best part of it all was that the marketers at Wolverine had almost nothing to do with it— no branding, no customer relationship building, no calculating customer equity, nothing. All they had to do was just sit back and watch it happen. Ah, nirvana. Ah, paradise. Ah, marketing heaven. It was marketing in which the customers themselves do all the work and the marketers reap all the rewards. It's the perfect solution to the **P** problems. Forget the **P**s, says a vocal set of our gurus. All you need is one very beautiful **B**—and that stands for buzz.

WHAT IS BUZZ?

You know what buzz is, right? Sure, you say, it's just old-fashioned word-of-mouth endorsement. Well, yes and no. *Newsweek* says that buzz is "infectious chatter; genuine, street-level excitement about a hot new person, place or thing."[2] Emanuel Rosen, who wrote *The Anatomy of Buzz,* says he prefers this broader definition: "Buzz is all the word of mouth about a brand. It's the aggregate of all person-to-person communication about a particular product, service, or company."[3]

Rosen provides the following example:

A kid stands outside a school leaning against the fence. He's about thirteen, wearing jeans and a baseball cap, and playing with a yo-yo. He's good. A younger kid walks by, carrying a backpack that may weigh as much as he does. He stops. His eyes follow the yo-yo that now spins in the air in ways that would make Newton go back and check his gravity theories.

> "Where'd ya get it?" the young kid asks softly.
> The older kid keeps working.
> "What kind is it?" the younger kid asks a little louder this time.
> "Yomega," says the older boy. "The Brain."
> "Brain?"
> "They call it 'The Brain.' It knows when to come back to your hand. It's cool."[4]

That, says Rosen, is an excellent example of the beginning of buzz. Add up all of the comments about "The Brain" and you've got Brain buzz.

> We live in a world where consumers actively resist marketing. So it's imperative to stop marketing at people. The idea is to create an environment where consumers will market to each other.
>
> *Seth Godin[5]*

From a marketer's perspective, writes Rosen, buzz is quite different from previous marketing strategies. Traditional marketing focused on identifying groups of consumers who might be interested in a product or service and targeting them. The marketing focus was on these customer groupings. Customer relationship management (CRM) changed the focus from customer groupings to relationships with individual customers. Buzz shifts the focus once again, this time from relationships with individual customers to interactions between customers themselves. And, says Seth Godin, buzz (which he calls the "ideavirus") does something else. It changes the marketing game in a way that all participants benefit.

> Traditional advertising is a game with winners and losers. If your product gets attention from the targeted consumer, you win "mindshare" and your customer loses time. When a customer is foolish enough to listen to an ir-

relevant ad, she loses time and doesn't even gain useful information. It's an old economy model in which every transaction has someone *taking* something. . . .

[The ideavirus is different from this model because it] creates a game in which everyone can win! If there's a great idea, and it moves through the hive [community of people sharing the idea] for free, everyone who touches it wins in several ways.

First, you as the consumer win for recommending it to a friend. This increases your status as a powerful [person]. . . . Because you respect your peers, you're not suggesting or pitching something that doesn't make your friends' lives better. Violate this respect and your power . . . goes way down.

Second, the recipient benefits as well. He benefits from the way the idea changes his life, and he benefits because he now has the ability to [pass the idea along to someone else], thus increasing his power.

Third, the creator of the idea succeeds because her idea propagates and because she can sell [her product/service] to people who are now open and receptive to her idea. [6]

(Note: Buzz goes by a number of different names such as "ideavirus," "viral marketing," and "evangelism," but a buzz by any name is still a buzz. See Exhibit 6.1 for some clarification.)

WHY BUZZ NOW?

Our gurus say there are several reasons why it is important and profitable to focus on generating buzz for your product today. Chief among these reasons are the following.

Reason to Buzz #1: Buzz Plays a Major Role in Purchasing Decisions Today for Many Types of Products and Services

Rosen says that initially he was skeptical about how much influence buzz had over purchasing decisions. Sure, buzz might be important in selling a high-tech product like software, but he questioned how much impact it had in other markets. That, he says, was before he conducted some research. Here is what he found:

EXHIBIT 6.1. **A Buzz by Another Name**

Our gurus use a variety of terms to refer to Buzz. Some of the most popular are the following:

Ideavirus—In his book *Unleashing the Ideavirus,* Seth Godin defines an Ideavirus as "a big idea that runs amok across the target audience . . . a fashionable idea that propagates through a section of the population, teaching and changing and influencing everyone it touches." Godin says that there are two key differences between an ideavirus and word of mouth. First, he says, an Ideavirus travels much faster than word of mouth since it is usually spread, in part, over the Internet. Second, since Ideaviruses travel so fast they have more lasting power than word-of-mouth. Each generation of recipients of the message is larger than the previous generation. In contrast, in the slow-moving word of mouth scenario, each generation can often be smaller than the generation before.

Viral Marketing—Godin defines viral marketing as a special case of an Ideavirus. He explains, "Viral Marketing is an ideavirus in which the medium of the virus *is* the product." A prime example of viral marketing is Hotmail. The company provides free e-mail, but each message contains the marketing message "Get Your Private, Free Email from Hotmail at www.hotmail.com." As customers use the product they spread the message/virus.

Evangelism—Guy Kawasaki, author of *Rules for Revolutionaries,* uses the term "evangelism" to refer to "the process of getting people not just to buy but to *believe* in your product, service, or company so much that they are compelled to make converts for you." He says that word of mouth is the precursor to evangelism, which is more proactive and aggressive.

Source: Seth Godin, Unleashing the Ideavirus *(Dobb's Ferry, NY: Do You Zoom, Inc., 2000), pp. 20 and 65; and Guy Kawasaki and Michele Moreno,* Rules for Revolutionaries *(New York: HarperBusiness, 1999), p. 84.*

- Sixty-five percent of customers who bought a Palm organizer told the makers of this device that they had heard about it from another person.
- Forty-seven percent of the readers of *Surfing* magazine say that the biggest influences on their decisions about where to surf and what to purchase come from a friend.
- Friends and relatives are the number-one source for information about places to visit or about flights, hotels, or rental cars, according to the Travel Industry Association. Of people they surveyed, 43 percent cited friends and family as a source for information.
- Fifty-seven percent of customers of one car dealership in California learned about the dealership by word of mouth. "This is not unusual," says Jim Callahan of the Dohring Company, which conducts surveys for about five hundred car dealerships around the country every year.
- Every year we hear about movies such as *The Blair Witch Project* or *There's Something About Mary* that are driven by word of mouth. Fifty-three per-

cent of moviegoers rely to some extent on a recommendation from someone they know, according to a study by Maritz Marketing Research. No matter how much money Hollywood pours into advertising, people frequently consult with each other about what movie to see.

- Seventy percent of Americans rely on the advice of others when selecting a new doctor, according to the same study. Sixty-three percent of women surveyed for *Self* magazine cited "friend, family or co-worker referral" as one of the factors influencing over-the-counter drug purchases.[7]

Reason to Buzz #2: There's Too Much Noise Today

Rosen notes that advertising experts estimate that consumers are exposed to as many as fifteen hundred ads every day. Their response is to tune out most of them in self-defense. (See our discussion of the ineffectiveness of advertising in Chapter 3.) Consequently, you have little chance of breaking through the clutter. However, consumers do listen to their friends, and buzz rises above the noise when nothing else can.

Reason to Buzz #3: People Don't Trust You

Rosen says the depth of consumer skepticism was brought forcibly home to him at a trade show he once attended:

I remember once standing at our booth at a trade show. We were about four weeks away from releasing a new version of our software. A young scientist stopped by the booth, and I showed him how the new software worked. He was impressed, but when I told him that this version was going to be released in a month, he turned around before I could say anything, muttered "Vaporware," and walked away. It didn't matter to him that I'd just showed him a working version (which had been under development for more than a year). As far as he was concerned, this software didn't exist, and he obviously didn't believe that it was going to be released in four weeks.[8]

◉ OUR VIEW

Message to Rosen—"Vaporware is real." We know. We have some clinging tenaciously to our hard disks. You couldn't remove it with a pickax. We've got even more in our junk software drawer. Does anybody know how to re-cycle CDs?

Consumer distrust is widespread. Rosen cites a survey by the public re-lations firm Porter Novelli showing that only 37 percent of the public trusted software and computer companies. It was even worse for other in-dustries. Only 28 percent of consumers felt that pharmaceutical companies were "very or somewhat believable." Only 18 percent felt car manufactur-ers could be trusted and only 16 percent felt that way about insurance com-panies. In short, says Rosen, people find the buzz from their friends much more believable than the hype from some PR or advertising firm.

Reason to Buzz #4: The Internet

Thanks to the Internet, writes Rosen, people are connected today like never before. They can talk and chat—"What camera's good?" "Should I get that DVD?" And they can get information—"How does Similac stack up against breast-feeding?" Godin makes a similar point:

> Think back. Really far. Ten years ago.
>
> How many people did you have regular telephone contact with ten years ago? Probably ten or twenty or thirty in your personal life, and maybe 100 at work?
>
> Now, take a look at your e-mail inbox or your instant messenger buddy list. How many people do you hear from every week?
>
> We're far more connected than we ever were. And now, we've got sec-ond or third or fourth order connections. There's an e-mail in my box from someone who is married to someone I went to summer camp with twenty years ago who got my e-mail address from a third friend.
>
> Another message is from a former employee, telling me about a doctor who's about to lose his license for trying radical medical treatments, and how her mother-in-law will suffer if this guy can't practice any longer.
>
> It's hard for me to imagine either person contacting me if they had to walk across the village and bang on the door of my hut or pick up the phone and call me. But the moment you connect to the Internet, you connect, at some level, to all of us. And the connections make ideas travel. Fast.[9]

Thanks to the Internet, buzz is like word of mouth on steroids. Consider, say our gurus, how much more limited non-Internet-enabled word of mouth is to Internet-rich buzz. Old word-of-mouth spread slowly. You met a friend on the street or at the office. You inserted a remark in a piece of snail mail. You dropped a hint in a phone conversation. You couldn't reach very many people and basically you reached them one at a time. Because word-of-mouth was slow and the number of people involved was small, writes Godin, it was hard for the ideavirus to become truly infectious. As people stop spreading the contagion, the virus begins to die. Consequently, with word-of-mouth, each generation of message receivers and senders is typically smaller than the previous.

With Internet-enabled buzz you have an entirely different story. Each buzzing person can reach many more people and they can do so quickly. Think about it, says Godin, you probably have 100, maybe 1,000 e-mail addresses in your address book. How difficult would it be to send a buzz to all of them? It wouldn't be hard at all, and if you don't believe the gurus, try this. Type the following e-mail message:

> Hi. I'm just reading the best book about marketing that I have ever read in my life. Really, it's outstanding. It's *The Guru Guide™ to Marketing*, by Joseph Boyett and Jimmie Boyett. Go buy a copy today. I promise you, you'll be glad you did. Signed [Insert your name here]

Now, send that message off to everyone in your address book. See how easy that was? And, by the way, we thank you, our publisher thanks you, and Colonel Parker thanks you.

Reason to Buzz #5: The New Consumer Wants Authenticity

In their book *The Soul of the New Consumer,* David Lewis and Darren Bridger report on the rise of a group of new consumers that they say are redefining the marketplace in almost every industry. These consumers cross gender, ethnic, income, and practically every other "line," but according to Lewis and Bridger, they share several common characteristics. They lack
Time—They constantly complain of not having enough time in the day to satisfy all the demands made upon them.
Attention—If they can't understand or see the personal relevance of something quickly, they move on to something else.
Trust—They don't believe manufacturers, retailers, and service providers.

They are

Individualistic—As Lewis and Badger put it, they "swim alone or in small groups rather than moving with the synchronized shoals of Old Consumers."[10]

Involved—They don't just want to buy eggs. They want to know a lot about the eggs they buy. Are the eggs free range? How were the chickens treated? Are the vegetables organic? Were the clothes stitched with child labor? Was the shampoo tested on animals?

Independent—They hate the hard sell, challenge established thought, and demand to participate in a dialogue.

Informed—They "check labels, study contents, compare prices, scrutinize promises, weigh options, ask pertinent questions and know their legal rights."[11]

Most of all, these new consumers want *authenticity*—the real thing. Lewis and Bridger note that the Japanese distinguish between *miryokuteki hinshitsu* (quality that fascinates) and *atarimae hinshitsu* (quality that is expected). New consumers want *miryokuteki hinshitsu,* and when it comes to finding it, they know that buzz is a much more reliable source than corporate hype.

SHOULD YOU BUZZ?

Let's say you buy the argument that buzz is in and hype is out. Or maybe you're just intrigued about the idea of letting the customer do all the marketing work for a change. Regardless of your motive, how do you know if buzz is right for you? Rosen says the answer depends on your product, on the kind of customers you are going after, and on your marketing strategy.

Products that Buzz

According to Rosen, some products naturally generate more buzz because they are the kind of products people want to talk about. He gives the following examples:

- **Exciting products,** such as books, records, and movies. Customers I [Rosen] interviewed said things like "I fell in love with it" or "It grabbed me" to describe their first encounter with certain products they later talked about.

- **Innovative products.** People talk about them both because these products may provide new benefits and because people are impressed by the ingenuity of the creators. The early web browsers—Mosaic and later Netscape—generated incredible buzz because people saw the usefulness of these tools and admired the creativity of the people who invented them.

- **Personal experience products.** When personal experience is needed to assess the product or the service, buzz can be expected. Hotels, airlines, cars, books—all fall under this category.

- **Complex products** like software or medical devices. Here the motivation derives from the need to reduce risk. When people don't understand products, they have to talk in order to make sense of them.

- **Expensive products,** such as computers or consumer electronics. Risk is the major motivation here, too.

- **Observable products,** such as clothes, cars, and cellular phones. People tend to talk about what they see. If your product is invisible to them, they are less likely to discuss it.[12]

Other examples of products people like to talk about include:

- **Products that evoke an emotional response,** such as a scary movie like *Psycho* or *The Blair Witch Project.*

- **Products that advertise themselves,** such as the first wheeled suitcases.

- **Products that leave traces behind after they are used,** such as Magnetic Poetry.

- **Products that become more useful as more people use them,** such as the telephone, fax machine, or e-mail.

- **Products that are compatible with the "preexisting structure" in people's minds,** such as the Palm handheld PDA device. Rosen argues that people got excited about the Palm because it did the things people envisioned a handheld device doing, like keeping track of addresses, schedules, contacts, and so on. It was a "neat device" you wanted to tell your friends about because it did what you always thought such "neat devices" were supposed to do.

- **Products that do the rest,** such as the camera that carries the notice "You push the button. We do the rest." A device that simplifies things—does the rest—is worth telling people about.[13]

People that Are Buzzable

Some people are more susceptible to buzz than others. For example, says Rosen, people between the ages of 18 and 24 are more tuned into buzz than people over 55. So are new immigrants and scientists. In other words, if your target consumers are 18-to 24-year-old nuclear physicists who have just arrived in this country, you've got a lot of reason to buzz.

A Buzzable Marketing Strategy

Finally, says Rosen, you are a good candidate for buzz if it fits with your overall marketing strategy. For example, if you market your product in a business-to-business environment in which purchasing decisions are central ized, generating a lot of buzz at the consumer level might not do you much good. On the other hand, if those end users have influence over the central-ized purchasing decision in some way—for example, they participate in evaluating competing products—then buzz might be a good strategy.

Your Product Must Exceed Expectations

There is one final thing to consider when deciding if you're right for buzz, says Rosen, and that is just how good your product or service is. It had bet-ter be great, or at least exceed expectations. Otherwise, warns Rosen, you'll get buzz all right—but the wrong kind.

THE ART AND SCIENCE (?) OF BUZZ

Assuming you have decided that you do have a product or service that is buzzable, the question becomes how to make it happen. You'll recall that in the Hush Puppies example at the beginning of this chapter buzz just hap-pened. In fact, the marketers at Wolverine were some of the last people to be buzzed. They didn't start the buzz or control it once it was started. When the buzz works for you, that's a nice position to be in. You don't have to do anything and your product takes off like a rocket. You just get the credit.

But let's suppose that you aren't so lucky. Your product/service isn't going to buzz on its own. Is there something you can do to get the buzz started? Our gurus' answers are likely to be "Yes," "Maybe," "We think so," "We aren't sure but we've got some ideas." Comforting? Not exactly, but the fact is that no one completely understands buzz. As Godin puts it:

> To date, no one has come up with a repeatable formula for creating viruses [buzz] in a reliable way. There are precious few people who are serial virus [buzz] starters.
>
> My hope was that . . . I could answer your question about *how*. Alas, I don't know. I know it when I see it, but I fear the rest is art.[14]

In spite of the fact that, as Godin freely admits, at least for now (1) buzz creation is more art than science, (2) very few gurus have ever successfully created buzz themselves, and (3) almost no one has successfully buzzed twice, our gurus, including Godin, still offer their how-to advice. We will summarize some of the best of that advice in the next two sections on why people buzz and who buzzes, followed by an examination of some of our gurus' tips for buzz success.

Why We Buzz

Why do people buzz? Rosen answers that it is for a very simple reason; it's in our genes. Rosen says we buzz for the following reasons:

- **We're programmed from birth to do it**—"Sharing information is an effective survival mechanism for ravens, bees, ants, and . . . people. We may no longer need to trade knowledge about bison hunting, but we're still programmed to do so. And when it comes to certain survival issues, like hunting for a job, we do count on tips from others."[15]
- **We buzz to connect**—Rosen says that talking helps us establish and maintain alliances and social ties. It's the friendly thing to do, analogous to one monkey picking fleas off another. Since most people don't have fleas and anyway it might look strange to be caught rummaging though your best friend's hair, we chat about things like who's doing what with, to, or about someone else and what it all means. We are always looking for topics for this connecting process, and products are great conversation starters. "What aftershave are you wearing?" "So, what do you use for stuffing?" "Where did you stay in New York on your last trip? Did you like it?"

Rosen says another reason we talk about products, such as the latest electronic gadget we bought or the latest book we read, is to send a message to people about how wealthy, smart, or sophisticated we are. "Words," he writes, "are often the currency we exchange to manage an important asset: our reputation. And products help us do that."[16]

- **We buzz to make sense of the world**—Remember what we said about the proliferation of brands in Chapter 2? In the early 1970s there were zero web sites; now there are over 4.7 million and the number of sites is increasing every day. Colgate made 2 types of toothpaste in the 1970s. They produce 17 types today. Styles of SUVs—8 in the 70s, 38 today, and so on. Rosen says that proliferation of choices has made life complex and confusing. Plus, every day there are scores of new products we have to make sense of—Do they work? Are they worth the price? Making sense of all of these options is hard. In such a world, anything like buzz that helps us make sense of these options, well, makes sense.
- **We buzz to reduce risks**—Buzz offers the additional benefit, says Rosen, of reducing risks, costs, and uncertainty. He notes that when he moved recently, he had to leave his doctor behind and find a new one. He asked his new neighbors and business associates to recommend a doctor they liked. In short, he checked the doctor buzz. He notes that 70 percent of Americans ask the advice of others before choosing a physician. Even though these people are rarely qualified to judge the professional competence of a physician, we feel better knowing that most of a doctor's patients consider him or her competent.
- **We buzz because it makes economic sense to do so**—Rosen notes that another reason we buzz is because sometimes it benefits us if we can convince other people to buy the products or adopt the technical standards we do. After all, if we use Microsoft Windows and Word, it's a lot easier for us to share information with others if they use the same products. We might even engage in some negative buzz and try to discourage people from using an alternative and even better product because it would be costly for us to have to switch to match their standard.
- **We buzz to relieve tension**—Rosen notes that sometimes people buzz just to let off steam or to vent anger. They've had a negative experience with a company and they want to get even. Think about it.

How often have you told someone about a negative experience you had with a piece of software or a software company?

Who Buzzes?

As we suggested in the last section, everyone buzzes. So the answer to the question, Who buzzes? is obvious. We all do. On the other hand, say our gurus, we don't all buzz equally. Some people buzz better, louder, more consistently, and with more authority than others. Who are these super-buzzers? For an explanation we will turn to guru Gladwell, the author of *The Tipping Point.*

Remember Paul Revere? No, not the sixties pop group. The Paul Revere we're thinking about is the one that had a featured role in that unfortunate misunderstanding Americans had with the British back in the late 1700s. Remember the Longfellow poem?

LISTEN, my children, and you shall hear
Of the midnight ride of Paul Revere,
On the eighteenth of April, in Seventy-Five;
Hardly a man is now alive
Who remembers that famous day and year.
He said to his friend, "If the British march
By land or sea from the town to-night,
Hang a lantern aloft in the belfry arch
Of the North Church tower, as a signal light,—
One, if by land, and two, if by sea;
And I on the opposite shore will be,
Ready to ride and spread the alarm
Through every Middlesex village and farm. . . . [17]

Paul Revere. That fateful night he jumped on his horse and did just what the poem said he did. He rode through every Middlesex village—Charlestown, Medford, North Cambridge, Menotomy—all the way from Boston to Lexington—buzzing like crazy. "The British are coming! The British are coming!" and boy did he cause a lot of stir. People were jumping out of bed, grabbing their rifles, and engaging in all kinds of goings on. And the next day—well, it wasn't a good day for the British.

Paul Revere's ride was a classic case of very successful buzz, says Glad-well. Revere started a true word-of-mouth epidemic. But what made Revere so successful? Gladwell admits that Revere had a pretty sensational bit of news that was important to everyone along his route, but, argues Gladwell, it wasn't just the news. In fact, someone else was riding that night carrying the same news as Revere and he wasn't nearly as successful in buzzing.

> At the same time that Revere began his ride north and west of Boston, a fellow revolutionary—a tanner by the name of William Dawes—set out on the same urgent errand, working his way to Lexington via the towns west of Boston. He was carrying the identical message, through just as many towns over just as many miles as Paul Revere. But Dawes's ride didn't set the countryside afire. The local militia leaders weren't alerted. In fact, so few men from one of the main towns he rode through—Waltham—fought the following day that some subsequent historians concluded that it must have been a strongly pro-British community. It wasn't. The people of Waltham just didn't find out the British were coming until it was too late. If it were only the news itself that mattered in a word-of-mouth epidemic, Dawes would now be as famous as Paul Revere. He isn't.[18]

So why was Paul Revere so successful in buzzing that he created a firestorm of excitement, while William Dawes barely created a yawn with the same news? The answer, says Gladwell, is that "the success of any kind of social epidemic [highly successful buzz] is heavily dependent on the in-volvement of people with a particular and rare set of social gifts. Revere's news tipped [created a social epidemic] and Dawes's didn't because of the differences between the two men."[19] Some people, like Revere, have a par-ticular talent for buzzing that the rest of us don't possess, and they are im-portant people to know because their participation in your buzz marketing campaign is critical to your success. Gladwell refers to these particularly talented buzzers as connectors, mavens, and salesmen. Let's look at what Gladwell has to say about each of these talented buzzers.

Connectors

According to Gladwell, connectors are people who know a lot of other peo-ple. Of course, we all know people who know a lot of people—"Oh that's so-and-so, he knows everyone." Yet we underestimate both the importance of these people in buzzing and just how many people they can really buzz. As a way of illustrating his point, our guru offers a simple game that involves the following list of 250 names selected at random from the Manhattan phone book.[20] You play the game by reviewing the list and giving yourself one point for each person you know who has one of these surnames. To score a point, you must know the person's name and they must know yours. Take a moment, review the names, and give yourself one point for each name you know, including multiple points for people with the same last name. For example, let's say you know three people whose last name is Bell. In that case, you get three points.

Algazi	Brendle	Delakas	Gladwell
Alvarez	Butler	Dillon	Greenup
Alpern	Calle	Donaghey	Gannon
Ametrano	Cantwell	Daly	Ganshaw
Andrews	Carrell	Dawson	Garcia
Aran	Chinlund	Edery	Gennis
Arnstein	Cirker	Ellis	Gerard
Ashford	Cohen	Elliott	Gericke
Bailey	Collas	Eastman	Gilbert
Ballout	Couch	Easton	Glassman
Bamberger	Callegher	Famous	Glazer
Baptista	Calcaterra	Fermin	Gomendio
Barr	Cook	Fialco	Gonzalez
Barrows	Carey	Finklestein	Greenstein
Baskerville	Cassell	Farber	Guglielmo
Bassiri	Chen	Falkin	Gurman
Bell	Chung	Feinman	Haberkorn
Bokgese	Clarke	Friedman	Hoskins
Brandao	Cohn	Gardner	Hussein
Bravo	Carton	Gelpi	Hamm
Brooke	Crowley	Glascock	Hardwick
Brightman	Curbelo	Grandfield	Harrell
Billy	Dellamanna	Greenbaum	Hauptman
Blau	Diaz	Greenwood	Hawkins
Bohen	Dirar	Gruber	Henderson
Bohn	Duncan	Garil	Hayman
Borsuk	Dagostino	Goff	Hibara

Hehmann	Leifer	Popper	Silverton
Herbst	Leung	Potter	Silverman
Hedges	Levine	Purpura	Silverstein
Hogan	Leiw	Palma	Sklar
Hoffman	Lockwood	Perez	Slotkin
Horowitz	Logrono	Portocarrero	Speros
Hsu	Lohnes	Punwasi	Stollman
Huber	Lower	Rader	Sadowski
Ikiz	Laber	Rankin	Schles
Jaroschy	Leonardi	Ray	Shapiro
Johann	Marten	Reyes	Sigdel
Jacobs	McLean	Richardson	Snow
Jara	Michaels	Ritter	Spencer
Johnson	Miranda	Roos	Steinkol
Kassel	Moy	Rose	Stewart
Keegan	Marin	Rosenfeld	Stires
Kuroda	Muir	Roth	Stopnik
Kavanau	Murphy	Rutherford	Stonehill
Keller	Marodon	Rustin	Tayss
Kevill	Matos	Ramos	Tilney
Kiew	Mendoza	Regan	Temple
Kimbrough	Muraki	Reisman	Torfield
Kline	Neck	Renkert	Townsend
Kossoff	Needham	Roberts	Trimpin
Kotzitzky	Noboa	Rowan	Turchin
Kahn	Null	Rene	Villa
Kiesler	O'Flynn	Rosario	Vasillov
Kosser	O'Neill	Rothbart	Voda
Korte	Orlowski	Saperstein	Waring
Leibowitz	Perkins	Schoenbrod	Weber
Lin	Pieper	Schwed	Weinstein
Liu	Pierre	Sears	Wang
Lowrance	Pons	Statosky	Wegimont
Lundh	Pruska	Sutphen	Weed
Laux	Paulino	Sheehy	Weishaus

So how did you do? Gladwell says he has given this test to over 400 people from all professions and walks of life. As you might expect, the results are varied. In a group of college students, the average score was 21. A group of academics at a conference—middle aged, mostly white, many Ph.D.'s—averaged 39. A group of journalists averaged 41. Across all 400, says Gladwell, about two dozen people scored under 20, twelve scored over 90 and four of these twelve scored over 100. The interesting thing about these experiments, says Gladwell, is that regardless of the group—students, academics, journalists, and so on—there were always at least some people who scored in the high-end 90+ range. These were the connectors—the handful of people in every group who have a real knack for getting to know people. They are important to buzz for that reason, but, adds Gladwell, there is something else about these people that make them effective buzzers. Connectors are important to buzz not just because of the number of people they know, but also because of the variety of people they know. Gladwell says the parlor game "Six Degrees of Kevin Bacon" illustrates this point very well.

> The idea behind the game is to try to link any actor or actress, through the movies they've been in, to the actor Kevin Bacon in less than six steps. So, for example, O.J. Simpson was in *Naked Gun* with Priscilla Presley, who was in *Ford Fairlane* with Gilbert Gotffried, who was in *Beverly Hills Cop II* with Paul Reiser, who was in *Diner* with Kevin Bacon. That's four steps. Mary Pickford was in *Screen Snapshots* with Clark Gable, who was in *Combat America* with Tony Romano, who, thirty-five years later, was in *Starting Over* with Bacon. That's three steps.[21]

Of course, you have to know a whole lot of movie trivia to play this game. Fortunately, a computer scientist at the University of Virginia has done the work for us. Don't ask us why he did this, but Gladwell says someone by the name of Brett Tjaden input data for a quarter million or so actors and actresses and came up with scores for various actors to find out who was best connected, that is, had the shortest number of steps to reach them from any other actor or actress. For example, Kevin Bacon's connection score is exactly 2.878498 steps. In other words, it takes a little less than 3 steps to reach Bacon from almost anyone. (Aren't you glad that you now know that?) Martin Sheen did even better at 2.671420 steps, and Donald Sutherland's score was even better than that at 2.632921 steps. Who was tops? Christopher Lee at only 2.599102 steps. According to the University of Virginia computer, Lee is at the center of the Hollywood universe. He knows everyone, or at least should.

Those of you old enough to have gone to the movies in the early fifties will remember Lee as the British-born actor in a string of horror films—*The Curse of Frankenstein, Dracula, Horror of Dracula, The Mummy,* and so on. The younger set may remember him for his roles in the 1999 film *Sleepy Hollow* and the 2001 release of *The Lord of the Rings.* Lee has been playing roles in films for half a century. That gives him an advantage over Bacon, because he's older and has had more roles and therefore more opportunity to build connections. But there is something more, as Gladwell points out. Connectors, like Lee, have a wider range of contacts. Lee appeared in a lot of horror films, that's true, but he has also done adventures (*The Three Musketeers*), comedy (*Police Academy II*), drama (*A Tale of Two Cities*), mystery (*Sherlock Holmes and the Deadly Necklace*), and fantasy (*The Lord of the Rings*). It's not just the number of contacts he has, it's the breadth of contacts due to the wide range of types of films in which he has appeared.

Compare Lee's experiences with that of John Wayne, another actor who appeared in a large number of movies. Wayne's score is 2.777828, behind those of Rip Torn (2.721335), Robert DeNiro (2.705463), and more than 170 other, often less-well-known actors. Wayne's connection problem was variety. As Gladwell notes, John Wayne made a lot of movies, but more than half of them were Westerns. His range of contacts was more limited than Lee's. Connectors not only meet a lot of people, they are involved in such a variety of cultures and subcultures that the breadth of their contacts is extremely wide. That was one of Paul Revere's strengths, adds Gladwell:

Here, then, is the explanation for why Paul Revere's midnight ride started a word-of-mouth epidemic and William Dawes's ride did not. Paul Revere was . . . a Connector. He was, for example, gregarious and intensely social. When he died, his funeral was attended, in the words of one contemporary newspaper account, by "troops of people." He was a fisherman and a hunter, a card player and a theater-lover, a frequenter of pubs and a successful businessman. He was active in the local Masonic Lodge and was a member of several select social clubs. . . .

Had Revere been given a list of 250 surnames drawn at random from the Boston census of 1775, there is no question he would have scored well over 100.

After the Boston Tea Party, in 1773, when the anger of the American colonists against their British rulers began to spill over, dozens of committees and congresses of angry colonists sprang up around New England.

They had no formal organization or established means of community. But Paul Revere quickly emerged as a link between all those far-flung revolutionary dots. He would routinely ride down to Philadelphia or New York or up to New Hampshire, carrying messages from one group to another. Within Boston as well, he played a special role. There were, in the revolutionary years, seven groups of "Whigs" (revolutionaries) in Boston, comprising some 255 men. Most of the men—over 80 percent—belonged to just one group. No one was a member of all seven. Only two men were members of as many as five of the groups: Paul Revere was one of those two.[22]

See Exhibit 6.2 for a different way of thinking about connectors.

Mavens

Paul Revere was a connector, there is no doubt about that. Being a connector, when he rode through every Middlesex village and farm, the chances are he knew which doors to knock on to spread the alarm. That made him a very effective buzzer, but there was more. Revere, says Gladwell, was also

---

EXHIBIT 6.2. Network Hubs

In his book *The Anatomy of Buzz*, Emanuel Rosen uses the term "network hubs" to refer to people who have lots of contacts like Gladwell's connectors. Rosen says there are four types of network hubs:

Regular Expert Hubs—These are normal people who are important sources of buzz because they have a particular expertise; for example, your friend Tom is a regular expert hub because he keeps track of the latest movies and always knows what is worth seeing and what isn't.

Mega Expert Hubs—These are celebrities, analysts, members of the press, and so on who have links to a lot of people in addition to a recognized and widely accepted expertise; for example, Peter Drucker on management.

Regular Social Hubs—Again, these are normal people but instead of deriving their influence from what they know they derive it from being charismatic, trusted, and oh so social; for example, your official or unofficial neighborhood social chairperson.

Mega Social Hubs—Celebrities who are known and respected not so much for their expertise but because people genuinely like and trust them; for example, Oprah Winfrey.

Source: Emanuel Rosen and Roger E. Scholl, The Anatomy of Buzz: How to Create Word-of-Mouth Marketing (New York: Random House, 2000), pp. 44–47.

a person who accumulated knowledge, or, as they say in Yiddish, he was a maven.

Connectors know people—lots of people. Mavens know about things. They know, or find out first, what is going on. Connectors, says Gladwell, need mavens to tell them what to buzz about.

> It's possible that Connectors learn about new information by an entirely random process, that because they know so many people they get access to new things wherever they pop up. If you look closely at social epidemics [successful buzz], however, it becomes clear that just as there are people we rely upon to connect us to other people, there are also people we rely upon to connect us with new information. There are people specialists, and there are information specialists.[23]

It so happened that Paul Revere was both a people specialist and an information specialist. He had been actively engaged in ferreting out the information he later buzzed about on that fateful night. For example, writes Gladwell, Revere had set up a secret group in the fall of 1774 for the express purpose of monitoring British troop movements.

Of course, many people collect information. There is no shortage of curiosity in the population. What makes mavens unique is that they don't want to hoard the information they gather. They delight in passing it along. Mavens pass information along because they want to help others, and that, says Gladwell, turns out to be quite appealing. Mavens are trying to help, not persuade. Of course, persuasion is important in successful buzz, but that takes a different type of person. Gladwell calls that type the salesman.

Salesmen

Connectors connect. Mavens joyfully share information. Salesmen convince us to use the information in a certain way. Gladwell reports on two studies that he says provide some interesting insight into what makes salesmen so persuasive.

In the first study, researchers videotaped the nightly news programs of Peter Jennings (ABC), Tom Brokaw (NBC), and Dan Rather (CBS) during the 1984 presidential campaign between Ronald Reagan and Walter Mondale. Then they deleted the sound and showed the broadcasts to a randomly chosen group of volunteers. The volunteers had no idea what the news anchors were talking about but were asked to rate the emotional content of the anchors' expressions on a scale of 1 to 21 – 1 being "extremely negative" to 21 being "highly positive." When the researchers analyzed the results they discovered that when Dan Rather was talking about Walter Mondale the volunteers gave him an average score of 10.46. When he talked about Ronald Reagan, his score was 10.37. In other words, the volunteers rated Rather's emotional expression as almost perfectly neutral between the two candidates. Tom Brokaw's scores were similar—11.21 for Mondale and 11.50 for Reagan. But when it came to Peter Jennings, there was an obvious difference. Jennings's scores were much more positive for Reagan—17.44 versus just 13.38 for Mondale. Wanting to know if the differences between the three anchors had any impact on their viewers, the researchers surveyed regular viewers of the three networks in various cities. The results showed that viewers who watched the Jennings broadcast were more likely to have voted for Reagan. (Note: Gladwell says that ABC vigorously disputes this study, although he claims the same researchers repeated the study in the next election between Michael Dukakis and George Bush with similar results.)

Gladwell's second study that illustrates the subtleties of persuasion is less controversial. He describes it this way:

> A large group of students were recruited for what they were told was a market research study by a company making high-tech headphones. They were each given a headset and told that the company wanted to test to see how well they worked when the listener was in motion dancing up and down, say, or moving his or her head. All of the students listened to songs by Linda Ronstadt and the Eagles, and then heard a radio editorial arguing that tuition at their university should be raised from its present level of $587 to $750. A third were told that while they listened to the taped radio editorial they should nod their heads vigorously up and down. The next third were told to shake their heads from side to side. The final third were the control group. They were told to keep their heads still. When they were finished, all the students were given a short questionnaire, asking them questions about the quality of the songs and the effect of the shaking. Slipped in at the end was the question the experimenters really wanted an answer to: "What do you feel would be an appropriate dollar amount for undergraduate tuition per year?"[24]

You can probably guess the results. That's right. The students who shook their heads up and down said they thought the tuition should be increased.

Those who shook their head side to side said it should be decreased. Those who kept their heads still said they thought the current tuition was about right.

So what's going on here? What do these two studies tell us about persuasion? Gladwell says he thinks they tell us three things. First, they tell us that little things can make a big difference. Just the act of nodding made a big difference in how the students responded to the question about raising tuition. Second, the studies remind us that nonverbal clues are important. Jennings wasn't trying to be anything other than neutral, but somehow his viewers seemed to be picking up some subtle clues from his facial expression. Finally, and perhaps most importantly according to Gladwell, the studies show that persuasion works in ways that most of us non-mavens never recognize. If asked, writes Gladwell, the students would never have admitted that their opinions were swayed by so insignificant a thing as the motion of their heads. And, we can imagine that few, if any, ABC viewers would admit that Peter Jennings's facial expressions might have influenced their vote.

Of course, these subtleties of persuasion haven't gone unrecognized in the marketing and sales literature. Books on salesmanship often report on studies that have shown that the most successful salesmen mirror the posture and talking styles of those they are seeking to persuade. Unfortunately, as Gladwell reports, when less-successful salesman are taught to do the same thing, that is, adopt the customer's posture, mannerisms, talking style, and so forth, it doesn't work. Those who were less successful remained so. In fact, they come across as phony.

Salesmen are different. They aren't phony; they have the gift. "What we are talking about," writes Gladwell, "is a kind of super-reflex, a fundamental physiological ability of which we are barely aware. And like all specialized human traits, some people have much more mastery over this reflex than others."[25]

MAKING BUZZ HAPPEN

Earlier we said that buzz, at least as it stands now, is more of an art than a science. We added that no one has come up with a reliable formula for making buzz happen. Therefore, we can't give you our gurus' step-by-step guidance. The best we can do is give you some tips for buzz success drawn from their writings.

Finding Hubs, Connectors, Mavens, and Salesmen

One question you might ask is where to find these connectors, mavens, and salesmen that our gurus say are so important. Rosen offers the following suggestions:

- **Let them identify themselves**—The nice thing about people who are connectors, mavens, and salesmen is that they are active. Mavens are constantly seeking information. Connectors are constantly connecting. Salesmen are constantly trying to persuade. One way to find them is just to look and listen. For example, the guy who hangs around your booth at the trade show and keeps asking all those questions that regular customers never think to ask just might be a maven out foraging for input.
- **Identify categories of people who might be connectors, mavens, or salesmen in different contexts**—Let's say you want to find some people who would be good connectors, mavens, and/or salesmen for your new super-duper baby food product. Where might they be found? Think carefully now. Who talks to young mothers about nutrition for their infants? If you said pediatric nurses, you've got the idea.
- **Spotting connectors, mavens, and salesmen in the field**—Rosen says if you want to tap into network hubs (connectors, etc.) at the street level, you just need to get out on the street and talk to people. Ask them who is socially active and whose opinion is respected. Rosen says you should listen to what people have to say about themselves. For example, you find out a physician has a practice in two or more clinics or two or more towns. He might be a connector. If you hear someone describe themselves as "wearing two hats," says Rosen, you might just have located a connector.

Getting Connectors, Mavens, and Salesmen Buzzing

Let's assume that you have identified some connectors, mavens, and salesmen. Now the question becomes one of getting them to buzz. Our gurus suggest the following:

- **Make sure the connectors, mavens, and salesmen get the information first**—These network hubs, as Rosen calls them, always want to be the first to know about something new, exciting, or different. Make sure they find out. Why do you think record companies give sneak previews to DJs?

- **Give them ammunition**—Buzzers need something to buzz about. Give it to them. Let's say you're a buzzer about off-road vehicles and you just happen to get an invitation to an exciting, action-packed, weekend, off-road Jeep Jamboree. What are you going to talk about to your followers Monday morning? Rosen bets you won't be asking them what they did all weekend. You'll be buzzing about what you did.

- **Give 'em a good story to tell**—There is nothing that generates buzz so much as an outrageous story. Hollywood publicists have known this for years, and, says Rosen, you should take a lesson from them. As an example Rosen cites the publicity stunt Mel Brooks pulled off for his 1974 film *Blazing Saddles*. The media was invited to cover a free cocktail party and advance showing of the movie Brooks was holding for some special guests. When the TV crews and journalists showed up to cover the event they discovered that the "special guests" were 250 horses and their owners who were there to watch the movie, eat oats and "Horse d'Oeuvres," and visit the "Horsepitality Bar."[26]

- **Make it easy**—Finally, here is a piece of advice from Godin. He says that one of the most effective things you can do to get buzz to take off, or as he puts its for the ideavirus to become an epidemic, is to just make it enormously easy and effortless for buzzers to buzz about your product, service, or company. Godin says one of his favorite examples of a company that did this is Vindigo. (See http://www.vindigo.com/.) Vindigo's product is an application for the Palm that provides a directory of restaurants, entertainment, stores, and so on in major U.S. cities. You plug in where you are by major city and major street/cross street and Vindigo will show you restaurants, stores, movie houses, and so on that are nearby. You can even get ratings, operating/show times, ticket information, and so forth, and it is all available on your handheld Palm. As Godin notes, it is a cool product, particularly for people who travel a lot, but what is so cool about the product from a buzz standpoint isn't the obvious. What is important for buzz is a small button down on the bottom of the screen along with the words "eating," "shopping," and "entertainment." The word is "give." The buzzwise Vindigo designers made buzz about their product not just easy but instant and effortless. Let's say you're a connector or maven and you're showing this great new Palm application to someone. They ask where they can get it. Instead of writing out a long URL for them that they might or might not ever use, you simply push the "give" button. Suddenly, instantly the entire application is copied to your friend's Palm. It's the effortless, 60-second buzz.[27]

REACHING THE TIPPING POINT

So there you have it. You locate the right connectors, mavens, and salesmen. You make sure that they get the scoop about your product or service first. You give them a good story to buzz. Most of all, you make it easy for them. And, voilà, you have it! You find the holy grail of buzz. Buzz about your product or service reaches what Gladwell calls "the tipping point."

Gladwell traces the idea of the tipping point back to the 1970s. He writes:

> The expression first came into popular use in the 1970s to describe the flight to the suburbs of whites living in the older cities of the American Northeast. When the number of incoming African Americans in a particular neighborhood reached a certain point—20 percent say—sociologists observed that the community would "tip": most of the remaining whites would leave immediately. The Tipping Point is the moment of critical mass, the threshold, the boiling point.[28]

Fax machines and cell phones are two well-known products that reached their respective tipping points, says Gladwell:

> Sharp introduced the first low-priced fax machine in 1984, and sold about 80,000 of those machines in the United States in that first year. For the next three years, businesses slowly and steadily bought more and more faxes, until, in 1987, enough people had faxes that it made sense for everyone to get a fax. Nineteen eighty-seven was the fax machine Tipping Point. A million machines were sold that year, and by 1989 two million new machines had gone into operation. Cellular phones have followed the same trajectory. Through the 1990s, they got smaller and cheaper, and service got better until 1998, when the technology hit a Tipping Point and suddenly everyone had a cell phone.[29]

EXHIBIT 6.3. **The Mathematics of the Tipping Point**

Malcolm Gladwell says that one of the best ways to understand how tipping points occur is to imagine the outbreak of a hypothetical flu epidemic. It might occur somewhat like this:

> Suppose, for example, that one summer 1,000 tourists come to Manhattan from Canada carrying an untreatable strain of 24-hour virus. This strain of flu has a 2 percent infection rate, which is to say that one out of every 50 people who come into close contact with someone carrying it catches the bug him- or herself. Let's say that 50 is also exactly the number of people the average Manhattanite—in the course of tiding the subways and mingling with colleagues at work—comes into contact with every day. What we have, then, is a disease in equilibrium. Those 1,000 Canadian tourists pass on the virus to 1,000 new people on the day they arrive. And the next day those 1,000 newly infected people pass on the virus to another 1,000 people, just as the original 1,000 tourists who started the epidemic are returning to health. With those getting sick and those getting well so perfectly in balance, the flu chugs along at a steady but unspectacular clip through the rest of the summer and the fall. But then comes the Christmas season. The subways and buses get more crowded with tourists and shoppers, and instead of running into an even 50 people a day, the average Manhattanite now has close contact with, say, 55 people a day. All of a sudden, the equilibrium is disrupted. The 1,000 flu carriers now run into 55,000 people a day, and at a 2 percent infection rate, that translates into 1,100 cases the following day. Those 1,100, in turn, are now passing on their virus to 55,000 people as well, so that by day 3 there are 1,210 Manhattanites with the flu and by day 4 1,331 and by the end of the week there are nearly 2,000, and so on up, in an exponential spiral, until Manhattan has a full-blown flu epidemic on its hands by Christmas Day. That moment when the average flu carrier went from running into 50 people a day to running into 55 people was the tipping point. It was the point at which an ordinary and stable phenomenon—a low-level flu outbreak—turned into a public health crisis. If you were to draw a graph of the progress of the Canadian flu epidemic, the tipping point would be the point on the graph where the line suddenly turned upward.

Gladwell offers the following sources for additional information on the phenomenon of tipping points:

Jonathan Crane, "The Epidemic Theory of Ghettos and Neighborhood Effects on Dropping Out and Teenage Childbearing," *American Journal of Sociology* 95, no. 5 (1989): 1226–1259.

Mark Granovetter, "Threshold Models of Collective Behavior," *American Journal of Sociology* 83 (1978): 1420–1443.

Mark Granovetter and R. Soong, "Threshold Models of Diffusion and Collective Behavior," *Journal of Mathematical Sociology* 9 (1983): 165–179.

Thomas Schelling, "Dynamic Models of Segregation," *Journal of Mathematical Sociology* 1 (1971): 143–186.

Thomas Schelling, *Micromotives and Macrobehavior* (New York: W. W. Norton, 1978).

Source: Malcolm Gladwell, The Tipping Point: How Little Things Can Make a Big Difference *(Boston: Little Brown & Company, 2000), pp. 260–261.*

(See Exhibit 6.3 for Gladwell's explanation of the mathematics of tipping points.)

So that's what buzz is really all about—reaching the tipping point. As Godin puts it, "somehow a magic moment appears when the entire population goes from blissful unawareness of your offering to total and complete infatuation,"[30] but, he adds, there is only one problem. The odds are your product or service is never going to tip, because most of the world's population—about seven billion—aren't going to be interested in your product or service no matter what it is. They certainly aren't going to get so interested they go nuts about it. As he adds, "even if you just boil it down to the United States, or to Republicans with Internet access, it's pretty clear that large [groups of people] rarely tip about anything."[31]

OUR VIEW

For example, take our own household. One of us is very interested in—or as the other would say, obsessed by—genealogy. She and her genealogy cohorts tipped all over www.ancestry.com and www.familysearch.org. The other of us just doesn't get it. She retorts that he's just afraid of what he might find out about his ancestors. Regardless, the point Godin makes is that chances are you aren't going to have a product or service of universal interest, so tipping (except in restaurants) is probably something you aren't going to experience. Fortunately, says Godin, you don't have to tip to win. He cites eBay as an example:

> By almost any measure, eBay is a winner. Its employees are millionaires and billionaires. Early investors are delighted. Users are happy, with time spent on the service going up all the time.
>
> But has eBay tipped? Certainly not in terms of awareness among the general population. When asked to name an online service, only a tiny fraction of the population picks eBay as their first choice. But it gets even more obvious when you ask people where they go to buy and sell used junk. The vast majority of people are still using classified ads and garage sales, not eBay.[32]

The good news, says Godin, is that you can win without having buzz about your product or service ever reach the tipping point.

And you, dear reader, what do you think? Is BUZZ the future of marketing, or is it branding, CRM, or customer equity? In the future will we all be praying for tipping points? Or is the future a little bit of all of the above—maybe even some wild idea we haven't uncovered? Drop us an e-mail at boyett@jboyett.com and let us know what you think. In the meantime, we wish you good branding, buzzing, and relating. May your **P**s be prosperous and your customer equity strong.

Joseph H. Boyett

Jimmie T. Boyett

KEY POINTS

- Buzz is the aggregate of all person-to-person communication about a particular product, service, or company.

- Buzz shifts the focus of marketing from customer groupings (traditional marketing) and customer relationships (customer relationship management) to interactions between customers.

- Buzz is important now because of the following reasons:

  - Buzz plays a major role in purchasing decisions today for many types of products and services.

  - There is so much advertising today that it is hard to break through the noise and get the attention of customers.

  - People don't trust marketers and companies to tell the truth about their products and services.

  - The Internet provides people with an easy way to communicate and share information.

  - The new consumer wants authenticity and knows that buzz is a much more reliable source of information concerning what is authentic and what is not more than corporate hype.

  - Buzz is right for you if your product is exciting, innovative, must be experienced to be evaluated, complex, expensive, and/or observable.

○—➔ Buzz is more of an art than a science. To date, no one has come up with a repeatable formula for how to generate buzz.

○—➔ People buzz for the following reasons:

- They are programmed to do it.

- They want to connect with others.

- They need to make sense of a complex world.

- They want to reduce risks, costs, and uncertainty.

- Because it makes economic sense for them to do so.

○—➔ Three types of people are critical to making buzz happen:

- **Connectors**—people who know lots of people.

- **Mavens**—people who accumulate knowledge and information and who want to share their knowledge with others.

- **Salesmen**—people who are very persuasive.

○—➔ The keys to making buzz happen are

- Find connectors, mavens, and salesmen by letting them identify themselves; by identifying categories of people who might be connectors, mavens, or salesmen because of their position or role in society; and/or by going out into the field and asking people for names of those who are most influential.

- Make sure connectors, mavens, and salesmen get the information about a product or service first and have a good story to tell. Make it easy for them to buzz.

○—➔ The ultimate goal of buzz is to reach the tipping point where the entire population goes from being blissfully unaware of your product or service to being totally and completely infatuated with it.

○—➔ Buzz about most products/services will never reach the tipping point because not enough people in the population will be interested in them.

○—➔ A product/service can still win even if buzz about it never reaches the tipping point.

The Gurus

David Aaker is professor emeritus of marketing at the Haas School of Business, University of California, Berkeley, and vice chairman of the consulting firm Prophet Brand Strategy. Professor Aaker received a B.S. degree from MIT and an M.S. and Ph.D. from Stanford University. He has published more than 80 articles and 12 books, including *Managing Brand Equity, Building Strong Brands, Developing Business Strategies, Strategic Market Management,* and *Brand Leadership.* He can be reached by e-mail at aaker@haas.berkeley.edu or by fax at (510) 643-1420.

Harry Beckwith is the author of the best-sellers *Selling the Invisible* and *The Invisible Touch.* In addition, he is the founder and director of Beckwith Partners, a positioning and branding firm, and a guest lecturer. Mr. Beckwith is a Phi Beta Kappa graduate of Stanford University. He can be reached through Beckwith Partners at Suite 600, Lumber Exchange Bldg., Ten South Fifth Street, Minneapolis, MN 55402, or by e-mail at invisible@bitstream.com. His company maintains an Internet site at http://www.beckwithpartners.com.

Robert Blattberg is the Polk Brothers Distinguished Professor of Retailing and director of the Center of Retail Management at Northwestern University's Kellogg Graduate School of Management. He joined the Kellogg faculty in 1991, after many years at the University of Chicago. Professor Blattberg is author or coauthor of a number of books including *Customer Equity, The Marketing Information Revolution,* and *Sales Promotion.* He can be reached by mail at Marketing Department, Kellogg School of Management, Leverone Hall 4th Floor, 2001 Sheridon Road, Evanston, IL 60208-2001, or by e-mail at r-blattberg@nwu.edu. He also maintains an Internet site at www.customerequity.com.

Neil H. Borden was the Richard S. Reynolds Professor of Business Administration at the University of Virginia (UVA) until his retirement in May 1997. He had been a member of the UVA faculty since July 1963 and is currently assigned to the dean's office. Borden is the author of the *Advertising in Our Economy* and the classic book *The Economic Effects of Advertising*.

Professor Borden can be reached by mail at Faculty Pavilions, Room 165, Charlottesville, VA 22904-4321, or by e-mail at nhb@Virginia.edu.

Marc Braunstein is a cofounder of the marketing consulting firm Firebrand and coauthor of *Deep Branding on the Internet*. Though educated at the University of Washington with a degree in neurobiology, he began his career as a copywriter for a Chicago-based advertising agency. He later moved to New England to open and manage a Milwaukee-based agency and ultimately founded Firebrand with coauthor Edward Levine. He can be reached by e-mail at mbraunstein@firebrand.com.

Darren Bridger is coauthor of *The Soul of the New Consumer* and a researcher at the David Lewis Consultancy. He can be reached through the Internet site http://www.dlcltd.com or by fax at +44 (0) 1892-542827.

Kevin J. Clancy, coauthor of *Counterintuitive Marketing,* is chairman and CEO of the marketing investment strategy firm Copernicus. He received B.A. and M.A. degrees from City University of New York and a Ph.D. in sociology from New York University and served on the faculties of Boston University's School of Management and the Wharton School.

Mr. Clancy's extensive list of publications on advertising, marketing, and social science research include *The Marketing Revolution, Marketing Myths That Are Killing Business, Simulated Test Marketing,* and *Uncover the Hidden Power of Television Programming*. He can be reached by mail at Copernicus Marketing Consulting and Research, 450 Lexington Street, Auburndale, MA 02466, or by e-mail at kclancy@copernicusmarketing.com.

Steven Cristol is a consultant in brand strategy and coauthor of *Simplicity Marketing and Essentials of Media Planning: A Marketing Viewpoint*.

Adam Curry, coauthor of *The Customer Marketing Method,* was the founder and chief technology officer of the marketing communications company Think New Ideas, Inc. He has served on Internet advisory boards and is a well-known radio and MTV guest. He can be reached by e-mail at adam@curry.com.

Jay Curry is chairman of the Customer Marketing Institute and consultant in the area of direct marketing. Born and raised in New York State, Curry received a B.A. from Bates College and an M.S. from Boston University School of Public Communication. He is the cofounder of the Amsterdam-based consulting company MSP Associates, coauthor of *The Customer Marketing Method,* and author of *Know Your Customer* and *Customer Marketing: How to Increase the Profitability of Your Customer Base.* He can be reached by e-mail at Jay@customermarketing.com. In addition, the Customer Marketing Institute also maintains an Internet site at http://www.customer-marketing.com, and MSP Associates has a site at http://mspassociates.com.

David d'Alessandro is CEO of John Hancock Financial Services and coauthor of *Brand Warfare.* He can be reached through the corporate offices at 200 Clarendon Street, Boston, MA 02117.

Frank W. Davis Jr., coauthor of *Customer Responsive Management: The Flexible Advantage,* is a professor of marketing, logistics, and information technology at the University of Tennessee Knoxville. He can be reached by mail at 316 SMC, College of Business Administration, the University of Tennessee, Knoxville, TN 37996, or by e-mail at fwdavis@utk.edu.

Scott M. Davis is a managing partner for the consulting company Prophet Brand Strategy and author of *Brand Asset Management.* In addition, he is an adjunct professor at Northwestern University's Kellogg Graduate School of Management and guest lecturer at other graduate schools. He received his bachelor's degree in marketing management from the University of Illinois and a master's degree in marketing, finance, and management strategy from Kellogg. Mr. Davis is a contributing writer for *BrandWeek* and has published articles in the *Journal of Consumer Marketing,* the *Journal of Product and Brand Management, Marketing News, Management Review,* and *New Product News.*

He can be reached by mail at Prophet Brand Strategy, 221 North LaSalle Street, Suite 2400, Chicago, IL 60601, or by fax at (312) 879-1940. Prophet Brand Strategy maintains an Internet site at http://www.prophet. com.

George S. Day is the Geoffrey T. Boisi Professor of Marketing at the Wharton School of the University of Pennsylvania. He is also the codirector of the Mack Center for Technological Innovation. Professor Day received his

B.A.Sc. from the University of British Columbia, Canada, M.B.A. from the University of Western Ontario, Canada, and his Ph.D. from Columbia University. Prior to joining the Wharton faculty in 1991, he taught at the University of Toronto, the International Management Development Institute (IMEDE), Switzerland, Stanford University, and the University of Western Ontario, Canada. He also held visiting appointments at the Massachusetts Institute of Technology, Harvard University, and the London Business School. Day's publications include *Essentials of Marketing Research, The Market Driven Organization, Wharton on Dynamic Competitive Strategy,* and *Market Driven Strategy.*

He can be reached by mail at 1478 Steinberg Hall-Dietrich Hall, University of Pennsylvania, Philadelphia, PA 19104-2129, or by e-mail at dayg@wharton.upenn.edu.

Laura Day is the author of *Practical Intuition for Success* and has been teaching a seminar of the same name for more than 10 years. Her other works include *Intuition for Success* and, most recently, *The Circle: How the Power of a Single Wish Can Change Your Life.* She can be reached through her Internet site http://www.practicalintuition.com.

Frank Delano is the president and CEO of the brand image and naming firm Delano & Young. In addition to his books, *Brand Slam* and *The Omnipowerful Brand,* he has published articles in *Harvard Business Review, Advertising Age, ID Magazine,* and *Crain's New York.* He can be reached by mail at Delano & Young, Inc., 420 West 42nd Street, 12th Floor, New York, NY 10036, or by e-mail at fdelano@attglobal.net. He also maintains an Internet site at http://www.frankdelano.com.

Gary Getz is a managing principal at the northern California firm Integral, Inc. and coauthor of *Customer Equity.* He has also been published in *Fortune Magazine, Harvard Management Update, The Handbook of Business Strategy, Planning Review,* and the *European Management Journal.* Mr. Getz holds a B.S.E. in chemical engineering from Princeton University and an M.B.A. from Harvard. He can be reached by mail at Integral, Inc., 104 Mount Auburn Street, Floor 3R, Cambridge, MA 02138-5019, through the Integral Internet site at http://www.integral-inc.com, or through http://www.customerequity.com.

Malcolm Gladwell is the author of the best-seller *The Tipping Point.* He is a former business and science writer for the *Washington Post* and is currently a staff writer for the *New Yorker.* Gladwell, who was born in England and grew up in Canada, graduated with a degree in history from the University of Toronto. He can be reached by e-mail at Malcolm@gladwell.com and maintains an Internet site at http://www.gladwell.com.

Marc Gobé is president and CEO of the brand image firm d/g* and author of *Emotional Branding.* He has taught at the École Superieure de Dessin Industriel in Paris and speaks at Columbia University and conferences on marketing and design. He can be reached through the Internet site http://www.dga.com.

Seth Godin is vice president of direct marketing for Yahoo! He is also the founder of Yoyodyne, the first company to use on-line direct-mail marketing, which Yahoo! subsequently bought. Godin, who graduated from Tufts University with a degree in computer science and philosophy and from Stanford Business School, worked as a brand manager at Spinnaker Software along with Arthur C. Clarke and Michael Crichton. His publications include *Permission Marketing, Unleashing the Ideavirus, The Guerrilla Marketing Handbook, Guerilla Marketing for the Home-Based Business, Emarketing,* and *Get What you Deserve!: How to Guerrilla Market Yourself.* He can be reached by e-mail at Seth@permission.com.

Ian Gordon is a management consultant and director of Convergence Management Consultants. He has written more than 40 articles, and his books include *Beat the Competition, Relationship Marketing,* and *Competitor Targeting.* He can be reached by e-mail at igordon@converge.on.ca or through his Internet site http://www.relationshipmarketing.ca. The mailing address for Convergence Management Consultants is 1054 Centre Street, Suite 289, Thornhill, Ontario L4J 8E5 Canada.

Sam Hill is president of Helios Consulting and coauthor of *The Infinite Asset* and *Radical Marketing.* In addition, he has published articles in *Strategy & Business, Wall Street Journal,* the *Financial Times,* and *Estrategia & Negocios.* He holds a degree in engineering from the University of Georgia and an M.B.A. from the University of Chicago. Mr. Hill can be reached by mail through the Chicago offices of Helios Consulting Group at 8120

Lawndale Avenue, Skokie, IL 60076. In addition, his company maintains an Internet site at http://www.heliosconsulting.com.

Robert D. Hisrich, author of *Marketing: A Practical, Managerial Approach,* holds the Mixon Chair for Entrepreneurship at Case Western Reserve University's Weatherhead School of Management. Prior to joining the faculty at Weatherhead, he was a professor at MIT's Sloan School of Management and set up an entrepreneurship program at the University of Tulsa.

Professor Hisrich holds a B.A. from DePauw University and an M.B.A. and Ph.D. from the University of Cincinnati. His other publications include *Entrepreneurship, Cases in International Entrepreneurship, Sales and Sales Management, Marketing Decisions for New and Mature Products,* and articles in journals like the *Handbook of Technology Management* and *Business Venturing.* He can be reached by e-mail at Robert.Hisrich@ weatherhead.cwru.edu.

Arthur M. Hughes is vice president for strategic planning of M\S Database Marketing (msdbm). He is the author of *Strategic Database Marketing* and *The Complete Database Marketer.* Mr. Hughes can be reached by mail at msdbm, 10866 Wilshire Blvd., Suite 650, Los Angeles, CA 90024, or through the Internet site http://www.msdbm.com.

Erich A. Joachimsthaler is CEO of the New York-based consulting firm the Brand Leadership Company and coauthor of *Brand Leadership.* In addition, he is a visiting professor at the Darden School, University of Virginia, and author of more than 40 articles and case studies published in such journals as *Harvard Business Review, MIS Quarterly,* and *Sloan Management Review.* He can be reached by mail at the Brand Leadership Company, 584 Broadway, Suite 510, New York, NY 10012, or by e-mail at infor@brandleadership.com. His company maintains an Internet site at http://www.brandleadership.com.

Guy Kawasaki is founder, CEO, and chairman of Garage.com, an Internet site that helps entrepreneurs and investors create, build, and fund promising early stage technology companies. Prior to founding Garage.com in 1997, Kawasaki served as chief evangelist of Apple Computer (1995 to 1998) and as CEO of Fog City Software, Inc. He holds a B.A. from Stanford University and an M.B.A. from the University of California, Los Angeles.

Kawasaki is a columnist for *Forbes Magazine* and author or coauthor of seven books, including *Rules for Revolutionaries, New Rules for the New Economy, Selling the Dreams,* and *How to Drive Your Competition Crazy.* He can be reached by e-mail at Kawasaki@garage.com, through the Internet site http://www.garage.com, or through Garage.com's corporate offices at 420 Florence Avenue, Palo Alto, CA 94301.

Duane Knapp is president of the consulting firm Brand Strategy™, Inc. and author of *The Brand Mindset.* His articles have appeared in publications like the *Journal of Commerce, BrandWeek, Risk Management,* and *Washington CEO.* He can be reached through the Internet site http://www. brandstrategy.com or by mail at Brand Strategy, 2415 T Avenue, Suite 210, Anacortes, WA 98221.

Philip Kotler is the S.C. Johnson & Son Distinguished Professor of International Marketing at Northwestern University's Kellogg Graduate School of Management. Professor Kotler received an M.A. in economics from the University of Chicago and a Ph.D. in economics from MIT.

Kotler's extensive publications list includes *Kotler on Marketing, Value-Added Public Relations, Principles of Marketing,* and *The New Marketing Era.* He can be reached by e-mail at p-kotler@nwu.edu, or through the graduate school at Kellogg Graduate School of Management, 2001 Sheridan Road, Leverone/Andersen Complex, Evanston, IL 60208-2001.

Peter C. Krieg is cofounder and president of the marketing investment strategy firm Copernicus Marketing Consulting and Research and coauthor of *Counterintuitive Marketing.* Mr. Krieg is a graduate of the University of Notre Dame. He can be reached by mail at Copernicus Marketing Consulting and Research, 315 Post Road West, Westport, CT 06880, or by e-mail at pkrieg@copernicusmarketing.com. The firm maintains an Internet site at http://www.copernicusmarketing.com.

Chris Lederer is a cofounder of Helios Consulting and coauthor of *The Infinite Asset.* He holds a B.S. in economics from Washington and Lee and an M.B.A. from Columbia Business School. He can be reached by mail through the New York office of Helios Consulting Group at 188 Grand Street, 2nd Floor, New York, NY 10013. His company maintains an Internet site at http://www.heliosconsulting.com.

Katherine Lemon is an assistant professor in Boston College's school of management and a coauthor of *Driving Customer Equity*. Before joining the faculty at Boston College, she was a visiting assistant professor at Harvard University and an assistant professor at Duke University. Her articles have appeared in such journals as the *Journal of Marketing, Marketing Management, California Management Review,* and *Marketing Science*. She can be reached by mail at the Wallace E. Carroll School of Management, Boston College, Fulton Hall, 140 Commonwealth Avenue, Chestnut Hill, MA 02367, or by e-mail at Katherine.lemon@bc.edu.

Edward H. Levine is a cofounder and CEO of the marketing consulting firm Firebrand and coauthor of *Deep Branding on the Internet*. He can be reached through the Firebrand Internet site http://www.firebrand.com.

Jay Conrad Levinson is chairman of Guerrilla Marketing International and author of the series of Guerilla books that include *Guerilla Marketing, Mastering Guerrilla Marketing, Guerrilla Selling, Guerrilla Negotiating,* and *Guerrilla Financing*. Mr. Levinson taught an extension course based on the Guerrilla concept at the University of California, Berkeley, and now conducts Guerrilla Marketing Workshops. He can be reached by e-mail at GMINTL@aol.com or by mail at Guerrilla Marketing International, P.O. Box 1336, Mill Valley, CA 94942. The company's Internet site is at http://www.gmarketing.com.

David Lewis is the chairman of the consumer research firm David Lewis Consultancy and coauthor of *The Soul of the New Customer*. In addition, he hosts a BBC radio series and lectures on management topics like the relationship between suppliers and their customers. He holds a doctorate in psychology from the University of Sussex and has published other books, including *Information Overload, Ten-Minute Time and Stress Management,* and *How to Get Your Message Across*. Dr. Lewis can be reached by e-mail at david@dlcltd.com or through his Internet site at http://www.dlcltd.com.

Karl B. Manrodt is an assistant professor of information systems and logistics at Georgia Southern University and coauthor of *Customer Responsive Management*. He holds a B.A. from Wartburg College, an M.S. from Wright State University, and a Ph.D. from the University of Tennessee, Knoxville. He can be reached by e-mail at kmanrodt@gasou.edu.

Chuck Martin was the founding publisher and COO of *Interactive Age,* the first publication to be launched electronically. Prior to that venture, he was an associate publisher of *Information Week* and editor in chief of *Personal Computing.* He was also corporate technology editor for Time, Inc., worked for five daily newspapers, and hosted a daily television show on the Financial News Network.

Following the establishment of *Interactive Age,* Martin became vice president for publishing and advertising in IBM's telecommunications and media industry solution unit, after which he became president of the Net Future Institute, which focuses on the future of electronic commerce. Martin is an associate of the Alliance for Converging Technologies, now Digital 4Sight, president of the Digital Estate Group LLC, and author or coauthor of *Max-e-Marketing in the Net Future, The Digital Estate,* and *Net Future.* He can be reached by e-mail at chuckmartin@worldnet.att.net, or through the Internet site http://www.netfutureinstitute.com.

Regis McKenna is chairman of the management and marketing consulting firm The McKenna Group. He is also an independent investor in web startups like Weblogic, Graham Technologies, and Real Time Knowledge Systems. McKenna's books include *The Regis Touch, Relationship Marketing,* and *Real Time.* He can be reached by mail at the McKenna Group, 2350 West El Camino Real, Suite 200, Mountain View, CA 94040, or by e-mail at Regis@mckenna-group.com. The company also maintains an Internet site at http://www.mckennagroup.com.

Mary Modahl is vice president of marketing at Forrester Research, Inc., and author of *Now or Never: How Companies Must Change Today to Win the Battle for Internet Consumers.* She can be contacted through Forrester's Internet site at http://www.forrester.com or by e-mail at marymodahl@forrester.com.

Adam Morgan left the advertising business after the success of his book *Eating the Big Fish.* He is now a consultant in brand management. Morgan spent four years as planning director, North America, for TBWA Chiat/Day, the well-known advertising agency behind the Energizer Bunny campaigns and Nissan's "Enjoy the Ride." He can be reached at eatbigfish.com.

Frederick Newell is a pioneer in the field of database marketing and a partner in the international consulting firm Seklemian/Newell. His books include *Loyalty.com* and *The New Rules of Marketing*. He can be reached by e-mail at frednote@aol.com.

Don Peppers is an independent consultant and speaker in the areas of marketing technology, business development and customer retention. His publications include *Enterprise One-to-One, The One-to-One Fieldbook, The Complete Toolkit for Implementing a 1-to-1 Marketing Program, The One-to-One Future,* and *The One-to-One Manager.* Peppers can be contacted through his web site, http://www.1to1.com, or by e-mail at don.peppers@ 1to1.com.

Faith Popcorn is founder of Faith Popcorn's BrainReserve, a New York-based marketing consulting firm. She is the author of *The Popcorn Report, Clicking,* and *EVEolution.* She can be reached by mail at Faith Popcorn's BrainReserve, 59 East 64th Street, New York, NY 10021, or by e-mail at Faith@faithpopcorn.com. Her company also maintains an Internet site at http://www.faithpopcorn.com.

Stan Rapp is chairman and CEO of McCann Relationship Marketing (MRM) Worldwide. He is also coauthor of *Max-e-Marketing in the Net Future, The Great Marketing Turnaround, Maximarketing, Beyond Maximarketing,* and *The New Maximarketing.* Mr. Rapp can be reached by mail at MMR Worldwide, 750 Third Avenue, New York, NY 10017, or by e-mail at stan_rapp@mccann.com. MRM also maintains an Internet site at http//www.mrmworldwide.com.

Frederick Reichheld is a director emeritus of the consulting firm Bain & Company, a Bain Fellow, and founder of the firm's loyalty practice. He is also the author of *The Loyalty Effect* and the editor of *The Quest for Loyalty.* You can contact Mr. Reichheld by mail through the Boston offices of Bain & Company at Two Copley Place, Boston, MA 02116, or by e-mail at Loyalty.Rules@Bain.com. The company also maintains an Internet site at http://www.Bain.com.

Al Ries is chairman of Ries & Ries, an Atlanta-based marketing firm, and coauthor of *The 22 Immutable Laws of Branding.* He is a graduate of Depauw University and has authored or coauthored several other books, including *Positioning: The Battle for Your Mind, Marketing Warfare, Bottom-*

up Marketing, and *The 11 Immutable Laws of Internet Branding.* Mr. Ries can be reached by mail at Ries & Ries, 2195 River Cliff Drive, Roswell, GA 30076, or by e-mail at alries@ries.com. His company also maintains an Internet site at http://www.ries.com.

Laura Ries is president of Ries & Ries, an Atlanta-based marketing firm that she cofounded with her father, Al Ries. Laura is a graduate of Northwestern University and coauthor of two books, *The 22 Immutable Laws of Branding* and *The 11 Immutable Laws of Internet Branding.* Ms. Ries can be reached by mail at Ries & Ries, 2195 River Cliff Drive, Roswell, GA 30076, or by e-mail at lauraries@ries.com. Her company also maintains an Internet site at http://www.ries.com.

Martha Rogers is an associate professor in marketing at Bowling Green State University and partner in the Rogers and Peppers Group. Dr. Rogers has also worked as a copywriter and advertising executive, and she served on the National Advertising Review Board. Her publications include *The One-to-One Future, The One-to-One Fieldbook, The One-to-One Manager,* and *Enterprise One-to-One.*
  Rogers can be contacted through her web site, http://www.1to1.com, or by e-mail at Martha.rogers@1to1.com.

Emanuel Rosen is a former vice president of marketing for the Silicon Valley company Niles Software. After selling his stock in the company and retiring, he wrote the best-seller *The Anatomy of Buzz.* He can be reached by e-mail at emanuel@emanuel-rosen.com and maintains an Internet site at http://www.emanuel-rosen.com.

Roland Rust holds the David Bruce Smith chair in marketing at the University of Maryland. He has a B.A. from DePauw University and an M.B.A. and Ph.D. from the University of North Carolina at Chapel Hill. Professor Rust has authored, coauthored, or edited six books, including *Driving Customer Equity, Service Quality, Service Marketing, Return on Quality, Advertising Media Models,* and *Readings in Service Marketing.* In addition, his articles have appeared in the *Journal of Advertising, Journal of Marketing, Journal of Retailing,* and *Marketing Science.* He can be reached by mail at Robert H. Smith School of Business, University of Maryland, Van Munching Hall, College Park, MD 20742, or by e-mail at rrust@rhsmith. umd.edu.

Bernd Schmitt is a professor of business at Columbia Business School and executive director of the Center on Global Brand Leadership. He is the author of *Experiential Marketing* and the coauthor of *Marketing Aesthetics* and *Build Your Own Garage.* In addition, he has published more than 50 articles and is an independent consultant. Professor Schmitt can be reached by e-mail at bhs1@columbia.edu, and he maintains an Internet site at http://www.meetschmitt.com.

Don E. Schultz, author of *Integrated Marketing Communications,* is president of the consulting firm Agora, Inc., and a senior partner with Targetbase Marketing International and the Targetbase Institute. He is also professor of integrated marketing communication at Northwestern University's Medill School of Journalism and author or coauthor several other books, including *Strategic Brand Communication Campaigns, Essentials of Advertising Strategy, The New Marketing Paradigm,* and *Communicating Globally.* He can be reached by mail at Medill School of Journalism, Northwestern University, 1845 Sheridan Road, Evanston, IL 60208, or by e-mail at dschultz@northwestern.edu.

Evan I. Schwartz is a former editor at *Business Week* and a contributor to *Wired* magazine and the *New York Times.* He is also the author of *Digital Darwinism, Webonomics,* and *The Last Lone Inventor.* He can be reached through his web site, http://www.digataldarwinism.com, or by e-mail at evan@webonomics.com.

Peter Sealey, coauthor of *Simplicity Marketing,* is a principal of Los Altos Group, Inc., and former chief marketing officer of the Coca-Cola Company. He is an adjunct professor of marketing at the University of California's Haas School of Business and codirector of the Center for Marketing and Technology. He holds a B.S. from the University of Florida, two master's degrees from Yale University and the Claremont University, and a Ph.D. from Claremont. Mr. Sealey can be reached by e-mail at sealey@ haas.berkeley.edu.

Patricia Seybold is the founder and CEO of the Patricia Seybold Group, a strategic e-business and technology consulting firm. She is also the author of *The Customer Revolution* and *Customers.com.* Ms. Seybold can be reached through the Internet site http://www.psgroup.com, by mail at Patricia Seybold Group, 85 Devonshire Street, 5th Floor, Boston, MA 02109, or by e-mail at feedback@psgroup.com.

Alex Simonson is president of Simonson Associates and a professor of marketing at Seton Hall University, on leave as a professor of marketing at Georgetown University School of Business. He holds a Ph.D. in marketing from Columbia Business School, a J.D. from New York University School of Law, and an A.B. from Columbia University.

Dr. Simonson, who is a coauthor of *Marketing Aesthetics,* is also a member of the editorial board of the *Trademark Reporter,* the *Intellectual Property Strategist,* and the *Journal of Public Policy and Marketing.*

He can be reached through Simonson Associates at 441 Stockton Place, First Floor, Englewood, NJ 07631, or by e-mail at inquiries@simonson associates.com.

Jacquelyn Thomas is an assistant professor at Emory University's Goizueta Business School and coauthor of *Customer Equity.* She holds B.A., M.S., and Ph.D. degrees from Northwestern University and taught at Stanford University before joining the Emory faculty. Professor Thomas can be reached by mail at Goizueta Business School, 1300 Clifton Road, Atlanta, GA 30322, or by e-mail at Jacquelyn_thomas@bus.emory.edu.

Daryl Travis is the CEO of Brandtrust, a brand consulting company, and an advertising executive. He is the coauthor of *Emotional Branding* and can be reached by mail at Brandtrust, 900 North Michigan Avenue, Suite 1100, Chicago, IL 60611.

Jack Trout is president of Trout & Partners, a Greenwich, Connecticut-based marketing firm, and coauthor of several books, including *Positioning: The Battle for Your Mind, Differentiate or Die, The 22 Immutable Laws of Marketing, Big Brands Big Trouble,* and *The Power of Simplicity.* He can be reached by mail at Trout & Partners, 8 Wahneta Road, Old Greenwich, CT 06870, or by e-mail at jtrout@troutandpartners.com.

Lars Tvede is cofounder and senior vice president of the marketing firm the Fantastic Corporation and author of *Marketing Strategies for the New Economy.* His other works include *The Psychology of the Financial Markets, International Market Information, Business Cycles,* and *Data Broad-*

casting. Mr. Tvede can be reached through the Internet site http://www.
fantastic.com.

Fred Wiersema is a fellow with the business strategy and technology solutions firm DiamondCluster International and cofounder of the firm's Center for Market Leadership. Mr. Wiersema is also the author of *The New Market Leaders* and coauthor of *The Discipline of Market Leaders.* He can be reached by mail at Center for Market Leadership, 10 St. James Avenue 16th Floor, Boston, MA 02116, or by e-mail at fdw@wiersema.com.

Valarie Zeithaml is a professor and area chair of marketing at the Kenan-Flagler Business School, University of North Carolina at Chapel Hill. She holds a B.A. from Gettysburg College and an M.B.A. and Ph.D. from the University of Maryland. Professor Zeithaml is a coauthor of *Driving Customer Equity* and author of numerous articles, some of which appear in the *California Management Review, Marketing Management, Journal of the Academy of Marketing Science,* and *Journal of Marketing Research.* She can be reached by mail at the Kenan-Flagler Business School, the University of North Carolina at Chapel Hill, Campus Box 3490, McColl Building, Chapel Hill, NC 27599-3490, or by e-mail at valariez@unc.edu.

Sergio Zyman is founder and CEO of Z Marketing, a marketing strategy firm. He is the author of *The End of Marketing as We Know It* and coauthor of *Building Brandwidth.* He can be contacted by e-mail at Sergio@ zmarketing.com. His company maintains an Internet site at http://www. zmarketing.com.

Notes

Chapter I

[1] Paul Temporal and K.C. Lee, *Hi-Tech Hi-Touch Branding: Creating Brand Power in the Age of Technology* (New York: John Wiley & Sons, 2000), p. 115.

[2] Ian H. Gordon, *Relationship Marketing: New Strategies, Techniques and Technologies to Win the Customers You Want and Keep Them Forever* (Etobicoke, Ontario, Canada: John Wiley & Sons, 1998), p. 1.

[3] Sergio Zyman, *Building Brandwidth: Closing the Sale Online* (New York: Harper-Collins, 2000), pp. 153–157.

[4] Susan Kuchinskas, "The End of Marketing," *Business2.com,* November 14, 2000, pp. 136–139.

[5] Ibid., p. 136.

[6] Sergio Zyman, *The End of Marketing as We Know It* (New York: HarperCollins, 1999), p. 229.

[7] David Lewis and Darren Bridger, *The Soul of the New Consumer* (Naperville, IL: Nicholas Brealey Publishing, 2000), p. 1.

[8] Ibid.

[9] Peter Drucker, *The Post-Capitalist Society* (New York: HarperCollins, 1993), p. 1.

[10] Robert D. Hisrich, *Marketing* (Hauppauge, NY: Barron's Educational Series, Inc., 2000), pp. 2–3.

[11] Ibid., p. 3.

[12] Don E. Schultz, *Communicating Globally: An Integrated Marketing Approach* (Lincolnwood, IL: NTC Business Books, 2000), p. 53.

[13] Richard S. Tedlow and Geoffrey Jones, eds., *The Rise and Fall of Mass Marketing* (New York: Routledge, 1993), p. 150.

[14] Seth Godin, "Change Agent," *Fast Company,* July 2001, p. 84.

[15] Philip Kotler, *Kotler on Marketing: How to Create, Win, and Dominate Markets* (New York: Free Press, 1999), p. 19.

[16] Harry Beckwith, *Selling the Invisible: A Field Guide to Modern Marketing* (New York: Warner Books, 1997), p. 3.

[17] Jay Conrad Levinson, *Mastering Guerrilla Marketing: Secrets for Making Big Profits from Your Small Business* (New York: Houghton Mifflin Co., 1999), pp. 31–33.

[18] Zyman, *Building Brandwidth,* p. 37.

[19] This discussion of the Four Ps is based upon Kotler, *Kotler on Marketing,* pp. 94–120, and Hisrich, *Marketing,* pp. 2–6. Also see Neil H. Borden, "The Concept of the Marketing Mix," *Journal of Advertising Research,* June 1964, pp. 2–7.

[20] Borden, "The Concept of the Marketing Mix," p. 2.

[21] This list of activities in the marketing mix is based upon Kotler, *Kotler on Marketing,* p. 96, and Hisrich, *Marketing,* p. 5.

[22] Kotler, *Kotler on Marketing,* p. 95.

[23] Ibid.

[24] Faith Popcorn and Lys Marigold, *EVEolution: The Eight Truths of Marketing to Women* (New York: Hyperion, 2000), p. 199.

[25] Lars Tvede and Peter Ohnemus, *Marketing Strategies for the New Economy* (Chichester, West Sussex, England: John Wiley & Sons, 2001), p. 76.

[26] Seth Godin, "The New P's of Marketing," *Sales & Marketing Management,* February 2001, p. 45.

[27] Stan Rapp and Chuck Martin, *Max-e-Marketing in the Net Future: The Seven Imperatives for Outsmarting the Competition in the Net Economy* (New York: McGraw-Hill, 2001), p. 13.

[28] Kotler, *Kotler on Marketing,* p. 99.

[29] Ibid.

[30] Ibid., pp. 97–98.

[31] Wunderman used the term "prodices" in 1996 in an address to the Direct Marketing Association.

[32] Frederick Newell, *Loyalty.com: Customer Relationship Management in the New Era of Internet Marketing* (New York: McGraw-Hill Professional Publishing, 2000), p. 269.

[33] Ibid., pp. 273–274.

[34] Gordon, *Relationship Marketing,* p. 13.

[35] Ibid.

[36] Levinson, *Mastering Guerrilla Marketing,* p. 81.

[37] Seth Godin, *Permission Marketing: Turning Strangers into Friends, and Friends into Customers* (New York: Simon & Schuster, 1999), p. 21.

[38] Marc Braunstein and Edward Levine, *Deep Branding on the Internet: Applying Heat and Pressure Online to Ensure a Lasting Brand* (Roseville, CA: Prima Publishing, 2000), p. 43.

[39] Kotler, *Kotler on Marketing,* p. 210.

[40] Ibid., pp. 210–213.

[41] Lewis and Bridger, *The Soul of the New Consumer,* p. 149.

[42] Ibid., p. 148.

[43] Kevin J. Clancy and Peter C. Krieg, *Counterintuitive Marketing: Achieve Great Results Using Uncommon Sense* (New York: Free Press, 2000), pp. 130–131.

[44] Ibid., p. 131.

[45] Don E. Schultz, "Consumer Marketing Changed by Advent of 29.8/7 Media Week," *Marketing News,* September 24, 2001, pp. 11–12.

[46] Kotler, *Kotler on Marketing,* p. 100.

[47] Gordon, *Relationship Marketing,* p. 8.

[48] Ibid., p. 13.

[49] Evan I. Schwartz, *Digital Darwinism: 7 Breakthrough Business Strategies for Surviving in the Cutthroat Web Economy* (New York: Broadway Books, 1999), p. 56.

[50] Ibid., pp. 56–57.

51 Mary Modahl, *Now or Never: How Companies Must Change Today to Win the Battle for Internet Consumers* (New York: HarperBusiness, 1999), p. 82.

52 Ibid., pp. 82–84.

53 Ibid., p. 84.

54 Ibid., p. 88.

55 Kotler, *Kotler on Marketing,* pp. 5–7.

56 Ibid., p. 9.

57 George S. Day, *The Market Driven Organization: Understanding, Attracting, and Keeping Valuable Customers* (New York: Free Press, 1999), pp. 22–23.

58 Ibid., pp. 23–25.

59 Ibid., p. 25.

60 Peter Drucker, *Management: Tasks, Responsibilities, Practices* (New York: Harper & Row, 1974), p. 61.

Chapter 2

1 Marc Gobé, *Emotional Branding: The New Paradigm for Connecting Brands to People* (New York: Allworth Press, 2001), p. 305.

2 Clancy and Krieg, *Counterintuitive Marketing,* p. 317.

3 David A. Aaker, *Managing Brand Equity: Capitalizing on the Value of a Brand Name* (New York: Free Press, 1991), p. 7.

4 Scott M. Davis, *Brand Asset Management: Driving Profitable Growth through Your Brands* (San Francisco: Jossey-Bass, 2000), p. 31.

5 Duane E. Knapp and Christopher W. Hart, *The Brand Mindset: Five Essential Strategies for Building Brand Advantage Throughout Your Company* (New York: McGraw-Hill, 2000), p. 8.

6 Adam Morgan, *Eating the Big Fish: How Challenger Brands Can Compete Against Brand Leaders* (New York: John Wiley & Sons, 1999), p. 27.

7 Daryl Travis, *Emotional Branding: How Successful Brands Gain the Irrational Edge* (Roseville, CA: Prima Venture, 2000), pp. 20–22.

8 David F. d'Alessandro, *Brand Warfare: 10 Rules for Building the Killer Brand* (New York: McGraw-Hill, 2001), p. xiv.

9 Travis, *Emotional Branding,* p. 8.

10 Ibid., pp. 8–9.

11 Davis, *Brand Asset Management,* pp. 5–6.

12 D'Alessandro, *Brand Warfare,* p. 17.

13 Ibid., p. 150.

14 Davis, *Brand Asset Management,* p. xviii.

15 Clancy and Krieg, *Counterintuitive Marketing,* pp. 64–65.

16 Aaker, *Managing Brand Equity,* pp. 15–16.

17 Clancy and Krieg, *Counterintuitive Marketing,* pp. 68–69.

18 Ibid., p. 69.

19 Zyman, *Building Brandwidth,* p. 77.

20   Jack Trout and Steve Rivkin, *Differentiate or Die: Survival in Our Era of Killer Competition* (New York: John Wiley & Sons, 2000), p. 8.

21   Clancy and Krieg, *Counterintuitive Marketing,* p. 110.

22   Davis, *Brand Asset Management,* p. 109.

23   Trout and Rivkin, *Differentiate or Die,* p. 95.

24   Ibid., pp. 95–105.

25   Ibid., pp. 109–110.

26   Ibid., p. 116.

27   Trout actually lists "hotness" as a separate form of differentiation. We felt it was similar enough to being "preferred" to include here.

28   Trout and Rivkin, *Differentiate or Die,* pp. 153–154.

29   Ibid., p. 161.

30   Steven M. Cristol and Peter Sealey, *Simplicity Marketing: End Brand Complexity, Clutter and Confusion* (New York: Free Press, 2000), pp. 1–2.

31   Ibid., p. 48.

32   Godin, *Permission Marketing,* pp. 97–103.

33   Harry Beckwith, *The Invisible Touch: The Four Keys to Modern Marketing* (New York: Warner Books, 2000), p. 124.

34   Frank Delano, *The Omnipowerful Brand: America's #1 Brand Specialist Shares His Secrets for Catapulting Your Brand to Marketing Stardom* (New York: AMACOM, 1999), pp. 40–46.

35   Ibid., p. 50.

36   Kotler, *Kotler on Marketing,* p. 64.

37   Ibid., p. 65.

38   Knapp and Hart, *Brand Mindset,* pp. 117–118.

39   Ibid., pp. 113–114.

40   Adapted from Gobé, *Emotional Branding,* p. 70.

41   Bernd Schmitt and Alex Simonson, *Marketing Aesthetics: The Strategic Management of Brands, Identity, and Image* (New York: Free Press, 1997), pp. 11–12.

42   Kotler, *Kotler on Marketing,* pp. 69–70.

Chapter 3

1   David Aaker and Erich Joachimsthaler, *Brand Leadership: Building Assets in the Information Society* (New York: Free Press, 2000), p.138.

2   Ibid., p. 141

3   Sam Hill and Chris Lederer, *The Infinite Asset* (Boston: Harvard Business School Press, 2001), pp. 3–5.

4   Ibid., p. 7

5   Ibid., pp.7–8

6   Ibid., pp. 7–8.

7   Ibid., pp. 8–9.

8   See Hill and Lederer, *The Infinite Asset,* p. 37 for an explanation of these conclusions.

[9] Al Ries and Laura Ries, *The 22 Immutable Laws of Branding* (New York: HarperCollins, 1998), p. 11; cited Hill and Lederer, *The Infinite Asset*, p. 70.

[10] Hill and Lederer, *The Infinite Asset*, p. 72.

[11] Ibid., p.74.

[12] Ibid., p. 81–82.

[13] Ibid., pp. 84–85.

[14] Ibid., p. 93.

[15] Ibid., p. 96.

[16] Ibid., pp. 109–110.

[17] Ibid., p.128.

Chapter 4

[1] Some of the explanations and illustrations used in this chapter appeared previously in Joseph H. Boyett and Jimmie T. Boyett, *The Guru Guide™ to the Knowledge Economy* (New York: John Wiley & Sons, 2001), pp. 164–231.

[2] See Don Peppers and Martha Rogers, *The One-to-One Future: Building Relationships One Customer at a Time* (New York: Currency/Doubleday, 1993), pp. 10–11.

[3] Ibid., pp. 15–17.

[4] Patricia Seybold, *The Customer Revolution: How to Thrive When Customers Are in Control* (New York: Crown Business, 2001), pp. 1–3.

[5] Ibid., pp. 11–12.

[6] Ibid., p. 13.

[7] Don E. Schultz, "Learn to Differentiate CRM's Two Faces," *Marketing News*, November 20, 2000, p. 11.

[8] Newell, *Loyalty.com*, pp. 16–17.

[9] Frederick Reichheld and Thomas Teal, *The Loyalty Effect* (Boston: Harvard Business School Press, 1996), pp. 36–39.

[10] Ibid., p. 37.

[11] Ibid., p. 43.

[12] Ihid., p. 45.

[13] Ibid., p. 48.

[14] Ibid., pp. 48–49.

[15] Ibid., pp. 49–50.

[16] Ibid., p. 35.

[17] Seybold, *The Customer Revolution*, p. 86.

[18] Arthur Hughes, *Strategic Database Marketing: The Masterplan for Starting and Managing a Profitable, Custom-Based Marketing Program*, 2d ed. (New York: McGraw-Hill, 2000), p.58.

[19] This discussion of the calculation of customer lifetime value is adapted from Arthur M. Hughes, *The Complete Database Marketer: Second-Generation Strategies and Techniques for Tapping the Power of Your Customer Database*, rev. ed. (Chicago: Irwin, 1996), pp. 233–250.

[20] Don Peppers, Martha Rogers, and Bob Dorf, *The One-to-One Fieldbook: The Complete Toolkit for Implementing a 1-to-1 Marketing Program* (New York: Currency/Doubleday, 1999), p. 25.

[21] Ibid.

[22] Ibid., pp. 28–29.

[23] Gordon, *Relationship Marketing,* p. 53.

[24] Jay Curry and Adam Curry, *The Customer Marketing Method: How to Implement and Profit from Customer Relationship Management* (New York: Free Press, 2000), p. 8.

[25] Ibid., p. 122.

[26] Newell, *Loyalty.com,* p. 103.

[27] Adapted from Peppers, Rogers, and Dorf, *One-to-One Fieldbook,* p. 95.

[28] Godin, *Permission Marketing,* pp. 44–45.

[29] Peppers, Rogers, and Dorf, *One-to-One Fieldbook,* pp. 128–130.

[30] Seybold, *The Customer Revolution,* p. 170.

Chapter 5

[1] Roland T. Rust, Valarie A. Zeithaml, and Katherine N. Lemon, *Driving Customer Equity: How Lifetime Customer Value Is Reshaping Corporate Strategy* (New York: Free Press, 2000), p. 1.

[2] Ibid., p. 15.

[3] This discussion is based upon Rust, Zeithaml, and Lemon, *Driving Customer Equity,* pp. 15–22.

[4] Ibid., pp. 20–21.

[5] Robert Blattberg, Gary Getz, and Jacquelyn S. Thomas, *Customer Equity: Building and Managing Relationships as Valuable Assets* (Boston: Harvard Business School Press, 2001), p. 70.

[6] Ibid.

[7] This discussion is based upon Clancy and Krieg, *Counterintuitive Marketing,* pp. 190–193.

[8] Ibid., p. 190.

[9] Ibid., pp. 30–44.

[10] Ibid., pp. 30–31.

[11] Ibid., p. 31.

[12] Ibid.

[13] Roland T. Rust, Katherine N. Lemon, and Valarie A. Zeithaml, "Where Should the Next Marketing Dollar Go?" *Marketing Management,* September-October 2001, pp. 25–26.

[14] Rust, Zeithaml, and Lemon, *Driving Customer Equity,* p. 9.

[15] Ibid., p. 81.

[16] Ibid., p. 95.

[17] See Grahame R. Dowling and Mark Uncles, "Do Customer Loyalty Programs Really Work?" *Sloan Management Review,* Summer 1997, pp. 71–82, for a discussion of switching and what some researchers call "polygamous loyalty."

[18] For a complete discussion of calculating "share of wallet," see Rust, Zeithaml, and Lemon, *Driving Customer Equity*, pp. 38–44.

[19] Ibid., p. 63.

[20] Ibid., p. 163.

[21] Ibid., p. 65.

[22] Blattberg, Getz, and Thomas, *Customer Equity*, p. 31.

[23] Ibid., p. 36.

[24] http://www.customerequity.com/ce_in_depth/acquisition/actman_qual.html.

[25] Blattberg, Getz, and Thomas, *Customer Equity*, pp. 35–36.

[26] Ibid., p. 39.

[27] Ibid., pp. 39–40.

[28] Ibid., p. 74.

[29] Ibid., p. 95.

[30] Ibid., p. 118.

[31] Ibid., pp. 103–108.

[32] See the discussion of difficulties in obtaining the data for customer equity calculations at http://www.customerequity.com/ce_in_depth/ce_calculations/.

Chapter 6

[1] Malcolm Gladwell, *The Tipping Point, How Little Things Can Make a Big Difference* (Boston: Little Brown & Company, 2000), pp. 3–4.

[2] Emanuel Rosen and Roger E. Scholl, *The Anatomy of Buzz: How to Create Word-of-Mouth Marketing* (New York: Random House, 2000), p. 7.

[3] Ibid.

[4] Ibid., pp. 6–7.

[5] Seth Godin, *Unleashing the Ideavirus* (Dobb's Ferry, NY: Do You Zoom, Inc., 2000), p. 20.

[6] Ibid., pp. 44–45.

[7] Rosen and Scholl, *Anatomy of Buzz*, pp. 5–6.

[8] Ibid., p. 16.

[9] Godin, *Unleashing the Ideavirus*, pp. 38–39.

[10] Lewis and Bridger, *The Soul of the New Consumer*, p. 15.

[11] Ibid., p. 18.

[12] Rosen and Scholl, *Anatomy of Buzz*, pp. 25–26.

[13] Based upon Rosen and Scholl, *Anatomy of Buzz*, pp. 104–114.

[14] Godin, *Unleashing the Ideavirus*, p. 193.

[15] Rosen and Scholl, *Anatomy of Buzz*, pp. 30–31.

[16] Ibid., p. 33.

[17] William Harmon, ed., *The Top 500 Poems* (New York: Columbia University Press, 1992), p. 584.

[18] Gladwell, *Tipping Point*, p. 33.

[19] Ibid.

20 This game and the discussion of connectors is based upon Gladwell, *Tipping Point,*
   pp. 38–59.
21 Ibid., pp. 46–47.
22 Ibid., pp. 56–57.
23 Ibid., p. 59.
24 Ibid., p. 77.
25 Ibid., p. 83.
26 Rosen and Scholl, *Anatomy of Buzz,* p. 181.
27 See Godin, *Unleashing the Ideavirus,* pp. 119–121, for Godin's description of the Vindigo product.
28 Gladwell, *Tipping Point,* p. 12.
29 Ibid., p. 12.
30 Godin, *Unleashing the Ideavirus,* p. 170.
31 Ibid., p. 171.
32 Ibid.

Bibliography

Aaker, David A. *Building Strong Brands.* New York: Free Press, 1996.

———. *Managing Brand Equity: Capitalizing on the Value of a Brand Name.* New York: Free Press, 1991.

Aaker, David A., and Erich Joachimsthaler. *Brand Leadership: Building Assets in the Information Society.* New York: Free Press, 2000.

Ambler, Tim. *Silk Road to International Marketing: Profit and Passion in Global Business.* London: Financial Times Management, 2000.

Bacon, Frank R., Jr. and Thomas W. Butler Jr. *Achieving Planned Innovation®: A Proven System for Creating Successful New Products and Services.* New York: Free Press, 1998.

Bean, Roger, and Russell Radford. *Powerful Products: Strategic Management of Successful New Product Development.* New York: AMACOM, 2000.

Beckwith, Harry, *The Invisible Touch: The Four Keys to Modern Marketing.* New York: Warner Books, 2000.

———. *Selling the Invisible: A Field Guide to Modern Marketing.* New York: Warner Books, 1997.

Bishop, Bill. *Global Marketing for the Digital Age.* Lincolnwood, IL: NTC Business Books, 1999.

Blattberg, Robert, Gary Getz, and Jacquelyn S. Thomas. *Customer Equity: Building and Managing Relationships as Valuable Assets.* Boston: Harvard Business School Press, 2001.

Borden, Neil H. "The Concept of the Marketing Mix." *Journal of Advertising Research,* June 1964, pp. 2–7.

Boyett, Joseph H., and Jimmie T. Boyett. *The Guru Guide™ to the Knowledge Economy.* New York: John Wiley & Sons, 2001.

Braunstein, Marc, and Edward Levine. *Deep Branding on the Internet: Applying Heat and Pressure Online to Ensure a Lasting Brand.* Roseville, CA: Prima Publishing, 2000.

Brondmo, Hans Peter. *Eng@ged Customer: The New Rules of Internet Direct Marketing.* New York: HarperCollins Publishing, 2000.

Brown, Stephen. *Marketing: The Retro Revolution.* Thousand Oaks, CA: Sage Publications, Inc., 2001.

———. "Torment Your Customers (They'll Love It)." *Harvard Business Review,* October 2001, p. 83.

Bruner, Rick E., Leland Harden, and Bob Heyman, with Mia Amato, eds. *Net Results.2: Best Practices for Web Marketing.* Indianapolis: IN: New Riders Publishing, 2001.

Buchholz, Andreas, and Wolfram Wördemann. *What Makes Winning Brands Different? The Hidden Method Behind the World's Most Successful Brands.* Chichester, West Sussex, England: John Wiley & Sons, 2000.

Carpenter, Phil. *Ebrands: Building an Internet Business at Breakneck Speed.* Boston: Harvard Business School Press, 2000.

Clancy, Kevin J., and Peter C. Krieg. *Counterintuitive Marketing: Achieve Great Results Using Uncommon Sense.* New York: Free Press, 2000.

Clifton, Rita, ed. *The Future of Brands: Twenty-Five Visions.* New York: New York University Press, 2000.

Cohan, Peter S. *E-Profit: High-Payoff Strategies for Capturing the E-Commerce Edge.* New York: AMACOM, 2000.

Cooper, Robert G. *Product Leadership: Creating and Launching Superior New Products.* Reading, MA: Perseus Books, 1998.

Cristol, Steven M., and Peter Sealey. *Simplicity Marketing: End Brand Complexity, Clutter and Confusion.* New York: Free Press, 2000.

Crosby, John V. *Cycles, Trends, and Turning Points: Practical Marketing & Sales Forecasting Techniques.* Lincolnwood, IL: NTC Business Books, 2000.

Curry, Jay, and Adam Curry. *The Customer Marketing Method: How to Implement and Profit from Customer Relationship Management.* New York: Free Press, 2000.

d'Alessandro, David F., and Michele Owens. *Brand Warfare: 10 Rules for Building the Killer Brand.* New York: McGraw-Hill Professional Publishing, 2001.

Davis, Scott M. *Brand Asset Management: Driving Profitable Growth through Your Brands.* San Francisco: Jossey-Bass, 2000.

Day, George S. *The Market Driven Organization: Understanding, Attracting, and Keeping Valuable Customers.* New York: Free Press, 1999.

Day, Laura. *Practical Intuition for Success: A Step-by-Step Program to Increase Your Wealth Today.* New York: HarperCollins Publishers, Inc., 1997.

Delano, Frank. *The Omnipowerful Brand: America's #1 Brand Specialist Shares His Secrets for Catapulting Your Brand to Marketing Stardom.* New York: AMACOM, 1999.

Dolnick, Barrie. *The Executive Mystic: Psychic Power Tools for Success.* New York: HarperBusiness, 1998.

Dowling, Grahame R., and Mark Uncles. "Do Customer Loyalty Programs Really Work?" *Sloan Management Review,* Summer 1997, pp. 71–82.

Drucker, Peter. *Management: Tasks, Responsibilities, Practices.* New York: Harper & Row, 1974.

———. *The Post-Capitalist Society.* New York: HarperCollins, 1993.

Fox, Jeffrey J. *How to Become a Rainmaker: The Rules for Getting and Keeping Customers and Clients.* New York: Hyperion, 2000.

Frank, Thomas. *One Market Under God: Extreme Capitalism, Market Populism, and the End of Economic Democracy.* New York: Doubleday, 2000.

Gerbert, Philipp, Dirk Schneider, and Alex Birch. *Age of E-tail: Conquering the New World of Electronic Shopping.* Milford, CT: Capstone Publishing, Inc., 2000.

Gladwell, Malcolm. *The Tipping Point: How Little Things Can Make a Big Difference.* Boston: Little Brown & Company, 2000.

Gobé, Marc. *Emotional Branding: The New Paradigm for Connecting Brands to People.* New York: Allworth Press, 2001.

Godin, Seth. "Change Agent." *Fast Company,* July 2001, p. 84.

———. "The New P's of Marketing." *Sales & Marketing Management,* February 2001, p. 45.

———. *Permission Marketing: Turning Strangers into Friends, and Friends into Customers.* New York: Simon & Schuster, 1999.

———. *Unleashing the Ideavirus.* Dobb's Ferry, NY: Do You Zoom, Inc., 2000.

Gordon, Ian H. *Relationship Marketing: New Strategies, Techniques and Technologies to Win the Customers You Want and Keep Them Forever.* Etobicoke, Ontario, Canada: John Wiley & Sons, 1998.

Grönstedt, Anders. *Customer Century: Lessons from World-Class Companies in Integrated Communications.* New York: Routledge, 2000.

Gutzman, Alexis D. *The E-Commerce Arsenal.* New York: AMACOM, 2001.

Halter, Marilyn. *Shopping for Identity: The Marketing of Ethnicity.* New York: Schocken Books, 2000.

Hartman, L.P. *Perspectives in Business Ethics.* Chicago: Irwin McGraw-Hill, 1998.

Herbig, Paul A. *Handbook of Cross-Cultural Marketing.* Binghamton, NY: International Business Press, 1998.

Hill, Sam, and Chris Lederer. *The Infinite Asset: Managing Brands to Build New Value.* Boston: Harvard Business School Press, 2001.

Hill, Sam, and Glenn Rifkin. *Radical Marketing: From Harvard to Harley, Lessons from Ten That Broke the Rules and Made It Big.* New York: HarperCollins Publishers, 1999.

Hisrich, Robert D. *Marketing.* Hauppauge, NY: Barron's Educational Series, Inc., 2000.

Holden, Philip. *Ethics for Managers.* Aldershot, Hampshire, England: Gower Publishing Limited, 2000.

Hughes, Arthur M. *The Complete Database Marketer: Second-Generation Strategies and Techniques for Tapping the Power of Your Customer Database.* Rev. ed. Chicago: Irwin Professional Publishing, 1996.

———. *Strategic Database Marketing: The Masterplan for Starting and Managing a Profitable, Custom-Based Marketing Program.* 2nd ed. New York: McGraw-Hill, 2000.

Iacobucci, Dawn, ed. *Kellogg on Marketing: The Kellogg Marketing Faculty, Northwestern University.* New York: John Wiley & Sons, 2001.

Jensen, Bill. *Simplicity: The New Competitive Advantage in a World of More, Faster.* New York: HarperCollins, 2000.

Kawasaki, Guy, and Michele Moreno. *Rules for Revolutionaries*. New York: Harper-Business, 1999.

Kilbourne, Jean. *Deadly Persuasion: Why Women and Girls Must Fight the Addictive Power of Advertising*. New York: Free Press, 1999.

Kinnard, Shannon. *Marketing with E-Mail*. Gulf Breeze, FL: Maximum Press, 2000.

Knapp, Duane E., and Christopher W. Hart. *The Brand Mindset: Five Essential Strategies for Building Brand Advantage throughout Your Company*. New York: McGraw-Hill, 2000.

Kotler, Philip. *Kotler on Marketing: How to Create, Win, and Dominate Markets*. New York: Free Press, 1999.

Kuczinskas, Susan. "The End of Marketing." *Business2.com*, November 14, 2000, pp. 136–139.

Kuczmarski, Thomas D. *Managing New Products: Using the MAP System to Accelerate Growth*. 3rd ed. Chicago: Innovation Press, 2000.

Kunde, Jesper. *Corporate Religion*. London: Pearson Education Limited, 2000.

Laczniak. Eugene R., and Patrick E. Murphy. *Ethical Marketing Decisions: The Higher Road*. Needham Heights, MA: Allyn & Bacon, 1993.

Lemon, Katherine N. "What Drives Customer Equity?" *Marketing Management*, Spring 2001, p. 21.

Levinson, Jay Conrad. *Mastering Guerrilla Marketing: Secrets for Making Big Profits from Your Small Business*. New York: Houghton Mifflin Co., 1999.

Levitt, Theodore. *The Marketing Imagination*. New York: Free Press, 1986.

Lewis, David, and Darren Bridger. *The Soul of the New Consumer*. Naperville, IL: Nicholas Brealey Publishing, 2000.

Lindstrom, Martin. *Brand Building on the Internet*. Dover, NH: Kogan Page (U.S.) Limited, 2000.

Marconi, Joe. *Brand Marketing Book: Creating, Managing, and Extending the Value of Your Brand*. Lincolnwood, IL: NTC Business Books, 2000.

————. *Future Marketing: Targeting Seniors, Boomers, and Generations X and Y*. Lincolnwood, IL: NTC Business Books, 2001.

McCarthy, E. Jerome. *Basic Marketing: A Managerial Approach*. 7th ed. Homewood, IL: Richard D. Irwin, Inc., 1981.

Modahl, Mary. *Now or Never: How Companies Must Change Today to Win the Battle for Internet Consumers*. New York: HarperBusiness, 1999.

Moore, Geoffrey A. *Crossing the Chasm: Marketing and Selling High-Tech Products to Mainstream Customers*. New York: HarperBusiness, 1999.

Morgan, Adam. *Eating the Big Fish: How Challenger Brands Can Compete Against Brand Leaders*. New York: John Wiley & Sons, 1999.

Murphy, Tom. *Web Rules: How the Internet is Changing the Way Consumers Make Choices*. Chicago: Dearborn Financial Publishing, 2000.

Newell, Frederick. *Loyalty.com: Customer Relationship Management in the New Era of Internet Marketing.* New York: McGraw-Hill Professional Publishing, 2000.

Parmerlee, David. *Developing Successful Marketing Strategies.* Lincolnwood, IL: NTC Business Books, 2000.

Patrick, Jerry. *How to Develop Successful New Products.* Lincolnwood, IL: NTC Business Books, 1997.

Peppers, Don, and Martha Rogers. *The One-to-One Future: Building Relationships One Customer at a Time.* New York: Currency/Doubleday, 1993.

Peppers, Don, Martha Rogers, and Bob Dorf. *The One-to-One Fieldbook: The Complete Toolkit for Implementing a 1-to-1 Marketing Program.* New York: Currency/Doubleday, 1999.

Popcorn, Faith, and Lys Marigold. *EVEolution: The Eight Truths of Marketing to Women.* New York: Hyperion, 2000.

Rapp, Stan, and Chuck Martin. *Max-e-Marketing in the Net Future: The Seven Imperatives for Outsmarting the Competition in the Net Economy.* New York: McGraw-Hill, 2001.

Reichheld, Frederick R. *Loyalty Rules! How Today's Leaders Build Lasting Relationships.* Boston: Harvard Business School Press, 2001.

Reichheld, Frederick, and Thomas Teal. *The Loyalty Effect.* Boston: Harvard Business School Press, 1996.

Ries, Al, and Laura Ries. *The 11 Immutable Laws of Internet Branding.* New York: HarperBusiness, 2000.

———. *The 22 Immutable Laws of Branding: How to Build a Product or Service into a World-Class Brand.* New York: HarperCollins, 1998.

Ries, Al, and Jack Trout. *The 22 Immutable Laws of Marketing: Violate Them at Your Own Risk.* New York: HarperBusiness, 1993.

Rosen, Emanuel, and Roger E. Scholl. *The Anatomy of Buzz: How to Create Word-of-Mouth Marketing.* New York: Random House, 2000.

Rust, Roland T., Katherine N. Lemon, and Valarie A. Zeithaml. "Where Should the Next Marketing Dollar Go?" *Marketing Management,* September-October 2001, pp. 25–26.

Rust, Roland T., Valarie A. Zeithaml, and Katherine N. Lemon. *Driving Customer Equity: How Lifetime Customer Value Is Reshaping Corporate Strategy.* New York: Free Press, 2000.

———. "Driving Customer Equity: Linking Customer Lifetime Value to Strategic Marketing Decisions." *Working Paper, Report No. 01–108.* Cambridge, MA: Marketing Science Institute, 2001.

Schlegelmilch. B. *Marketing Ethics: An International Perspective.* London: International Thomson Business Press, 1998.

Schmitt, Bernd H. *Experiential Marketing: How to Get Customers to Sense, Feel, Think, Act, and Relate to Your Company and Brands.* New York: Free Press, 1999.

Schmitt, Bernd, and Alex Simonson. *Marketing Aesthetics: The Strategic Management of Brands, Identity, and Image.* New York: Free Press, 1997.

Schreiber, Alfred L., with Barry Lenson. *Multicultural Marketing: Selling to the New America: Position Your Company Today for Optimal Success in the Diverse America of Tomorrow.* Lincolnwood, IL: NTC Business Books, 2001.

Schultz, Don E. *Communicating Globally: An Integrated Marketing Approach.* Lincolnwood, IL: NTC Business Books, 2000.

———. "Consumer Marketing Changed by Advent of 29.8/7 Media Week." *Marketing News,* September 24, 2001, pp. 11–12.

———. "Learn to Differentiate CRM's Two Faces." *Marketing News,* November 20, 2000, p. 11.

———. "Marketers Still Tarnished by Outdated Skills." *Marketing News,* March 13, 2000, p. 2.

Schwartz, Evan I. *Digital Darwinism: 7 Breakthrough Business Strategies for Surviving in the Cutthroat Web Economy.* New York: Broadway Books, 1999.

Sewell, Carl, Paul B. Brown, and Tom Peters. *Customers for Life: How to Turn That One-Time Buyer into a Lifetime Customer.* New York: Pocket Books, 1998.

Seybold, Patricia B. *The Customer Revolution: How to Thrive When Customers Are in Control.* New York: Crown Business, 2001.

Shaw, William H. *Business Ethics.* Aldershot, Hampshire, England: Gower Publishing Limited, 1999.

Silverstein, Barry. *Business-to-Business Internet Marketing.* Gulf Breeze, FL: Maximum Press, 2000.

Sindell, Kathleen. *Loyalty Marketing for the Internet Age: How to Identify, Attract, Serve, and Retain Customers in an E-Commerce Environment.* Chicago: Dearborn Financial Publishing, 2000.

Spoelstra, Jon, and Mark Cuban. *Marketing Outrageously.* Marietta, GA: Bard Press, 2001.

Spulber, Daniel F. *The Market Makers: How Leading Companies Create and Win Markets.* New York: McGraw-Hill, 1998.

Sterne, Jim. *Customer Service on the Internet: Building Relationships, Increasing Loyalty, and Staying Competitive.* New York: John Wiley & Sons, 2000.

———. *World Wide Web Marketing: Integrating the Web into Your Marketing Strategy.* New York: John Wiley & Sons, 1998.

Stewart-Copier, Cynthia. *Dream Big!: A Woman's Book of Network Marketing.* Holbrook, MA: Adams Media Corporation, 2000.

Strauss, Judy, and Raymond D. Frost. *Marketing on the Internet: Principles of On-Line Marketing.* New York: Broadway Books, 1999.

Tannen, Deborah. *You Just Don't Understand: Women and Men in Conversation.* New York: Ballantine Books, 1990.

Tedlow, Richard S., and Geoffrey Jones (eds.). *The Rise and Fall of Mass Marketing.* New York: Routledge, 1993.

Temporal, Paul, and K.C. Lee. *Hi-Tech Hi-Touch Branding: Creating Brand Power in the Age of Technology.* New York: John Wiley & Sons, 2000.

Tharp, Marye C. *Marketing and Consumer Identity in Multicultural America.* Thousand Oaks, CA: Sage Publications, Inc., 2001.

Travis, Daryl. *Emotional Branding: How Successful Brands Gain the Irrational Edge.* Roseville, CA: Prima Venture, 2000.

Trepper, Charles H. *E-Commerce Strategies.* Redmond, WA: Microsoft Press, 2000.

Trout, Jack, and Steve Rivkin. *Differentiate or Die: Survival in Our Era of Killer Competition.* New York: John Wiley & Sons, 2000.

Turner, Marcia Layton. *How to Think Like the World's Greatest Marketing Minds.* New York: McGraw-Hill: 2001.

Tvede, Lars, and Peter Ohnemus. *Marketing Strategies for the New Economy.* Chichester, West Sussex, England: John Wiley & Sons, 2001.

Wiersema, Fred. *New Market Leaders: Who's Winning and How in the Battle for Customers.* New York: Free Press, 2001.

Zimmerman, Jan, and Jerry Yang. *Marketing on the Internet.* Gulf Breeze, FL: Maximum Press, 2000.

Zyman, Sergio. *Building Brandwidth: Closing the Sale Online.* New York: HarperCollins, 2000.

———. *The End of Marketing as We Know It.* New York: HarperCollins, 1999.

Index